HUNTER

HUNTER

J. A. HUNTER

WITH AN INTRODUCTORY NOTE BY

CAPTAIN A. T. A. RITCHIE, O B. E., M. C.

Safari Press Inc.
P. O. Box 3095, Long Beach, CA 90803

Hunter, J. A.

Safari Press, Inc.

1999, Long Beach, California

ISBN 1-57157-243-0

Library of Congress Catalog Card Number: 2005937189

10 9 8 7 6 5 4 3 2

Readers wishing to receive the Safari Press catalog, featuring many fine books on big-game hunting, wingshooting, and sporting firearms, should write to Safari Press Inc., P.O. Box 3095, Long Beach, CA 90803, USA. Tel: (714) 894-9080 or visit our Web site at www.safaripress.com.

Contents

Publisher's Note

In 1948 Mr. W. J. Holliday of Indianapolis returned to the United States from a hunting trip in Kenya, British East Africa. He brought with him a large and fascinating manuscript of notes concerning certain episodes in the life of a veteran African white hunter, the author of these autobiographical notes being one John A. Hunter (by coincidence of name and profession). The editors at Harper & Brothers read Hunter's manuscript with great interest and enlisted the aid of Daniel P. Mannix, himself a sportsman and writer, in arranging, cutting and supplementing Hunter's notes for book publication. Mr. Mannix traveled to Hunter's home in Kenya where he spent many weeks helping him to put into final shape the story of his startling and varied adventures, which we now offer you in *Hunter*.

Introductory Note

by Captain A. T. A. Ritchie, o.b.e., m.c.
Game Warden of Kenya, 1923-1949

It is no enviable task to write an introductory note to a book which, because of time and distance, one has not yet seen, and of which indeed one has little idea of the form and substance. And I would have refused to do so if I could. But I have a sense of deep and lasting gratitude to J. A. Hunter—"J. A." from now on—for the work he did for the Kenya Game Department during the twenty-six years I was in charge of it, and I feel I must take this chance to avow it. Further, it gives me an opportunity to tell something of Game Control, and thus sketch in outline the background to many of the experiences and exploits of which this book will doubtless tell.

Game Control is a large and complex subject, for the term includes all those measures necessary in a country rich in indigenous fauna to prevent a serious conflict between that fauna and mankind. The problems it poses are infinitely varied, and range from those widespread in area and significance to those of merely parochial importance. For instance, elephants, their numbers, size, strength, destructive feeding habits and conservatively migratory mode of life, make them a prime preoccupation of all East Africa Game Wardens, while the temerity of duiker in eating the rose bushes in the gardens of Government House gives rise to more localized trouble!

Game Control is an essential corollary of Game Preservation; for no human community will tolerate in its vicinity the existence of— much less subscribe to the protection of—species that are a perpetual source of danger or depredation; and if any general system of preservation is to persist, active intervention must always be ready and at hand.

In Kenya during the last thirty or forty years, the opening up of new country and the more intensive use of old have caused frequent and bitter clashes, the vested rights of pristine inhabitants on the one hand, and the impatient demands of intolerant immigrants on the other fomenting endless trouble.

It is obviously impossible, in a brief note such as this, to detail the multifarious methods and processes used to minimize such clashes and prevent them leading to unrestricted destruction, but they can be summarized generally under three headings: (1) Driving animals from where their presence is undesirable to unclaimed areas where they can find "*Lebensraum.*" (2) Where (1) is not possible, instilling discipline—usually by oft-reiterated and painful lessons!—so that animals will respect man and his husbandry, and thereby earn a provisional tolerance. (3) Where (1) and (2) are impossible or ineffective, local extermination may be inevitable.

The necessity for the killing of game animals on Control is often misunderstood, even by those interested in wild life and its conservation. I will try to clarify it. Killing may have to be undertaken for two main reasons: (a) deliberately to reduce the number of a particular species, on what may be called biological grounds, which may be necessary when such species is too numerous for its environment, either as a result of restriction of habitat or of the upset of the balance of nature; and (b) purely incidentally, in the course of trying to achieve (1) or (2) *supra,* i.e., to drive animals or to build up a correlation of ideas, or as in (3) when their continued existence is not tolerable. It is a fundamental principle that not one more animal must be killed on Control than is necessary to bring about any required result; and it is equally fundamental that no wounded animal be allowed to escape if human effort can possibly prevent it, though this law of decent behavior should of course obtain under all circumstances of hunting everywhere.

The class of Game Control work that has fallen to the lot of J. A.

has been almost invariably concerned with those animals that resent interference and coercion, and are ever ready to contest an issue. It has thus been work of extreme danger, much of it, for a Control Officer has often to deal with beasts that are malicious and cunning, rogues perhaps, or at least animals that have had previous and unpleasant experience of man. Further it must be remembered that Control work imposes one grave disadvantage; for while a big game hunter normally has almost complete freedom of choice—time, place, and other attendant conditions—hunting on Control involves taking on an animal on its ground, and on its own terms, which is indeed a different proposition!

It may well seem from this that J. A. has always been given the "dirty end of the stick." This is true, and it has been because he has wanted it, and because he has been fitted for it by his great qualities: unrivaled experience and knowledge of animal behavior, surpassing skill and speed in handling firearms, and most importantly perhaps an equable temperament and iron nerve, a formidable combination. It is not blood lust that has made him volunteer when dangerous game have had to be killed, for he has never enjoyed the taking of life; it is the thrill of the hunt and the danger of it that he revels in, and the practice of skill that alone maintains the thin line which separates superman from suicide.

I have said enough, for J. A. is a modest man and would resent panegyrics. In any case I can pay no greater tribute to his prowess than is provided by the fact that he is still alive; and when you have read this book you will probably understand better what this means.

A. T. A. R.

Kenya Colony, 1952

1

Rogue Elephant

Two natives were returning to their village one evening when they saw a great black mass standing motionless in the shadows of the huts. The men shouted to scare the thing away. At once the mass left the shadows and charged them at fearful speed. Then the men saw it was a huge bull elephant.

They ran for their lives, each going in a different direction. One man was wearing a red blanket and that blanket was his death warrant, for the elephant followed him. The villagers cowering in their huts listened to the chase, powerless to help their friend. They heard the man's screams as the elephant caught him. The great brute put one foot on his victim and pulled him to pieces with his trunk. Then he stamped the body into the ground and went away.

I was guiding two Canadian sportsmen through the Aberdare Forest in British East Africa when runners arrived from the chief of the murdered man's village to ask my help in killing the elephant. The natives in Kenya knew me well, for I had lived there many years as a white hunter—taking out sportsmen to shoot big game and killing dangerous animals at the request of the government. The chief sent me word that this bull was a rogue elephant that had been destroying farms and terrorizing the district for many months. If the animal were not destroyed, he was sure to kill someone else sooner or later.

I was under contract to my two sportsmen. They were brothers, Allen and Duncan McMartin, and we had been in the bush many weeks looking for bongo, a rare antelope not easily come by. If I took off time to track down the rogue, it would lessen the brothers' chances of getting a good trophy. Still, the McMartins told me to go ahead. I have seen other sportsmen who would not have been so generous. I started back at once with the runners, taking Saseeta, my Wakamba gunbearer who had been with me many years.

When we arrived at the village, I was met by the chief. His name was Ngiri and we were old friends. But we had little time to talk of past adventures for the village was in a panic. The natives were afraid to venture into the shambas, as their maize fields are called, and many of them would not even leave their huts although the wattle shacks would have been little enough protection against a rogue elephant. Ngiri told me the rogue moved from village to village, destroying the maize fields as he went, and unless he was killed the villagers would be in dire straits indeed.

With Saseeta, I went out to look for the body of the dead native. We picked up his tracks on the edge of the village where he had first seen the elephant and followed them through the bush. It was a sad sight to see how he had zigzagged and doubled, trying to throw off his pursuer. Well do I know how he felt, for I have often been chased by elephants. It is like running in a nightmare, for the wait-a-bit thorns hold you back and the creepers pull at your legs while the elephant goes crashing after you like a terrier after a rat. Not a second goes by but you expect to feel that snakey trunk close about your neck, yet you dare not look back for you must keep your eyes on the brush ahead.

We found what was left of the body, but there was no sign of the red blanket that the man had been wearing. The elephant had no doubt carried it off with him. This was not the first time I had heard of a native dressed in red being attacked by an elephant and I believe the color must attract them.

I was ready to start at once on the rogue's spoor but Ngiri told me to wait. The bull was sure to despoil another village that evening and runners would bring in word during the night. Then I could start out on the fresh spoor in the morning and save a day or more of hard tracking. Ngiri was right. I could only wait and hope that the rogue would ruin a shamba and not take another life.

A few hours before dawn, a runner arrived all breathless from a village in the uplands some five miles away. The rogue had entered the village in the evening but instead of going straight to the fields had wandered up and down among the huts. He stopped in front of one hut and stood there so long that he dropped a great mass of dung not six feet from the door. One can imagine the feelings of the wretched natives who were huddled together under the flimsy thatch roof while outside stood the rogue elephant, unafraid and forbidding in the darkness. After a time that must have seemed to the natives like an eternity, they heard the great beast move off in the direction of their shamba and listened despairingly while he destroyed the crop—their little all, the fruits of their sweat and labor. When he had gorged himself, he moved away into the bush to digest his feast and sleep during the day.

As soon as dawn broke, Saseeta and I started out for the village. We had a stiff, uphill climb of nine thousand feet and the going was hard on the lungs. In the village we picked up the bull's spoor at a trodden gap in the thorn-bush barricade around the shamba. The trail led us toward the deepest part of the great Aberdare Forest.

After the bright light of the open country, the forest seemed like a great building with a green roof and tree trunks for pillars. There was an eerie stillness about the place for the thick foliage deadened sounds. We walked noiselessly among the boles of the vast trees. I was glad there was little undergrowth. I could see twenty yards ahead; as much as one might ask or want.

I smelt the pungent odor of elephant droppings and saw ahead of us a pile of these unsightly dollops, surrounded by myriads of small forest flies. Saseeta kicked the heap and pointed to the kernels of undigested maize. The droppings were fresh. The bull was only a few hours ahead of us.

I had hoped to come up with the bull in this semi-open part of the forest. But he was cunning and had gone into the thicket to take his daytime rest. The tracks led us into a belt of dense bamboo, inter-growing with a tall plant like forest nettle that was anything but desirable to hunt in. We put up troops of Colibi and Sykes monkeys that bounded away through the trees and I prayed the rogue wouldn't hear their startled crashing. In any case, the rotting bamboo underfoot made it impossible to walk quietly. I tried to step in the deep impressions made by the bull but his great stride dwarfed the efforts of mere man. Every time a red-legged francolin or tiny duiker antelope burst out of the cover, my heart gave a jump and I clutched my rifle. This kind of work is very different from trophy hunting where you can locate a herd in open bush and pick your bull. If it hadn't been for my promise to Chief Ngiri, I would have turned back and tried again when the bull was in better country.

The bamboo opened out and we came on a spot where natives had been cutting wood. I swore to myself when I saw how the bull had shied away from the hated man smell and knocked the bamboos aside as he raced off through the grove. An elephant that has no fear of human scent at night in shambas will often grow panicky when he smells man in the jungle. So far the bull had been moving slowly, grazing as he went. Now he was trying to put as many miles as possible between him and the woodcutters' camp.

Saseeta and I looked at each other. He shrugged. It was hunting luck. Doggedly we set out on the great spoor which took us up an almost unbelievably steep slope to a high ridge. Here the tracks went through a tangle of wild briars and stinging nettles as if the rogue were determined to find the foulest cover in the whole Aberdare. The snarl was so bad we had to crawl under it on our hands and knees, a time-consuming business and hard on the back. Wriggling along, I suddenly came out into a place where the elephant had stopped to rest. I was most grateful to him for having moved on. Coming unexpectedly on a rogue when you are flat on your belly under a briar tangle is not pleasant.

Suddenly a distinct crackling sound came from ahead. Saseeta and I lay still. The noise came again. The bull was feeding in a grove of bamboo only a few feet ahead of us.

We crawled forward. Once in the bamboo, we could stand upright—a great relief. We moved toward the noises, stepping carefully on the ground already flattened by the bull's great imprints. The wind was uncertain. Cross drafts in the bamboo tossed it about in all directions. There was no way we could be sure of keeping downwind of the elephant and the growth was so thick we could move only by staying in his tracks. I knew we must be almost up with him but I could see little through the tall stalks of bamboo hemming us in on every side.

Saseeta stopped and pointed with his lips toward our left. I could still see nothing but I slowly raised my rifle. I was using a .475 Jeffery #2, double-barrel express—a reliable gun that has never failed me or I wouldn't be writing these notes. The crashing sounded again only a few feet away. I held my breath, waiting for a shot.

Suddenly the noises ceased. There was absolute silence. Saseeta and I stood motionless and I wished I could stop the noise of my heart. It sounded to me like a drum. Then we heard the bamboos crack and sway as the bull turned and ran through the grove at full speed. That accursed breeze had given him our scent.

Saseeta and I looked at each other. Poor fellow, there is no profanity in his language but I was more fortunate and swore for us both. But I did so silently, for even though the elephant was now far away, we never spoke in the bush unless absolutely necessary.

The sun was beginning to drop and I knew it must be about five o'clock. We had been going since dawn through very hard country, and the elephant was now definitely alarmed. He might go for miles before he stopped. A wise man would have given up and returned to camp, but I have never been very wise, as far as hunting is concerned and I motioned to Saseeta that we'd continue to track.

Light in the undergrowth was already failing but we had no trouble following the bull. He had trampled down the tough bamboos like so much grass in his fright. As we pressed on, the rotting surface of the ground became worse than ever. My shoes plunged through it, producing sounds that not even an unwary elephant would have stood for.

After an hour's tracking, Saseeta gave a low, birdlike whistle—the recognized bush signal for "attention." We stopped and listened. I could hear the bull moving through the bamboo to our left. He was going downwind, trying to pick up our scent. Then the sounds stopped and I knew he had paused to listen. Instead of our stalking the elephant, he was now stalking us, and in my experience an elephant is a better stalker than a man.

I again considered turning back but I hated to break my promise to old Ngiri. My chances of getting a shot at the rogue were now very slim but Saseeta and I kept on. He could not have caught our scent as yet for we didn't hear him crashing away. He was still standing there, probably testing the air with his raised trunk. If he waited a few more minutes, we would be up to him. My eyes ached from the constant strain of peering ahead through the greenish yellow bamboo poles.

Suddenly I saw an indistinct, shadowy shape through the bamboo. I stopped dead and slowly raised my rifle. In the thick cover I could not tell head from tail. There was no gleam of white or yellow ivory to guide me. I held my breath until I nearly strangled to avoid the slightest noise and I knew Saseeta behind me was doing the same. I wanted badly to fire but was afraid of only wounding him. If he moved a few feet one way or the other I could tell where to shoot.

Then a sudden breeze swept through the bamboo. In an instant the bull got our scent and was gone.

I felt a sickly feeling. If I had fired I might have brought him down. But if I had only injured him, he might have killed us both in the thick cover or raced off with the pain of the wound driving him for miles before he stopped. A wounded elephant is a terrible creature and I never like to shoot unless I can be sure of a kill.

There was no use in going on. Evening was falling and the camp many miles away. Saseeta and I slowly toiled back over the long route. In the village, everyone was bitterly disappointed at my failure. Hardly a word was spoken. Supper was served in complete silence.

After I had eaten and lit my pipe, I could regard the whole business more philosophically. The failures make hunting worth while. If you won every time, there would be no thrill to it. I hoped the natives whose shambas the rogue was destroying that night could view the affair equally impartially.

I went to bed and lay awake listening to the herd calls of the hyrax, a curious beast that looks like an overgrown guinea pig, and the steady beat of native drums in the village. I knew they were keeping up their courage by gulping quantities of home-made brew and I wished I could join them, but I needed a clear head for hunting in the morning. Then came the haunting grunt of a lion. The sound of the drums quickly petered out as the natives hurried to their huts. I heard the lion drinking at the stream a few feet from my camp and move off again. Then there was silence except for the occasional distant chatter of disturbed monkeys and the twitter of a drowsy bird. I fell asleep.

The next morning a heavy fog covered the forest. The grass was heavy with dew and the air was distinctly chilly. While I was drinking my hot tea, a half-naked runner rushed into camp. During the night the bull had raided a shamba three miles away and destroyed the crop. The rogue was so cunning that he never raided the same village twice in succession and this made hunting him far more difficult.

Saseeta and I started off at once. When we reached the raided village, some of the natives volunteered to go along as guides. We picked up the bull's trail. By now, I knew every toenail in his huge feet and was beginning to hate the sight of them. We followed him as fast as we could go. He was headed toward the hills and our guides assured me that the country was more open there. I hoped they were right.

The slopes were steep and I had to stop constantly for rests. I envied the local natives their remarkable staying power. Still, the brush was open and we made fair time. But this was too good to last. By noon we entered some of the most damnable cover it has ever fallen my lot to hunt in. Bamboo shoots and fallen stems were woven into a virtual mat. Boles of dead trees lay across the trail,

some four feet high. They were hard to climb over and worse to
crawl under. The elephant had taken all these obstructions in his
stride but we were not so fortunate. Moving quietly was impossible.
I scowled at Saseeta for making an unnecessary noise and a moment
later made a much louder noise myself.

We came on a spot where the bull had lain down at full length
to sleep. I could see the imprint of his hide on the soft earth. This
was encouraging, for if he had kept going, we never would have
caught up with him. At the same time, I hoped we would not meet
him in this thick stuff. We were in a secondary growth of bamboo,
the stalks barely half as high as the long poles we had struggled
through the previous day, and their tufted tops made it impossible
to see beyond muzzle range.

Gusts of wind began to spring up making the long bamboos clank
together. We moved forward with the greatest caution as it is difficult to tell whether wind-borne noises are caused by stems or by
beast. This was the last place I wanted to meet the rogue, for when
an elephant charges in bamboo, he knocks down the long, springy
stems in front of him and you may be pinned under them before
getting a chance to shoot. Even Saseeta, generally afraid of nothing,
made an ugly grimace when I looked back as if to say, "This is a
sticky business."

Suddenly we heard a movement in the bamboo ahead of us.
Saseeta and I both stopped dead and I raised my rifle, waiting for
the charge. Instead of the elephant, a magnificent male bongo broke
out of the cover and stood in front of us. This was the very trophy
the McMartins and I had been after for many long weeks. Yet I
could not shoot for fear of alarming the rogue. Often it happens
you see the best trophies when you can't collect them.

We passed the fern-clad banks of a mountain stream and saw
where the bull had been pulling up bracken with his tusks to get at
the roots. The roots of the bracken seem to possess a medicinal
quality that serves to keep the great beasts healthy. We knew the
bull must be just ahead of us now for the turned-over earth was still
moist.

While we were checking the signs, one of our native guides darted back to say he heard a noise in the bamboo ahead of us. This might mean much or little. Saseeta and I moved forward as quietly as possible. The wind was steady now and in our favor. We moved slowly through the high stalks. Then we heard the ripping noise of bamboo being torn apart. The bull was right ahead of us. He could not hear us above the noise of his own feeding, and if the wind held, we had him.

I saw his trunk appear above the stalks and pull a particularly succulent tip down to him. I crept along, trying to see through the stalks ahead and at the same time watch where I put my feet. Saseeta kept behind me, constantly testing the breeze with a small forest fungi puff. When shaken, these little puffballs give off a fine white powder almost like smoke and you can tell every shift of the wind by watching it. As we went deeper into the bamboo, the heavy growth cut off the breeze and the puffball dust hung motionless around Saseeta's hand. Then I saw the bull not fifteen yards from me.

I could hear him munching bamboo shoots as the line conveying elevator of his trunk hoisted them into his mouth. Between us was a network of bamboo poles through which I dared not shoot lest the bullet be deflected by one of the tough stems. Another of those terrible decisions. Should I take the chance and shoot? Or should I wait a few minutes and hope the bull would shift his position slightly and give me a shoulder shot? I would have to make up my mind quickly for we were so close that our smell would permeate to him in the absence of wind.

Suddenly the bull saw us. He did not run as he had the day before. Without the slightest hesitation or warning, he spun around and charged.

Almost before I could raise my rifle he was on top of us. His great ears were folded back close to his head and his trunk was held tight against the brisket. He was screaming with rage—a series of throaty "URRS" is the nearest I can describe the sound. I aimed the right barrel for the center of his skull, a point three inches higher than an imaginary line drawn from eye to eye, and fired. For an instant after the shot the bull seemed to hang in the air above me. Then he came down with a crash. He lay partly hidden by the bamboo, giving off high-pitched cries and low, gurgling sounds. I fired the second barrel through the center of his neck. Instantly the whole body relaxed, the hind legs stretched to their fullest. So ended the raider that had brought death and terror to Chief Ngiri's people.

Our local scouts had wisely vanished when the shooting started. Now they began to appear as if out of the earth. They gathered around the dead rogue and stood looking at him, so overjoyed that they could not speak. It must have seemed to them almost too good to be true that they could now work their fields in peace and security.

I sat down on one of the dead rogue's legs to fill my pipe. Everyone wanted to do something to express his gratitude, although all the poor fellows could do was to offer me a drink of cool water. Some of the sectional parts of the bamboo stems showed tiny openings bored by insects. The natives, selecting these sections, cut them down and pressed them on me. Each section contained a few mouthfuls of clean, cold water.

When I had finished my pipe, I examined the dead rogue's carcass. The ivory was very poor. The tusks were only about forty pounds each, whereas a really good bull will carry ivory weighing three times that much. Forest vegetation seems to lack calcium, for the forest elephants never have as good tusks as the bush dwellers. While examining the tusks, I found an old bullet hole at the base of the right hand tusk. With my knife I dug out a musket bullet, probably fired by an Arab ivory hunter years before. The bullet was embedded in the nerve center of the tusk and the pain must have been terrible. The constant suffering had driven the old bull mad and that was why he had become a rogue. No doubt the Arab who had fired the shot was now living comfortably with never a thought for the suffering he had caused to both man and beast.

We headed back toward camp. Everyone was in high spirits and elated with success. The leading scouts cut a path for us through the tangle with their knives, shouting and laughing as we progressed, a noisy contrast to the deathly stillness with which we had crept along that same trail a few hours before. As we came out into open country, I could see the hill slopes dotted with black figures who had heard the sound of the rifle shots and come hurrying to meet us. Our scouts yelled some guttural sounds across the valley. Native voices carry a surprising distance and I could see the black dots stop and then go scurrying back to the village with the good news.

Back in camp, a great welcome was given Saseeta and me. Even the old and sick tottered out of their huts to thank us. The white man had not failed them. I sent word to Chief Ngiri that the raider was dead and then sat down to a well-earned supper.

That evening, sitting in front of my campfire and smoking my pipe, I thought back over the many years I'd spent in Africa as a hunter. When I first came to Kenya, the game covered the plains as far as a man could see. I hunted lions where towns now stand, and shot elephants from the engine of the first railroad to cross the country. In the span of one man's lifetime, I have seen jungle turn into farm-land and cannibal tribes become factory workers. I have had a little to do with this change myself, for the government employed me to clear dangerous beasts out of areas that were being opened to cultivation. I hold a world's record for rhino, possibly another record for lion (although we kept no exact record of the numbers shot in those early days) and I have shot more than fourteen hundred elephant. I certainly do not tell of these records with pride. The work had to be done and I happened to be the man who did it. But strange as it may seem to the armchair conservationist, I have a deep affection for the animals I had to kill. I spent long years studying their habits, not only in order to kill them, but because I was honestly interested in them.

Yet it is true I have always been a sportsman. Firearms have been my ruling passion in life and I would rather hear the crack of a rifle or the bang of a shotgun than listen to the finest orchestra. I can-not say that I did not enjoy hunting, but looking back I truly believe that in most cases the big game had as much chance to kill me as I had to kill them.

I am one of the last of the old-time hunters. The events I saw can never be relived. Both the game and the native tribes, as I knew them, are gone. No one will ever see again the great elephant herds led by old bulls carrying 150 pounds of ivory in each tusk. No one will ever again hear the yodeling war cries of the Masai as their spearmen swept the bush after cattle-killing lions. Few indeed will be able to say that they have broken into country never before seen by a white man. No, the old Africa has passed and I saw it go.

This, then, is a record of the last great days of big-game hunting. Nowhere in the world was there game to equal the African game. Nowhere were there animals so big, so powerful or so numerous. Now that it is almost over, there may be some who wish to hear about the greatest hunting era in the world's history.

2

Scotland—John Hunter

I was born near Shearington in the south of Scotland, thirteen years before the close of the last century. My father had one of the finest farms in that part of the country, having three hundred acres of good farming land and three square miles of grazing. There was a tradition in the family that our name "Hunter" was derived from the profession of a remote ancestor, and certainly the love of hunting ran in our veins. My father was always out in the marshes that surround the Solway Firth with a fowling piece over his arm and my older brother was regarded as one of the best field naturalists in Scotland. My mother was the only non-sporting member of the family, her time being amply filled with trying to keep the household running.

But what was merely recreation to the rest of my family was the very breath of life to me. When I was little more than a baby I used to toddle after my father to pick up his cartridge cases after he fired and sniff the delicious odor of gunpowder that clung to them. When I grew older I spent all my days in the great Lochar Moss, a vast bog full of black game, duck and colonies of black-headed gulls that nested so thickly on the ground that you could hardly move without stepping on their eggs. By long experience I learned the pathways through the swamp and often while wandering there I would flush the red grouse from her clutch of eggs and the mallard from her dozen. I returned from these jaunts with my clothes in a sad state, for the thousands of circling birds would paint me with their droppings, and often I would sink up to my armpits in the mossy slime. My poor mother was driven to distraction, but I loved every moment of it and even today I could retrace, blindfolded, that network of paths through the great bog.

When I was eight, I borrowed father's gun while he was out one day and went shooting with it. This gun was an old Purdey and to my mind the Purdey shotgun is the finest firearm ever made by man. Today, a pair of matched Purdeys with case will cost you the better part of a thousand guineas in Kenya and they are well worth it, for nothing has ever equaled the beautiful precision of these matchless guns. Father got his Purdey secondhand from a friend who got it in turn from another man, and heaven only knows how many shots had been fired from it. But in spite of all that shooting, the breech action was still as tight as the day it left the shop and the gun's balance was a thing to delight the heart. The first day I took the gun out, I nearly shot off my foot with it. I was stalking partridge and in my excitement I happened to squeeze the trigger. When father heard what had happened, he was very put out but he did not forbid me the gun. Soon I learned to handle the lovely instrument correctly and spent every night in my room cleaning and oiling it until the barrels shone like dull silver and the old engraving on the breech was nearly rubbed away by so much polishing.

With the Purdey, I shot gray lag, pinkfoot and barnacle geese along the flats. I learned to stalk a flock of fowl while they were noisily guzzling the small mussels which were abundant in the wet sand and then stand stock still when the sound stopped and I knew the fowl were raising their heads to look about. At night I would lie in bed and listen to the cackling of wild geese overhead as they battled against the gale, and the sound was sweeter to me than the music of bagpipes. Then I would fall asleep dreaming of the morrow and the long tramps through the marshes.

Nor did I neglect my fishing. Many a day I spent whipping the waters of the Lochar stream with a split cane rod, and like as not I would be back that night with a torch and spear, for the salmon were dazed by the light and, if you were quick, you could harpoon one with a fast thrust. It was tricky work for the spear seems to bend as it enters the water and you must allow for what is known as "the angle of refraction."

As I grew older, some of the country folk introduced me to an ancient and honorable sport which has no better name given to it than poaching, yet it is a fine business requiring the greatest of skill. There were some noble poachers in the south of Scotland but I think I can say there was none my equal, for I spent every hour that was not given over to my Purdey and fishing rod learning how to set a snare or run a net. Many's the dark night I crawled through cover, my fine silk net twisted around my neck like a scarf, listening for the sound of the keepers' footfalls on the frosty ground. The keepers carried guns and were not slow to use them, putting the life of a pheasant or a rabbit higher than that of a man. But this only made the sport more exciting and I often think the practice I got as a lad dodging keepers stood me in good stead years later when I came to stalk big game. I worked with my lurcher, a very knowing dog of a breed originally developed by the gypsies for their poaching work. The dog warned me when the keepers were about and once he and I lay on our bellies while two keepers stood ten feet away and wondered together where I was hiding. Those were good days and I often think I got as much of a thrill bagging a rabbit behind the keeper's back as I did later bringing down a bull elephant with two hundred pounds of ivory in his tusks.

When I returned late at night, I often saw a light on in the house, which meant my parents had missed me and were sitting up to ask questions. I would hide my catch in the cellar behind barrels and creep up the back stairs. I got to know every creaking step in those stairs and how to avoid them. Then I would strip off my clothes and dive into bed. Later my parents would come up and seeing me apparently fast asleep mother would wonder, "Now where on earth can the lad have been?" I suspect father knew right well but he never betrayed me.

So I grew up, caring little for farming and less for the solid people in Shearington who, for the most part, were poor shots and could no more set a rabbit snare than they could flick a salmon fly into a pool thirty feet away. The only stone in my pudding was school. It was my habit to arrive late, for I hated to pass the marshes without a look around to see how the birds were moving. Our schoolmaster was a brutal man who used the birch and cane freely, but his favorite method of punishment was to cuff a boy's head, hitting him first on one side and then on the other until his ears turned black and blue and the child fell down nearly unconscious. Several of my schoolmates grew up partly deaf as the result of this treatment. I was a big lout and although our dominie thrashed me plentifully with his cane, he seldom dared to lay his hands on me. But one day when I was fourteen, I arrived in school covered with mud from one of my trips through the marsh. That was too much for the teacher and he fell upon me in a sort of wild rage, beating me with his fists and cuffing me until the blood ran out of my ears. I was truly afraid for my life, for he seemed like a madman, and snatching up my slate, I hit him as hard as I could. I had strong muscles from climbing trees after birds' eggs and handling my heavy gun. The man staggered back and nearly fell, clinging to a desk to support himself. I decided I had better leave school for the rest of the day and went back to my beloved Lochar Moss where I could be alone. When I returned home, I found the dominie had been there before me with the local minister. My parents were sore put out but when they heard my side of the story, father refused to punish me and mother simply begged that I spend more time with my books and less with the Purdey. From then on the master was afraid of me so it was little enough time I spent in school, preferring to be out with my fishing tackle or my gun.

My parents had always taken for granted that I would follow in my father's footsteps and become a farmer. Now I had little love for farming, or indeed for anything save hunting. Yet I considered farming better than being cooped up in an office, so I said nothing. But when I was eighteen, I got in a serious scrape. The lasses in that part of Scotland had changed little since the days of Robbie Burns and were not miserly with their favors. I had my share of good times, but, although I fancied myself a man of experience, I was still only a lad and I fell deeply in love with an older woman. Yet I think I would have gotten over my infatuation had not the local minister interfered. The minister went to my parents with a tale of my sins. I was summoned before the family council and ordered to give up the lady, but I defied them all and swore I would marry her. The minister departed, promising me hell and damnation while my poor parents did not know where to turn.

With the minister against me and my record none too good (except among those who were grateful for the gifts of game I had brought them during the bitter days of winter) I was an Ishmael in the community. Meanwhile, my parents were in mortal dread that I would fulfill my threat and marry the lady. One evening while I was sitting moody and sullen alone in my room, my father came up to see me.

"John, I've been talking to other members of the family about you," he said, sitting down on my bed and staring at his hands. "We've decided it would be nice if you took a trip somewhere . . . say to Africa. Some relations of ours have a cousin who is living there. He has a farm in Kenya near a town called Nairobi. If you were willing to go, I would buy you a half interest in the place."

I knew the relations father meant and an unco, tight-fisted lot they were. Whenever a farthing passed through their fingers it screamed for help. If their cousin were like them it was a hard time I'd have in Africa. But I cared nothing about that. There were lions in Africa and elephants and rhinoceros. That was the land for me. I was ready to leave that night and so I told my father.

As my father left the room, he hesitated a moment at the door. "Son, you may take the Purdey," he said. Then I knew that he had forgiven me all my sins.

A few weeks later I embarked for Mombasa on the east coast of Africa. I had the Purdey and a .275 Mauser rifle, a great, heavy thing that an uncle of mine had brought back from the Boer War. In Scotland, where the largest game we country folk ever hunted was a badger, it seemed like a monstrous weapon indeed.

When my father said good-by, he told me, "John, this trip will either make or break you. You would have nothing of our dull ways and wanted adventure. Very well, lad, here is your adventure. It will be hard in Africa but if you come back with your tail between your legs, never let me hear more of your fine talk. You will have been beaten, my lad, and from then on you must settle down to an honest job and work at it as other folks do."

I had small thoughts of that. I pictured myself returning some day, rich in ivory and with a dozen world records of big game to my credit. I would show these people what sort of lad it was that they had driven from their midst. I particularly looked forward to dropping in on my old friends the minister and the schoolmaster.

After a three months' voyage I reached Mombasa. To a raw Scotch lad like myself, it was like being picked up and set down in the middle of the Arabian Nights. For the first time in my life I saw palm trees growing, walked through native bazaars with leopard hides hanging up for sale and watched half-naked savages coming in from the jungles of the interior. In the bay, Arab dhows were setting sail across the Indian Ocean to Bombay. Most of the town was made of white-walled, thatched houses, but near the water front stood the old buildings, many of them dating back from the days when Mombasa was a great and proud Arab town. These buildings had carved teak doorways and great windows guarded by wrought-iron bars, all very strange and wonderful to me. Although it was the middle of winter, the tropical heat was heavy in the town and I sweated freely in my Scotch tweeds.

I was not able to stay long in Mombasa for I had to take the train north to Nairobi. I boarded the train in the evening and for the first part of the trip we traveled through tropical jungles. At the stations, natives offered bananas, oranges and grapefruit for sale, plucked fresh off the trees, a seeming miracle to me who had always regarded such fruits as something of a luxury.

When I awoke in the morning, the train had reached the uplands. On every side were great open plains, dotted with herds of wild game. A hunter's dream come true. I went nearly mad with excitement watching the strange beasts raise their heads calmly to watch

the train as it went by. I could identify only the long-necked giraffes, although there were a dozen different types of gazelles and
antelopes grazing along the tracks. In a few years I was to know all
these different kinds of game animals as well as I knew the various
types of duck and geese on Lochar Moss.

I arrived at Nairobi about noon. In those days, Nairobi was
largely a city of shacks although a few of the buildings had begun
to take shape. I stood on the station platform, listening to the other
passengers call to the native porters in Swahili, the lingua franca of
East Africa. I felt very lonely. My cousin was supposed to meet me
there and I longed to see him.

Then along the platform came striding a huge giant of a man, his
hair sprouting in every direction, and a dirty beard hanging down
from his chin. He carried two great revolvers strapped to his side
in the manner of an American cowboy and a knife stuck through his
belt. I stared at this monster in horror and hoped there were not
many like him in the country.

The man walked up to me and bellowed, "Are you John Hunter?"

"I am," said I, regretfully.

"I'm your cousin," he said with an oath. I was to learn he seldom
spoke without cursing. "Get in the rig."

We drove to his ranch some twenty miles away. My cousin talked
and swore the whole way, drinking from a bottle of rum he had on
the seat beside him. The man's talk brought the sweat out over me.
He had been the skipper of a windjammer that operated along the
African coast and judging from what he said, the ship was little better than a pirate. He told me fearful stories of keel-hauling and
flogging. I was soon to see that he was as brutal as his words. When
we reached his plantation, some native women were walking across
the fields, chattering and laughing together as women do.

"I've told those bloody natives to keep off my land," shouted my
cousin. Without more ado, he whipped out one of his great revolvers
and started shooting at them. The women fled screaming. One of
them tripped and fell. My cousin bellowed with laughter as the
bullets kicked up dust around her bare black behind. Whether any

of them were hit or not I cannot say but they all managed to escape while my cousin roared with delight at their terror.

My cousin's house was nothing but a mud-and-wattle hut with one room. This room had been divided into two compartments against my coming by hanging a strip of calico from a string that ran from wall to wall. This calico was a cheap, thin stuff, called "Americane" because it was made in the United States and shipped to Africa for trade with the natives. My cousin introduced me to his wife—a timid, thin woman who might once have been very pretty. She hardly dared to greet me and jumped nervously whenever my cousin spoke to her, as well she might, for it was a word and a blow with him. I was given one of the two compartments and a camp cot. I lay down on it, never more miserable in my life.

The next morning I went out with my cousin to look at the plantation. The place was in a miserable state of neglect. I knew enough of farming to realize that everything was being done wrong. My cousin was not a farmer and why he had taken it up was beyond me unless he was afraid to show his face along the seacoast. I tried to explain to him how fertilizer must be put in the soil and irrigation ditches dug but he would pay no attention to a young chap like me. The man's constant brutality was sickening. He kicked and struck his native boys seemingly for the pleasure of it, and when the time came to bring in the cows, he beat the poor creatures with a rawhide whip until they screamed like humans in their agony.

I stayed on the plantation for three months. I learned nothing of Africa during this time except how to speak Swahili. Although there are scores of native tribes in British East Africa, Swahili is the universal language, and nearly everywhere you go, there are at least some natives who can understand it. I could tell my cousin nothing about how to run a farm and the place was deteriorating daily. Every night I could hear him cursing his miserable little wife, and the curses were usually followed by blows. Yet I was only a boy and could do nothing. I held on, remembering what my father had said about coming back with my tail between my legs. I bitterly pictured myself crawling back to Shearington, asking my family to take me in and humbly apologizing to the minister and schoolmaster. How the old brutes would gloat! This was to be the end of all my fine dreams and ambitions. But at last flesh and blood could endure it no longer. I packed my few belongings and, getting a ride from a friendly farmer, returned to Nairobi.

What little money I had was in the Bank of India and there I went to get enough for my return passage. When the man behind the grill heard the Scotch burr in my voice, he looked at me curiously.

"What part of Scotland do you come from, lad?" he asked. There was a bit of a burr in his voice too.

"Shearington, seven miles from Dumfries," I told him.

"Why, you must know my brother, Major Cruickshanks of the Ayrshire Imperial Yeomanry."

Now it so happened I had been a trooper in the Ayrshire and Major Cruickshanks was my officer. He and I were good friends.

When the banker heard that, there was nothing for it but I must sit down with him and tell my adventures. When he heard that I was beaten and ready to go home, he would have none of it.

"A Scotsman is never licked, lad," he told me. "We'll have no more of that talk. I have a friend on the railroad and he'll give you a position as guard. That will tide you over until you find something more to your liking."

A week later I was put on the same Mombasa-Nairobi railroad on which I'd traveled three months before. They gave me a fine khaki uniform with a belt across the chest, but I cared nothing for such nonsense and never had the uniform on unless there was an official on the train. I found that as a railroad guard, I had a fine opportunity for shooting. Often we would see a lion on his kill beside the tracks, and in the early morning and evening we were as likely as not to pass a leopard. I carried my old Mauser in the chopbox where we kept our food and whenever we passed a likely-looking specimen, I would lean out the train window and bag him. Then I'd pull the Westinghouse release to stop the train, jump out with a native boy, and skin the beast. People were in no great hurry in those days and drivers were helpful. The engineer was a good sport and as he could watch the tracks ahead he would signal me with the whistle when there was game about. Three toots meant a leopard and two toots were a lion. If there was simply a passenger to be picked up, he gave one toot.

One day the engineer gave off a volley of toots. I looked out the window and saw my first herd of elephants grazing in the brush near the tracks. I had never seen an elephant before but I grabbed my rifle and jumped off the train. The engineer hurried over to stop me.

"I only meant you to look at them, not try to shoot one," he said to me. "Suppose they come for us?"

"Never fear, we'll knock them over like rabbits," I promised him.

Together we stole up on the herd. I had enough sense to stalk them from downwind and they had no idea what we were about. As we came up with them, the herd began to move with their grazing and drifted between us and the train. They did not keep in a body, but were scattered throughout the high brush. Suddenly they seemed to be on all sides of us, although none were actually downwind or they would have panicked from our scent. The engineer was a nervous man and he begged me not to shoot. "We'll be caught in the middle of a stampede. Let's get out of here," he pleaded.

I was not leaving there without a shot. I knew nothing about elephant shooting and did not realize that there are only a few places on an elephant where a .275 will penetrate. Still, I up with my Mauser and aiming for the shoulder of a bull carrying a nice pair of tusks, I squeezed the trigger.

The next instant hell broke lose. Elephants were running in all directions, trumpeting and screaming. The ground shook under our feet and some of them passed so close it seemed as though I could have touched them with a fishing rod. When the dust had settled, I found the engineer down on his knees praying. My bull had not dropped and I asked the man to help me spoor him. "If God in His infinite grace ever lets me get back to my engine, I'll never leave the train again," was all the man said. But my shot had told better than I thought. On our way back from Mombasa the next day I saw the dead bull lying not far from the tracks. I stopped the train and collected the tusks. I got five rupees a pound for the ivory, thirty-seven pounds for the two tusks, which was more than I made in two months as a guard.

For the first time I realized that it was possible for a man to make his living as a hunter—and a very good living, too. Such a thought had never occurred to me before. In Scotland, shooting was merely a recreation and that mostly for the very rich who could afford to raise pheasants and rent grouse moors. Being able to make my living with my gun seemed too good to be true, yet plenty of men in Nairobi were doing that very thing. One good point about being a railroad guard is that you get to meet people, and I made the acquaintance of some of the great white hunters of the period—to my mind, the most colorful group of men that ever lived.

There was Allan Black who decorated his hat with the tail tips of fourteen man-eating lions that he had killed. There was Bill Judd, one of the most famous ivory hunters in Africa, who was later killed by an infuriated bull. There was Fritz Schindelar, who always dressed in spotless white riding breeches and was said to be of royal blood. Fritz had been an officer in the Royal Hungarian Hussars and hunted lions from horseback, galloping alongside the big cats and shooting them with a carbine. He was finally killed by a lion that dragged him from the saddle. I met old "Karamojo Bell" who hunted elephant with a light .256 caliber rifle and knew the vital spots on the big bulls so perfectly that he needed no heavier weapon. I knew Leslie Simpson, an American hunter, reputed to be the greatest lion killer of his day, for in one year he had dispatched 365 lions. These men were my heroes and I longed to be like them.

3

Africa—Professional Hunter

I began my career as a professional hunter by shooting lions for their hides. Lion hides sold for a pound each in Mombasa and leopard skins for nearly as much. At that time, there were plenty of lions around the Tsavo area, some two hundred miles southeast of Nairobi. Lions were regarded as vermin, for they killed cattle and some were not adverse to picking up stray natives. In fact, a few years before, during the building of the railroad, lions killed so many of the Indian coolies working on the tracks that construction of the line had to be stopped until the man-eaters were hunted down and shot.

Personally, it has always been my belief that the coolies themselves virtually trained these animals to become man-eaters. The railroad company used to pay good sums to coolies who would volunteer to bury any of their comrades that died during the construction of the line. To save themselves trouble, these burial gangs would simply leave the corpses out in the bush to be eaten by the hyenas and lions. Lions are great scavengers and developed a liking for human flesh that made them a nuisance for many years.

Lion hunting was a dangerous business. Several of the tombstones in the Nairobi graveyard bear the simple inscription "killed by a lion." There were about forty professional lion hunters in the Nairobi area and at least half of them had been badly mauled at some time or other. Knowing next to nothing about these great cats, I set out with my old Mauser and a single native boy to make my mark as a famous lion hunter.

To hunt lions, you must understand how they think and behave. A man can understand dogs with fair ease, for dogs think much as humans do. But a lion is a cat and cats are curious beasts. They are temperamental creatures and highly subject to moods. Weather has a profound effect on them. Rainy weather makes them nervous, energetic, and keen. Very dry weather tends to make them lazy and indifferent. Lions hunt mainly at night. Darkness seems to act on them as a stimulant. The darker the night, the more likely lions are to be about. I never heard of a lion making a kill during the full moon. There are many cases of men meeting lions in the bush and scaring the animals off by shouting at them, yet I have also seen a lion charge a lorry and nearly knock it over in his attempts to get at the men inside. I will come to that story later.

Lions are fairly sociable animals and like to collect in groups. They do not take the keen pleasure in companionship that dogs do, but a lion likes to feel that he's not all alone. A group of lions is called a "pride," an old medieval term that was forgotten for centuries but has been revived in Africa and is now universally used. I have seen as many as eighteen lions in a pride, ranging from the grand old male down to the newborn cubs playing with their mothers' tails. Lions are polygamous and as each lioness comes into season, the lion will retire with her for a few days and then rejoin the pride. There may be several males in a pride, each with his own harem, but there is generally one head male and the others defer to him.

Although it would not be true to say that they hunt in packs, yet there is a certain organization about their work. The actual killing is frequently done by the lionesses or by young, active males. The old patriarch often holds back, directing the business and only throwing in his own weight and strength when necessary. A pride of lions on the hunt communicate with each other by deep grunts that have a strangely ventriloquial quality. It is almost impossible to tell where the noise comes from. Lions very seldom roar; I have heard the true roar only a few times in my life. They must have an amazing ability to see during the darkest night for I be-

lieve they hunt by sight rather than smell. They count on stampeding the game by their hunting grunts and sending it toward a spot
where the other lions are waiting. Of course, if they manage to get
close enough to their quarry, they will stalk and leap upon it much
as any cat does.

A pride of lions does not kill every night. After a kill, the lions
gorge themselves. Then they return to the carcass the next night
to finish it off. Often they will lie up the following night to digest
their food and rest. The third night, they will kill again.

There was little trouble about finding lions near Tsavo. The local
natives were only too glad to help me out. During the rainy season,
lions were apt to leave their usual range and wander great distances. At such times, they usually went alone rather than in
prides. Often a lion would find himself in a district where there
was no game. Then he would be forced to turn to the natives'
cattle for food. The natives keep their cattle penned up in thorn-
bush kraals at night and lions generally dislike entering these en-
closures. But they have an ingenious system of making the cattle
come to them. The lion moves upwind of the kraal and gives the
terrified cattle his scent. If the cattle do not stampede immediately,
the lion deliberately urinates on the ground. The strong odor of
the urine is enough to drive the cattle frantic with terror. They
stampede out of the kraal and scatter into the bush where the
lion can kill them at his leisure. I have no doubt that lions use a
similar method for stampeding herds of wild game.

When a native sent word that a lion had killed some of his
cattle, my boy and I would find where the lion had made the kill
and then start spooring the cat. On the sandy soil of the bush
country, spooring is fairly easy. The lion would generally be lying
up for the day in a patch of thick bush not too far away. We
could tell by his angry growls when we were getting close to him.
Then my boy would throw stones into the bush while the growls
rose in pitch and fury. Finally the lion would charge us, moving
so fast that a man often had time for only one shot.

There are few sights in nature more terrible than that of a

charging lion. He comes at a speed close to forty miles per hour, hitting top pace the instant he takes off. If a stalking lion can get to within fifty yards of an antelope, the antelope is doomed, for in spite of his great speed, the lion will overtake him within a dozen bounds. A man standing only thirty yards or so from a charging lion cannot afford to miss. A full-grown lion weighs some 450 pounds, and if he reaches you with the full force of his charge, he will knock you down as easily as a man overturns a mushroom with his foot.

I would stand with my rifle held ready while my boy was throwing stones to provoke the charge. When the charge came, I'd throw my rifle to my shoulder and fire instantly at the tawny shape that seemed to move with the speed of a shell. I have often thought that my early training with a shotgun, firing at waterfowl as they flashed across the Lochar Moss, was of great benefit to me in this type of hunting. If the shot is true, the lion often turns a somersault and comes smacking down maybe a dozen feet in front of you. If a man misses, he is indeed fortunate if he has time for a second shot before the lion is on him, with fangs busy and hind claws ripping him open.

Still, if a man trusts himself and his gun he can hunt lions under these conditions with no very great danger. But if he has to trouble about the shortcomings of someone else, the business becomes very uncertain indeed. During these early days, I formed a partnership with an older man who was considered to be a great lion hunter. This man's method of hunting was simple. He hunted by means of a "dumb killer." A dumb killer is a rifle lashed into position against a tree with a string leading from the trigger to a bit of bait. When a lion comes to eat the bait, he pulls the string and shoots himself.

The first time this man and I went out to visit his "dumb killers" we found that one of the guns had gone off but only wounded a lion. There were bits of hair and blood about but no sign of the lion. My partner shrugged and prepared to go on to the next dumb killer, but it had always been my feeling that no one should leave a wounded animal to die slowly in the bush. I insisted on spooring the lion, although my partner thought it was an unnecessary risk to follow a wounded lion into bush. Still, I prevailed and we started out on the blood spoor.

We followed the tracks until I saw by the quality of blood that the wounded animal must be very close. My partner said that he would climb a tree. He explained that he wished to look around for the lion.

I was willing enough to get rid of him as the man was so nervous I had no idea what he might do next and I dislike having a nervous man with a loaded gun behind me. I told him to go ahead and went on following the spoor.

While pushing my way through the cover, I suddenly saw the lion crouched in some high grass a few yards away watching me. It was a perfect shot and I slowly raised my rifle. I was about to fire when suddenly my friend's gun went off from the tree. The lion gave a scream of pain and came straight at me. I dropped my sights and fired without taking true aim, for there was no time. The lion fell dead almost at my feet.

My friend up the tree shouted, "John, are you alive?" "I am, and small thanks to you," I called back. When I came to examine the lion, I found that my helpful partner had done no more than shoot his tail off, thus not only provoking a charge at close quarters but ruining the hide. By a bit of luck, we happened to have another skin belonging to a mangy old beast that was worthless. We cut the tail off that specimen, sewed it onto the new skin, and did such a good job that the hide sold in Mombasa without a word being said.

After that experience, I decided to go back to hunting with my native boy. You must have some companion on these trips because you need two men to skin a lion. One man has to hold the legs apart while the other makes the incision. After several months we managed to reduce lion hunting to something of a system.

My boy and I would take the train to one of the small stations along the line and start out into the bush with no equipment but my rifle, cartridges, a skinning knife and a water flask. We would strike out through the bush until we came on a donga. Dongas are shallow ravines, usually filled with high grass and weeds which provide excellent cover. Lions often lie up in dongas during the heat of the day. I would take my stand on one side of a donga and my boy would walk along the other, throwing stones into the cover. If we heard any growls, he would continue his stone throwing until he flushed a lion. After shooting a lion, we would draw him and hang him by the hind legs to a tree limb before going on after another. I never killed more than four lions on one trip, for the green skins weighed forty pounds each and two of them were a good load for a man to pack out of the bush.

The main trouble with this type of hunting was that I never knew how many lions would bolt out of the cover when the boy started throwing stones. Once I was walking along the edge of a donga when I heard a sleeping lion snoring away in the high grass. I tossed in a stone to flush him. Instead of one lion, two came charging out straight at me. There was no time to think. I fired at one and saw him drop. The other gave a great leap and passed right over my head, knocking off my hat as he went.

These lions were not making a proper charge. The stone had frightened them and they were merely trying to escape. I just happened to be in their way.

After several months of this work, I began to fancy myself as a bushcraftsman. Like many another young lad, I became overconfident. In my opinion, every hunter goes through three stages. At first, he is nervous and unsure of himself. Then, as he masters the rudiments of bushcraft, he becomes cocky and feels that nothing can hurt him. Later, he learns what risks he must be prepared to take and which are nothing but plain foolishness. I was now in the second stage. I nearly lost my life learning the third lesson.

For some time I had been hunting with my native boy in the bush around Tsavo. Some seven miles from Tsavo was Kyulu Hill, where a blasting crew had set up camp to collect rock for the railway roadbed. Between the two places was a stretch of wild bush, completely uncrossed by trails or roads, and reputed to be very rich in lion. I decided to set out from Tsavo and walk to the hill, cutting through the bush and doing some shooting as I went.

Seven miles seemed an easy distance and I set out early in the morning, expecting to reach Kyulu by noon. I had no compass and did not even bother to take along a box of matches or a water bottle. I took my Mauser and a pocketful of ammunition. That was all. My native boy had gone to visit some relations of his so I was alone.

For a few miles all went well. The thick, umbrellalike thorn trees completely shut off the sun but that made walking cooler. There were plenty of rhino signs about and some lion. I was going along fine when I saw a line of footprints ahead of me. "Hello," I said to myself. "What's this?" for I was sure there was no one else in the bush. I stopped to examine them and found that they were my own. I was circling.

I was a cheeky youngster and a bit conceited, but at the sight of those footprints I lost all confidence in myself. That may sound like a small thing, but I tell you that when a man is alone in the bush with no one but himself to depend on, it is a terrible sensation. I felt panic for the first time in my life. I suddenly realized how much I had depended on my native boy, for natives seem to have a compass inside their heads and never get lost.

I sat down and tried to think. Then I made several attempts to climb the trees and see the sun but no one could force his way up through the four-inch thorns. I thought of backtracking myself to Tsavo but that would take many hours and I had no wish to spend the night in the bush. I decided to press on and run my chances of reaching Kyulu.

When night fell, I was still lost in the bush. I did not dare to stop for I was afraid that without water I would not survive another day in the barren brush. I struggled on. Rhino, suddenly flushed from the cover, went by me like express trains. That they missed hitting me was nothing short of a miracle. When dawn broke, I was nearly dropping from exhaustion but I saw no signs of coming to the end of the bush.

A few hours later, I came across my footprints again. Now I was completely lost, and there was no use trying to backtrack myself for I would be dead before I untangled the trail. I went on and on through the endless bush. Occasionally I came upon a rhino standing under a thorn tree. If he ran off, well and good. If he charged, I shot him, for I was too weak to run or dodge. I left them lying dead, caring nothing for the horns or hides although rhino horn was worth more than ivory, pound for pound.

Night fell again and I was still in the bush. I wandered about in a delirium, firing my rifle at anything I saw or fancied I saw in the darkness. When daylight came again I was out of my head. I remember feeling the thorn branches slapping me in the face as I staggered along but I no longer had any idea of what I was doing. I would have died that day if I had not stumbled upon a rhino watering hole, a foul mass of ooze and mud full of rhino droppings and pitted by holes made by their great feet. I fell into it and drank until I could drink no more.

After I had lain in the hole a couple of hours I felt better and kept on. But by evening I was as badly off as before. That night was another torture. By morning I was desperate from lack of food and mad with thirst. I was beginning to go out of my head again as I reeled on through the never-ending bush. I was running out of ammunition and when I came across a rhino I had to give way for him. Detouring around the brute in my enfeebled condition often lost me as much ground as I'd been able to cover in an hour.

Then I saw something shimmering through the bush like silver heat waves. At first I paid no attention. As I got closer, I stopped and forced my eyes to focus on the things. They were the telegraph wires that ran from the railroad to Kyulu. I fought my way through the brush toward them, still fearful it was only delirium. When I reached the telegraph poles I fell sobbing to my knees. I was saved. I had only to follow the line to Kyulu and the camp.

While I was recovering from the effects of this trip, I stayed in Nairobi. I had begun to achieve a small reputation as a white hunter and I was asked to many of the dances. At one of these events I met a Miss Hilda Banbury whose father owned a fine music shop in Nairobi. Hilda seemed to me the prettiest, gentlest girl I had ever laid eyes on. She seemed to like me too, but no one could have been more surprised than I when I asked her to be Mrs. Hunter and she said yes.

With the responsibility of this lovely young girl on me, I determined to turn over a new leaf and give up the risks and uncertainties of professional hunting. A relative in Scotland had died, leaving me a little money, and I decided to go into the transportation business. Nairobi had begun to grow rapidly and there was a great demand for goods. I invested my capital in mules, horses and wagons and started hauling freight for the settlers. I am a poor businessman, and although I worked hard, in a year I was bankrupt and had lost every penny I'd put into the venture.

I told Hilda the bad news. She took it very calmly, although there was a child on the way.

"Why, John, I've been waiting for you to lose that money," she told me cheerfully. "You were never meant for business. Now it's gone, you can be a white hunter . . . which you always wanted to be in the first place."

With faith like that, what can a man do? I went to see my friend, Leslie Simpson, the American white hunter. When Leslie heard I wanted to guide parties and needed a job at once, he rubbed his chin.

"Two American sportsmen have just arrived in town who want to take a safari across the Serengeti Plains," he told me. "There's a great extinct volcano in the heart of that country called Ngorongoro. According to the accounts, there is more game in that crater than any man has ever seen before. As far as I know, no regular safari has ever crossed the Serengeti although a few ivory hunters have been there and a strange man by the name of Captain Hurst is said to have a home in the crater. I told these Americans I didn't know of any man who would care to take them through, but if you want the job, it's yours."

I thanked Leslie and hurried home to tell Hilda I was starting on my career as a white hunter and guide.

4

Serengeti Safari

The following day I met my two American clients at their hotel. They were big, hearty chaps—successful business-men from the western part of the United States. "Captain, we want you to take us into fresh territory that hasn't been all shot out," one of them explained while his friend nodded approval. "What we want is trophies and we don't mind roughing it some to go where the high-class stuff is."

Aside from Leslie Simpson, these men were almost the first Americans I had met and the nasal twang in their voices was new to me, although my own Scotch burr must have seemed equally strange to them. Their slang was infectious. After an hour's con-versation I heard myself saying, "You bet, that's a whale of an idea," and when I returned home that evening, I called to Hilda, "Well, looks like everything's O.K." I couldn't understand why she stared at me in astonishment.

My clients were very keen to make the Ngorongoro trip. I ex-plained to them frankly I knew nothing about the place but that according to rumor the crater was the finest game country in Africa. I was concerned about crossing the great Serengeti Plains during the dry season. The plains are a vast, semi-desert country extending for hundreds of miles across southern Kenya and I had no notion where the water holes were or what game we would find as food for our native porters. I cautioned my clients that the trek would be hard and possibly dangerous but my warnings only served to make them more eager.

I was pleased with their enthusiasm but I knew well the difficulties of taking a safari across such country. I went to Leslie Simpson for advice and he came up with an excellent suggestion.

"I know an old-time Dutch hunter named Fourrie," he told me. "The chap's somewhat under a cloud because of ivory poaching and cattle running, but he's one of the few men who's been through that country. Fourrie is in Nairobi now and I believe he'd guide you to Ngorongoro."

Fourrie turned out to be a lean, shrewd-eyed man old enough to be my grandfather. Early in life, a rhino had taken him unexpectedly from behind and so lacerated his thigh muscles that he walked with a limp. Like many of the old ivory hunters, he had made and lost several fortunes—always sinking the money he made from a successful trip into a still bigger safari. As long as his luck held, the returns from these expeditions continued to grow but a few unsuccessful trips had wiped out all his profits. Fourrie had then taken to cattle running—driving herds past the government guards into districts where they could be sold for a high price. In spite of the old fellow's shaky morals, he was one of the finest bushcraftsmen I have ever seen. Down on his luck, he was glad to guide us to the crater for a few pounds.

We outfitted in Arusha, two hundred miles south of Nairobi en route to the Serengeti Plains. Our first consideration was porters. The only men available were the Wa-Arusha tribesmen, a miserable lot, lazy and cantankerous. They are an agricultural people, the women doing all the work while the men amuse themselves drinking and painting their bodies in weird designs with burnt bone and red clay. Fortunately, Leslie Simpson had loaned me one of his men to act as our head boy. This fellow's name was Andolo and he was the best field taxidermist in Africa, having been trained in the business some years before by an expedition sent out by the American Museum of Natural History in New York. I knew Andolo would be a great help in preserving our trophies and also act as a top sergeant to keep the unruly porters in order.

The modern white hunter can hardly realize the trouble and

difficulties inherent in the old-fashioned foot safari. Today, safaris are made by heavy-duty lorries. Riding comfortably in one of these powerful machines, you can carry plenty of equipment and need not worry about lack of food or the cruel heat of the sun. You can cover a hundred miles a day in comparative comfort while twenty miles a day was a long, hard grind on foot. Best of all, a lorry is not temperamental. Unlike a porter, a lorry will not suddenly desert you because it becomes homesick for its wife or because the going is too hard. Unless you have had to endure the emotional outbreaks of several dozen porters, you can hardly appreciate the sterling qualities of a lorry.

Our safari consisted of 150 porters. Everything we needed for the three months' trip would have to be carried on their heads. Nearly a third of them would be carrying food for the others. Even so, we would have to stop continually to shoot game to eke out our supplies. Although shooting game in Africa sounds simple, yet the animals must be stalked and this takes time and slows up the march. Also, you may find yourself in country where there is little or no game. Only a small amount of water could be carried and so we depended on finding water holes.

All the equipment had to be broken down into sixty-pound loads, the recognized weight for a porter to carry on his head. For food, I leaned heavily on tinned goods, which are very convenient although heavy. In addition to our tents, camp beds, mosquito nettings, cooking utensils, guns and ammunition, we took along several hundred pounds of salt for preserving the trophies.

Before we left Arusha, Fourrie suggested that we give the porters a big feast to put them in a good mood. As the Wa-Arusha have few cattle and are poor hunters, they seldom taste meat. As a result, they have a passion for it. We purchased a fat bullock and the porters prepared for a banquet. They invited all their friends and relatives. As everyone in the group is, at least, distantly related to everyone else, the entire tribe arrived for dinner.

Hours before the meal was due to begin, long streams of natives came pouring into our camp from all directions. The men wore

strips of greasy calico around their waists, loaded down with juju
charms purchased from the local witch doctor to protect them on
the journey. The women were mostly naked except for the grease
on their bodies and a few forest flowers stuck at important points.
The average native woman is far from engaging, especially if she
follows the fashion of shaving her head so the undulating bumps
of her skull can be seen. But several of these damsels were quite
handsome and possessed points which might be described as
indicative of good breeding. The group, waiting for the distribution of the meat, became very excited and worked themselves into a
noisy gabble that sounded like the chatter of monkeys. As they
grew gayer, they hurled all kinds of abusive epithets at each
other, ceaselessly and at a speed well-nigh incredible. Every sally
was greeted by bursts of uncontrolled laughter, the younger girls
rolling on the ground with delight.

One of the Americans said to me, "I don't figure we'll have any
trouble with these good-natured guys." I felt the same way but
Fourrie seemed more doubtful. The next morning his misgivings
were amply justified. The cool, early morning hours are the best
time to travel but long after sun-up our Wa-Arusha porters were
still sitting around their campfires leisurely eating breakfast.
Andolo, our head boy, became so angry he went around kicking
over the porters' kettles to make them hurry. Instantly the Wa-
Arusha went wild with rage. Some of the men fell to the ground,
chewing grass in their fury. The rest grabbed their knives and went
for Andolo. Fourrie and I had to hold them off with our rifles.
Andolo was so frightened that he wanted to return to Nairobi at
once and I had trouble persuading him to stay.

After this inauspicious beginning, we slowly got started. The
long line of sullen porters stretched out for half a mile. We had
been lucky enough to get a few donkeys to carry the heavier
loads and these patient beasts were a great help. Because of the
rough nature of the country, we did not take any wheeled vehicles,
although an oxcart or two would have made a vast difference.

Our first march was only a few miles so as to condition the

porters for the long trek ahead. Also, during the first day or so of a safari there are innumerable unforeseen quarrels and difficulties that make it impossible to move at any speed. In the night, some of the porters deserted. You must always count on losing a few men while you are still close to their native village. Fourrie and I had allowed for this and had hired enough porters so we could afford to let the missing men go.

As we went deeper toward the Serengeti, our porters settled down into some semblance of order. They had much to learn about safari duties. I had a great amount of trouble finding a competent camp cook. I had hired a likely-looking chap in Arusha. One evening I entered the cook tent to find him wiping the grease off an antelope roast he was cooking and smearing it on his own naked body. At the expression on my face, the man guiltily started rubbing the grease off his body and putting it back on the roast.

I wish people who write of Africa as though the whole land were a tropical glade full of shady trees and purling streams could have been with us on that bare, waterless waste. The country was nothing but unbroken, flat plains constantly fanned by strong currents of hot wind. There was no shade. Our sweat soaked through our clothes and then dried almost instantly in the intense heat, leaving deposits of salt over our khaki jumpers. On rare occasions when we came on pools of stagnant water the foul stuff semed to taste of various horrible smells. Our porters constantly demanded meat, but game was very scarce. There had been an outbreak of rinderpest in the district and the few surviving animals were nothing but skin and bones. The white skeletons of the others strewed the plains. In the evening, we pitched camp wherever we happened to stop and fell asleep listening to the hot wind howling over that miserable tract of desolation.

Several times during the interminable trek we would see that strange phenomenon of the desert, the mirage. Occasionally during the day the wind stopped. Then the heat waves would begin to gather. They appeared to race across the barren ground like an endless waving chain. Beyond them, the veldt would slowly turn to a watery plain before our eyes. I thought what a death trap this would be for a man lost on the desert as I had once been lost in the Tsavo bush. The poor fellow would stagger on and on in pursuit of that great lake of cool, fresh water which would constantly keep receding before him—just as the end of the rainbow moves away from an eager child looking for the legendary pot o' gold. The illusion of water was perfect, except that an animal would occasionally walk through the reflection. In the mirage light, small beasts like jackals were greatly exaggerated in size and the scrawniest gazelle seemed to carry record horns.

My two clients endured this long trek remarkably well. In fact, they actually seemed to enjoy the hardships. They trudged on day after day, cracking jokes with each other or me, and when we happened to find some Grant gazelles with good horns, they were delighted. These Grants were our first trophies and I was glad my clients were so pleased with them. Although the gazelles were as good as any I'd seen, Fourrie merely looked at them and smiled. "Wait until we reach the crater," was all he said.

We had traveled over one hundred miles and Ngorongoro was still not in sight. I began to be concerned. The porters were continually grumbling over the lack of meat and water and threatening to turn back. The country seemed to be growing worse. I spoke to Fourrie and he agreed that the porters were on the point of revolt. "But tomorrow, we'll reach N'garuka Springs," he promised me. "We can rest there a few days before pushing on to the crater."

I supposed the "springs" were nothing but another of the muddy, stinking, water holes we had encountered. Still there was nothing to do but keep on.

The next afternoon while we were plodding across the seemingly endless waste, Fourrie stopped and pointed ahead. I could hardly believe my eyes. Across the dirty brown of the desert was a splash of the purest emerald, as though a giant with a green paintbrush had dabbed the spot.

"N'garuka Springs," said Fourrie. "Fresh water and fig trees. We'll camp under the shade."

Our exhausted porters shouted with delight when they saw the oasis ahead. Our donkeys winded the water and galloped forward so desperately we were hard put to hold them. The whole safari broke into a clumsy trot as we neared the trees. When we reached the shade, the intense heat of the sun was cut off and the air was delightfully cool. A gin-clear stream ran beneath the tall boles, sparkling in the dappled shade. We drank and washed our hot faces in the stream and then lay on the banks, watching the precious stuff. Just to see and touch it was pure delight.

Hundreds of green pigeons were feeding on the figs and our sportsmen put in an hour of shooting while the boys pitched camp. These pigeons are very fast and a test for the best wing shot. Later, I found a herd of hippo in the stream although the water was so shallow it scarcely covered their broad backs. How the animals got there I have no idea. I shot one as meat for the porters. In an incredibly short space of time there was scarcely a vestige of flesh left.

We camped for ten days by the stream, resting and repairing minor damage caused by the trek. Then at daybreak one morning we regretfully left the wonderful spot and pushed on for Ngorongoro crater.

After some hard trekking, we saw ahead of us the tall, tree-covered slopes of the great extinct volcano. Ngorongoro rises nine thousand feet from the plains and the top was draped in mists. By evening we reached the foot of the great south wall of the volcano and camped there beside a little stream. We were in a tropical fairyland, surrounded by huge trees that formed a roof of branches above our heads. Brilliantly colored birds flitted between the great trunks. I remember especially the lovely plaintain eaters with their dark blue bodies and crimson wings. Bands of monkeys swung through the branches overhead, chattering at us. There were plenty of elephant and rhino spoors about and also many lion signs.

As we sat around our campfire that evening, we could hear lions giving their hunting grunts around us in the dark. Our donkeys began to bray with terror and jerk on their ropes. Fourrie and I moved them into the circle of light thrown by the campfire and tied them more securely. Fourrie told me that lions will seldom attack a tethered animal but try to make the creature stampede into the darkness and then pull him down. But I believe these lions were more curious than hungry. Lions are very inquisitive beasts. A pride of lions generally live in a certain definite district a few miles square which they regard as their own property. When humans enter the area the lions come over to see what kind of creature these strangers may be. After I had gone to bed, I could hear the lions padding around the camp, giving vent to their deep, soughing sighs. At times, I could even hear their deep breathing. But they made no attempt to attack the donkeys near the fire, and at last, curiosity satisfied, they moved away.

Our clients insisted on sleeping with revolvers tied to their wrists. Americans are very fond of these handguns, although I, myself, could never see much value to them. No handgun was ever made that could stop the charge of an elephant, rhino or even a lion. Then, too, accurate aiming with a handgun is almost impossible, for your hand tends to shake as you look along the sights and there is no stock to brace against your shoulder. However, I have seen some Americans who through long practice have become very expert with these interesting toys.

At dawn the next morning, we started the ascent of the crater. We followed the game trails, for animals are excellent surveyors and their paths are cleverly engineered to give the easiest climb. Nevertheless, our porters puffed and panted as they struggled up the steep slope through bamboo growths and mimosa bush. It was late afternoon before we reached the lip of the old volcano.

Every man in our party stopped dead as he arrived at the top and looked down on the vast crater, stretching away fifteen miles to the far edge of the encircling lip. All the tales I had heard of Ngorongoro were as nothing compared to the great herds spread out over those green fields as though shaken out of a giant pepper pot. The crater seethed with game. The grass was cropped as fine as a lawn by the thousands of beasts. In the distance the herds seemed to melt together into a trembling mass of white and fawn. There were zebra, eland, giraffe, topi, waterbuck, reedbuck, bushbuck, steinbok, Thomson gazelles, Grant gazelles, impala, wildebeest, duiker, oribi, and ostrich. This was how all the African veldt must have looked before the coming of the white man. Here in this isolated crater was the last great stronghold of game.

My two clients behaved like children suddenly turned loose in a candy store. They shot until their rifles were too hot to hold. The daylight hours were all too short to enable them to satisfy their passion for more hides and horn. "Trigger itch" had them in its grip. Later I was to discover that this is a common trait among Americans when first confronted by the abundance of African game after the shooting restrictions in their own country.

After their first enthusiasm had died down, my clients became determined to bag a world's record trophy. I must confess that I became sick of the sight of Rowland Ward's *Records of Big Game* on the breakfast table every morning. At that hour, a bowl of porridge looked far sweeter to me. Impala were particularly fine in the crater and we spent days studying the different beasts through a pair of binoculars, searching for a record head. At last we located our trophy, a fine animal with horns that looked to be well over thirty inches long. Beside him was standing another first-rate buck but slightly smaller. One of my clients took careful aim and fired, but, alas, it was the smaller antelope that fell. Here was a tragedy. We measured the long, curving horns in every way possible but twenty-eight inches was the best we could make out of them— an excellent trophy but still short of the record. To me, it was sportsman's luck and nothing could be done about it. But my clients were more determined. When we got back to camp, they held a long conference and then approached me with a proposition.

"Hey, captain, you can steam a gun stock to alter bend and cast, can't you?"

I admitted it.

"O.K., then. How about steaming these horns to stretch the ferrules and get a record?"

I don't know if this would have given us a new world's record or glue, but I declined to make the experiment.

Often in the early mornings when we were out after game, we would see a lion in the shade of an acacia tree. These crater lions were magnificent animals and it is my belief that no lions in Africa can equal them for size and manes. In a perfect climate with plenty of food around them, it is no wonder that they grow to be giants. Our sportsmen were eager to bag some of these fine specimens and I was no less keen. But I soon found out that hunting lions on the open floor of the crater was a very different matter from shooting them in dongas.

Today, with motorcars, the sportsman can drive up to a pride of lions, for the big cats have no fear of cars. Bagging lions in the flat, short-grassed crater on foot was another matter. Lions have excellent vision, and the moment they spotted us they did not take their eyes off our stalking figures for a moment. If we lay down on our bellies and tried to crawl closer, the lion would sit up on his hunkers like a dog to get a better view. If we tried circling, we might gain a few yards but the lion still had the situation well in hand and just as we got within range, he would rise and trot off. Once he was on the move, we would never come up with him, for a lion's skill in concealment is extraordinary. I have seen a big lion crouch low and take cover behind some grass that I thought would scarcely hide a hare.

Fourrie and I debated how best to approach these beasts. We decided that the easiest method was to dress one of our sportsmen in the skin of an ostrich and let him walk up to the lion, keeping downwind. This seemed an excellent plan. I shot an ostrich and instructed Andolo to skin the bird. He was halfway through his task when Fourrie strolled over.

"I've just thought of something," he remarked. "Ostrich is a lion's favorite food."

After reconsidering the matter, I decided to use some other method for getting the trophy.

We next tried baiting the lions. Either Fourrie or I would shoot an antelope and drag the animal near a patch of cover where I thought lions might be lying up for the day. We would slit open the game's belly to let out the stomach gases and increase the scent, taking care to place the carcass upwind of the cover. After putting out a number of these baits in the evening, we would return to them in the morning to see if lions had been feeding.

It was a simple matter to tell what types of animals had been at the kills. A lion always chews the gristly tops of the rib bones, for these are special tidbits for him. Also, a lion will urinate nearby and afterward scratch heavily with his hind claws, the scratch marks being very conspicuous. A leopard behaves in the same manner but leaves no claw marks. A hyena leaves chunks of splintered bone and his spoor will show the marks of his doglike claws.

We were always careful to see if any hairs from the lions' manes were sticking to the bait, for these hairs give you an idea of the lion's color. Black-maned lions are the most sought after as trophies. Some of these crater lions had manes that came down to their feet.

Unfortunately for our plans, there were so many scavengers in the district that the lions seldom had a chance to get at the baits. At night, hyenas and jackals would strip the carcasses nearly clean before the lions could reach the spot. During the day, the bait would be so covered by vultures that nothing could be seen but a wriggling mass of black feathers and scrawny necks. Sometimes a hyena would take a flying leap on top of this tangle and break a hole through by the mere weight of his body. We often saw leopards feeding beside the vultures. I have noticed that when leopards have finished, they will often grab one of the vultures and carry it off with them—I suppose as dessert.

A few scavengers at the bait is a good thing for they seem to give a lion confidence. The yapping calls of the jackals and the long *you-e-you* howl of the hyena attracts the big cats. But when there are so many that the meat vanishes before the lions can arrive, then baiting is useless. We tried covering the baits with thorn bushes but no matter how many of the spiky branches we piled on the kill, the scavengers always seemed able to pull them off.

Both stalking and baiting having failed, Fourrie and I set out to study the habits of these crater lions carefully and find out the best way to give our sportsmen a shot at them. After several days of watching the beasts, Fourrie said to me, "The lions seem to spend the nights hunting and feeding. Then at dawn they start back for the shelter of the reed beds. Why not put our clients in ambush among the reeds and waylay them on their return?"

We tried this plan and it worked well. Within a few days we had four magnificent lions; three fine black-maned specimens and one with a great platinum and orange mane that I considered the best trophy I had ever seen up to that time.

I have no hesitation in admitting the great debt I owed to Fourrie on this safari. The old Boer was as quick with his wits as with his trigger finger. One day after our clients had shot a lion, I told the boys to tie the hide on a donkey for transportation back to camp. The donkey paid no attention while the green skin was being strapped to his back. But once he was loose, he went crazy and raced over the plains bucking like a mad thing. He got rid of his furry load in a few bounds and then bolted off across the crater. I thought he was gone for good, but a few days later we saw him with a bunch of zebras, seemingly a member in good standing with the herd. Our boys tried to catch him, but when the zebras ran, the donkey stayed with them. Then Fourrie told us to hobble the rest of our donkeys and turn them loose. As soon as the fugitive saw his friends, he trotted over and joined them.

Fourrie also helped me out when our clients wanted to shoot elephant and rhino in the wooded slopes of the crater's walls. I hadn't expected to find such big game at Ngorongoro and had brought only a small supply of nickel-jacketed bullets. Our ordinary soft points did not have sufficient penetration power to pierce the thick skulls of elephant or rhino. Fourrie solved this problem by withdrawing the soft points and reversing them in the cartridges.

With this back-to-front method, the bullets' nickeled bases were foremost and gave us the necessary penetration power.

So far we had seen nothing of Captain Hurst, the lone Englishman, who had a small ranch in the crater. But while we were in Ngorongoro, a runner arrived from the District Commissioner in Arusha. The man had trotted the entire distance in spite of the heat and lack of water, carrying his message in the end of a cleft stick. The message said that Captain Hurst was dead. His native boys, not knowing we were in the district, had sent word to Arusha to find out what to do. The Commissioner asked me to investigate the circumstances of his death and bring back the man's belongings with me to Arusha.

We went to Captain Hurst's ranch and found his boys sitting around aimlessly waiting for instructions. The head boy told me that their master had been killed ten days before by an elephant. Hurst had wounded the animal with a shoulder shot. The bull had made off toward a thick clump of brush and Hurst, thinking to intercept the animal, had gone around the bush from the other side. He met the bull face to face. The elephant grabbed the man in his trunk before Hurst could raise his rifle.

Hurst's head boy told me, "The elephant carried bwana Hurst to the nearest tree and beat him against the trunk. The bwana screamed and the elephant beat him again. The bwana screamed a second time and the elephant dashed him against the tree still harder. Then the bwana did not scream any more so the elephant dropped him and went away."

There was no reason to doubt the boy's story.

Captain Hurst had lived in a little thatched cottage overlooking the crater. He could sit on his front porch in the evenings and watch the grandest collection of game that mortal man has ever seen grazing around him. The climate of Ngorongoro is about perfect. Although the mountain is only a few hundred miles from the equator, the high altitude keeps the crater cool and pleasant. In that wonderful spot it is always spring. The cold of winter or the heat of summer never reaches it. With game in plenty around him, a spring of cool water by the door, and forests full of fruit, a man could live there as happily as though in the Garden of Eden. Looking around me, I felt that I would be content to spend the rest of my life in Ngorongoro.

The captain had few possessions. Among them was a small flock of ostriches he kept in a thorn-bush corral. Apparently he had considered going into the ostrich-feather trade. I opened the gate of the corral to give the birds their liberty but they refused to leave. Finally I had to burn the corral to force them out. The stupid creatures returned as soon as the fire died down and stood on the hot ashes. Whatever happened to them I do not know, for they showed no sign of leaving the place even if they starved to death.

A more difficult problem was a fine pack of Australian kangaroo hounds that Captain Hurst had for lion hunting. These great dogs resembled large, rough-coated greyhounds. They were in poor shape, for the native boys had paid little attention to them since their master's death. I gave orders to have the pack fed, and the poor brutes seemed to understand my kind intentions for they followed me everywhere.

Our clients did not wish to return to Arusha with Captain Hurst's effects. They wanted to continue east across the Serengeti to Tabora where they could get a train to the coast. Their desires were naturally our first consideration. Fourrie and I agreed that we would go on with them to Tabora, and when our clients had left, Fourrie would remain there to arrange for the preparation and shipping of the trophies. I would return with the porters to Ngorongoro, pick up Captain Hurst's belongings and return to Arusha.

The trip down the east side of the crater and across the Serengeti to Tabora was accomplished without incident. There I said good-by to our clients and started back to Ngorongoro with the porters, leaving Andolo, our head boy, to help Fourrie prepare the trophies for shipment. Fourrie's last words were "Keep the porters full of meat and you'll not have any trouble with them." I found this an invaluable bit of advice.

Back in Ngorongoro crater, I stayed at Captain Hurst's cottage for a few days preparing for the long trip to Arusha. The kangaroo hounds were now in excellent shape and I could not resist spending a few days hunting with them. In lion hunting, the hounds made all the difference. As soon as the pack sighted a lion, on the plains, they would take off after him and bring him to bay, forming a circle around him. The lion was kept so busy slapping at the dogs that the hunter could walk up within a few yards of him and place his shots. The dogs were smart enough never to close with a lion and kept well away from his great paws. If the lion charged, the hounds would open to let him through and then chase him again, snapping at his flanks until they turned him. I collected five good lions, knowing that their hides would bring a good price in Nairobi. It never occurred to me that the day would come when lions would be carefully protected as a valuable game animal. In those days, we regarded them simply as a dangerous nuisance.

The lions got their revenge a few days later when we set out for Arusha. Among Captain Hurst's effects were a number of large milk cans, at that time a fairly valuable commodity in East Africa. We tied these cans on the backs of our donkeys and set out. Once on the Serengeti Plains, the heat was so intense that the boys begged me to camp by day and travel during the night. I reluctantly consented, although I had my doubts about night traveling. We rested during the heat of the day and set out again that evening.

We had gone only a few miles when the hounds began to bark. For a few minutes I could not imagine the cause. Then I heard the grunting of lions around us. They had winded our donkeys and were circling the safari looking for a chance to attack them. I shouted to bunch the donkeys together and form a ring around them. This we did, but the lions were not to be foiled. They deliberately moved upwind of us to give the donkeys their scent.

As soon as the donkeys smelt the lions, they went mad with terror. The boys clung to their heads, but the donkeys reared and bucked, kicking out with their heels with alarming accuracy. As the lions moved in closer, the terrified donkeys became impossible to hold. The whole place was in an uproar, the donkeys braying, the lions grunting, the boys yelling, and the tin milk cans clattering like gongs. I fired my rifle at the lions but got only savage growls as answers. The donkeys had become impossible to hold. I shouted to the boys to let the damned animals go. The beasts promptly bolted into the darkness, the milk cans on their backs sounding like a boiler factory. The hounds would have followed if I hadn't restrained them.

I knew the donkeys would be killed and eaten but there was nothing I could do. I told the boys we would spend the rest of the night at the spot and then sat down and lit my pipe, for there is much comfort in the weed. Afterward I scooped out a hollow in the sand for my bed, used my helmet for a pillow, and slept until dawn.

When it was light, I started out on the donkeys' trail. I soon came upon the spoor of ten lions, one male and nine females. To my surprise, I saw that the lions' tracks were headed in another direction. A few miles further on, I came on our donkeys huddled together on the open plain. There was no sign of the lions.

I backtracked the donkeys and found that the night before our terrified draft animals had charged right into the center of the pride of lions. The milk cans on the donkeys' backs had made such a racket that the lions had fled, not knowing what sort of creatures was attacking them. I believe this is the only case in history of donkeys defeating a pride of lions in combat.

Our safari reached Arusha without further trouble and I had Captain Hurst's property shipped on to his brother who lived in Nairobi. A few days later I happened to meet this gentleman. He told me that on his brother's death he had inherited a deed giving him a ninety-nine-year lease on Ngorongoro crater. "I have no use for the place," he told me. "I'll gladly rent it to you for forty-five rupees a year."

I talked the proposition over with Hilda. We agreed that the crater was so inaccessible that unless we chose to bury ourselves for life there, the lease would have no value. Ah, if we could only have foreseen that some day Ngorongoro crater would be a two days' trip from Nairobi by car and one of the show places of Africa! But then real estate seemed worthless. There were thousands of square miles to be had for the asking and no hint that some day the veldt would be covered by farms and that little towns would spring up like toadstools. To us, the only wealth was in ivory and hides. So I told Mr. Hurst that I could not accept his offer.

After this trip, I was definitely launched as a white hunter. I learned by painful experience the truth of an old white hunters' saying, "It's not the wild beasts that are the problem . . . it's the clients."

5

Clients, Brave and Otherwise

I spent much of my next twenty years as a white hunter, generally outfitting in Nairobi and going everywhere from the Belgian Congo to Southern Abyssinia. During those years I guided the Prince and Princess Schwarzenberg, the Baron and Baroness Rothschild, many of the lesser Continental nobility, a number of rajahs and maharajahs, and a scattering of American millionaires. I also guided many sportsmen in very moderate circumstances who had spent years saving up enough money so they could have a go at African big game.

Like most white hunters, I was usually employed by one of the big organizations in Nairobi that make a business of outfitting safaris for clients. Although I have worked for several of these organizations, I spent most of my time with Safariland, Inc., a company that has been in operation since the turn of the century and has arranged safaris for Radclyffe Dugmore, the Martin Johnsons, the Aga Khan, and in recent years MGM's *King Solomon's Mines*. Safariland keeps a number of white hunters on its payroll and during the boom years of the twenties, as soon as one of us returned from a safari, he was immediately sent out on another.

I never knew beforehand if my next client would be a nervous individual who merely wanted to camp a few miles outside of Nairobi so he could later boast of having been "on safari through the wilds of Africa" or a keen sportsman who was willing to risk his life to obtain a fine trophy. Whatever my clients wanted, I did my best to provide, whether it was a record head or an easy tour of the game country.

It has been said that a white hunter must combine "the expert lore of an Indian scout, the cool nerve of a professional soldier, and the ability to mingle easily with the rich and aristocratic." One of the most successful white hunters with Safariland put the matter to me somewhat differently. "Hunter," he said, "you must always remember that only ten per cent of your work is hunting. Ninety per cent is keeping your clients amused." Now I was never much of a clubman and so Safariland tried to send me out with sportsmen who were mainly interested in obtaining trophies. But during the rush seasons no such distinction could be made. Then I had to learn to study my clients and try to gratify their whims. This I did— up to certain limits.

Among my first aristocratic clients were a French count and his countess who wanted a few African trophies for their château in Normandy. It was fashionable for the European nobility to be able to say that they had been big-game hunting in Africa and we white hunters profited by the fad. With the help of Safariland, I arranged a luxury safari for the couple. I saw to it that we had big, comfortable tents divided up into several small dressing and bathrooms. The couple had eight trained native boys as their personal servants and I took along enough supplies to stock a small hotel. Before we left, the count made it clear that the only commodity he was interested in was a plentiful supply of whiskey. I took along more whiskey bottles than I did cartridges and it was well I did so. We could have done without the cartridges, but without the whiskey I fear I'd have had a dead count on my hands and no mistake.

A few days out, I spotted a fine black-maned lion and took my clients over to him. When the countess saw the lion, she screamed and wanted to go back to Nairobi. The count lifted his gun with shaking hands and then asked anxiously, "Suppose I shoot and don't kill, what does he do, eh?"

"He may charge, but I'll stop him with my rifle," I told the gentleman.

The count shook his head. "I think I need a drink," he said and off we went back to camp. That was all the lion hunting the count did. But that evening the couple called me in to have drinks with them.

"I have thought of a clever idea," said the count. "You are a hunter, no? So you go and hunt. I will stay here and you get me nice trophies to show my friends."

I agreed that this was an excellent suggestion, saving us all time and worry. I got them several good trophies and the countess posed on each one for photographs wearing her shooting togs and holding her rifle. She always asked me anxiously, "Hunter, how do I look?" I knew little about such matters but I always told her she looked very well indeed and my answer seemed to please her. The countess wanted her husband to pose on a few of the trophies, but he was seldom in a condition to sit up long enough for the camera to click. So she and I spent most of the time together, wandering about the veldt and having tea by the banks of a stream or under one of the big acacia trees.

One evening after I had turned in, the flap of my tent opened and the countess came in wearing a lace Parisian nightgown that covered her but poorly and carrying a beer glass full of whiskey. She sat down on the edge of my cot, offered me a drink, and then took one herself. "Hunter, my friend, I am lonely," she told me sadly. "Countess, where's your husband?" I asked her. She looked at me a long time. "Hunter, you Englishmen ask the strangest questions," she said and flounced out of my tent. For the next few days she was a bit cool toward me but when the safari was over, both she and the count kissed me as they said good-by. A very affectionate couple. I enjoyed meeting them.

It is a curious fact that some people lose their heads when they go into the bush and forget ordinary conventions. They seem to feel that they have escaped from civilization and all its responsibilities. Women succumb to this strange state of mind more often than men. I have seen carefully reared ladies whose conduct in the bush shocked even the broad-minded natives. There is much of the savage in all of us, but a man will work out his primitive instincts by shooting while a certain type of woman often turns to sex. Usually the white hunter is the object of her devotion. In the bush a white hunter cuts a fine figure. He is efficient, brave, and picturesque. These ladies never stop to think how this dashing individual would appear on the dance floors of London or in a Continental drawing room. One of the greatest scandals of Kenya came about as the result of a lady's unwise attachment to a white hunter.

This tragedy occurred near the turn of the century. The white hunter involved was internationally known, having established a reputation by killing several man-eating lions. One of the parties he guided consisted of a wealthy man and his attractive young wife. When the safari returned to Nairobi, the husband was not with them. The hunter announced that his client had shot himself with a revolver while delirious. However, the hunter could not stop his native boys from talking and the story got around that the man had met with foul play. The government sent a police officer to investigate. The officer backtracked the safari and found where the client had been buried. He dug up the body and discovered that the man had been shot in the back of the head by a heavy-caliber rifle. Meanwhile, the hunter and the dead man's wife had left the country. As far as I know, they were never heard of again. I believe that the American writer Ernest Hemingway based his famous story "The Short and Happy Life of Francis Macomber" on this incident.

After this case, the conduct of white hunters with their clients was carefully checked. Any suspicion of a scandal was enough to deprive a hunter of his license and ruin him for life. Although such careful supervision is no doubt a good thing, yet it occasionally puts a hunter in awkward positions.

I was once guiding a German baron who had a very handsome wife and was insanely jealous of her. He hired an ex-major in the German Army to stay with the lady at all times. This male chaperon earned his pay, for he never let the baroness out of his sight. The major was a trustworthy man but a bit heavy-footed and he made so much noise clumping along that he scared all the game away. This annoyed the baroness, who was a very keen sportswoman, but if she ordered the major away, he refused to go, looking suspiciously at the lady and me all the while. As the baron did not go out in the bush much, we usually had the major along and so we got little hunting done. One afternoon I mentioned to the baroness that there was a donga near the camp that usually held several lions. At supper that evening, she told her husband about the spot, adding, "Hunter says that the cover is so thick that taking three people would be dangerous."

She gave me a kick under the table as she spoke so I nodded my head and said, "Yes, I have my doubts if three can make it." I was always a poor liar so the major glared at us and said he was coming too, cover or no.

Next morning we started off to the donga. We put up no lion, but there was a fine warthog and the baroness wanted his tusks. The major stood on one side of the ravine and the baroness on the other, while I went in to drive the beast out.

I had taken only a few steps when I heard the baroness shout, "Hunter, come quick!" Thinking a lion had her, I ran to the spot throwing off the safety catch on my rifle. I burst through some little bushes and there was the baroness standing there stark naked except for her knickers. For an instant, I thought she was mad. Then I saw her desperately pulling safari ants off her body. These ants are terrible things, half an inch long, with jaws like pincers. I have been attacked by them myself in the bush and, like the baroness, I tore off my clothes to get at the creatures, for no one can stand the torture of their bites.

I spent several minutes pulling ants off the baroness. Then I had to scrape her body with the back of my knife blade to get out the insects' heads for the ants will let themselves be pulled apart rather than relax the grip. The lady had just gotten her clothes on again when the major came bursting through the bush on us.

"What's going on here?" he screamed.

"John and I were doing a little hunting together," said the baroness casually. The major glared at us but there was nothing he could say. Later, I sat down on the ground and shook as though

I'd had a close call with a rhino, for if the man had come upon us a few minutes before, he would have reported the matter to the baron and I would have lost my hunter's license for sure and certain. Under the circumstances no one would have believed either the lady or myself. Such are the perils of the veldt with clients.

I do not wish to give the impression that a white hunter's duties are merely to keep out of scrapes with beautiful women. Much of his work is the prosaic task of organizing the equipment necessary for a two or three months' trip "into the blue." In the case of a large safari, this is a tremendous undertaking. Some clients travel with a small city of tents equipped with generators to supply electricity. Each tent has its own bathtub, toilet facilities and an Electrolux icebox. To keep the cars and trucks in running condition, the equivalent of a small machine shop is taken along. Six- and seven-course meals that would not disgrace the best hotels in Paris or London are served regularly with a choice of several dishes and the best of wines. With such elaborate safaris, usually two or even three white hunters go along: one to handle the supplies and trucks, one to keep the clients entertained and one to find game.

As was only natural, the clients who wanted the luxury of these big safaris were seldom greatly interested in hunting. I remember guiding a rajah who refused to step out of his touring car to shoot a rhino which, I believe, carried a world's record horn. The rajah was afraid of getting the cuffs of his trousers wet in the tall grass. He insisted on trying to approach the animal in his car and the rhino took fright and galloped way.

Yet a short time after I was with this rajah, I had the privilege of guiding Commander Glen-Kidston, a British sportsman, who wanted to go to the Northern Frontier after oryx, a large straight-horned antelope. We took with us nothing but the barest essentials. In the desert country along the Abyssinian border the heat was so terrible that the rhinos scooped hollows in the sand during the day to bear the strain. The country was being continually raided by Abyssinian slave traders and bandits. We could hear their war parties go past our camp at night, but although they must have known we were there, they never bothered us. The local natives lived in such terror of strangers that the poor creatures urinated with fear when I spoke to them. Very few safaris ever penetrated that country and it was easy to see why. Water was more precious than gold. The natives dug in the ground for it and considered themselves well paid for an hour's hard work by a few mouthfuls of dirty seepages. At one camp, robbers stole our water bags. We had to punch holes in our cans of beans and drink the stale fluid out of them until we reached the next water hole. In return for all our trouble, Commander Glen-Kidston managed to bag what was at that time the world's record oryx and a greater kudu that was a Kenya record.

Until that time I had been receiving fifty pounds a month as a white hunter. After I returned from that safari, my salary was gradually increased to two hundred pounds. At that time, this was considered top salary for a white hunter.

I have always liked to guide sportsmen who were interested in getting fine trophies. I was guiding Mrs. Dorothy McMartin when she bagged a record Hunter's hartebeest. I helped Major Bruce to get a Thomson gazelle with 16 ¾-inch horns. I, myself, have shot a roan antelope with horns just one-half inch short of the record and have the head of a record suni gazelle that I collected in the Nyeri Forest. Yet I must say that in recent years the passion for "trophy hunting" has reached a point that I consider ridiculous. For a man to spend weeks or months hoping to get an animal with perhaps another quarter of an inch of horn or a half an inch more of span simply to see his name in Rowland Ward's *Records of Big Game* seems to me a bit foolish.

Records are often freak animals and the trophy instead of being a particularly fine specimen is actually deformed. Record rhino horns are often long, thin things like overgrown knitting needles, not at all an impressive trophy from my point of view. I prefer a really fine natural horn—thick, powerful, and of reasonable length. Such a trophy gives a far better idea of the animal and the strength of his weapon. By the same token, a buffalo with no boss —the boss being the thick, central base to which the horns proper are attached—will often have an extra length of horn. Yet such an animal bears no more relation to a true buffalo bull than a circus giant does to a strong, well-developed average man. These malformations may be of interest to a zoologist but I cannot see that they have a proper place among the trophies of a sportsman.

Some sportsmen carry their craze for world records to an amazing length. I remember talking to a man who had come back with a gigantic leopard skin measuring over ten feet. As an eight-foot leopard is very unusual, I could not believe my eyes when I saw this monster hide. Later when the owner was not around, I had the chance to examine the skin more closely. The man's native boys had very cleverly let into the center of the hide a four-foot strip of leopard skin from another trophy, matching the design so perfectly and doing such an expert job on the sewing, that not until I turned the skin over and examined the bottom did I detect the trick.

I soon learned to study my clients carefully before we started out into the bush. During my first few months as a white hunter, I would merely guide my client up to a good trophy and then expect him to do the rest. I found this was not a good practice. Some men would panic, others would show unwise boldness, many would fire wildly at the animal regardless of where they hit him. Then I would have a wounded rhino or elephant on my hands. So I tried to find out what sort of man I had as my client and laid my plans accordingly.

Sometimes having a client who is afraid of big game works out very well for the white hunter. I once guided a Swiss millionaire who was greatly impressed by the fine, 150-pound elephant tusk that hung in the Nairobi railway station. "I want you to find me an elephant like that," he informed me on our first meeting. I told the man that he was some thirty years too late, for big ivory like that is not common. However, it so chanced that after a few days in the bush we came on a bull carrying magnificent tusks, at least equal to those in Nairobi. After a careful hunt, we came up with him. My client fired. His bullet chipped the bull's right tusk and the elephant turned and ran. My client, thinking the elephant was charging him, bolted in the opposite direction. When I finally caught up with the man he was too paralyzed by funk to go after the bull. Yet he kept muttering, "Those tusks! I must have those tusks!" Finally I went after the bull myself and dropped him. My client was so delighted that he presented me with a fine car. I am enough of a Scotsman to find safaris like that very pleasant.

Other clients were brave to the point of rashness. While I was lion hunting with two Canadians, we went out one morning to visit our baits. We stopped at one bait and saw it was undisturbed. While we were looking at it, the wind shifted and carried our scent into a patch of tall grass a few yards away. Suddenly three heavy-maned lions stood up in the grass. They had been feeding on their own kill a short distance from our bait.

We were between the lions and a heavily bushed river bank. The lions rushed past us, intent on reaching the cover. Before I could move, the two Canadians had tumbled out of the car and were racing after the lions. The men and lions sprinted across the open ground that led to the river, the lions lashing themselves with their tails as they ran as though to whip up fresh energy. Then one lion veered to the left, racing across the plains in gigantic bounds. Instantly both sportsmen pulled up in their stride and threw up their magazine rifles. They fired at the two remaining lions, which tumbled head over heels like shot hares. These two young men played at hunting very much as they might have played at football.

Rashness in my clients was always a source of concern to me for no one knows what a wild animal may do. A professional hunter learns to expect a certain type of animal to behave in a certain way and nine times out of ten he will be right. But there is always the tenth animal and he is the danger. No one can say that an animal will never perform a certain action unless it is something that the animal is physically incapable of doing. Sometimes an animal will show completely unexpected ferocity. At other times, he will be remarkably tolerant of humans. Rhinos are generally considered to be among the most bad-tempered of all African big game, but I once saw a rhino deliberately avoid goring a man who was at his mercy.

I was guiding a rajah who never moved without his personal secretary and doctor. The doctor carried a regular medical clinic around with him, most of the drugs being potent aphrodisiacs as the rajah was afraid of losing his manhood from the hardships of African life. In the bush, the doctor became a sort of general factotum, struggling along under a heavy cinema outfit to record the rajah's triumphs, while his pockets bulged with bottles of medicines, packets of herbs, and pills.

On one occasion, we were hunting buffalo. The rajah and I were in front while the doctor and the secretary lagged behind. We came on a herd with a fine bull and the rajah fired. At the sound of the shot, the herd panicked and dashed off through the thorny bush. The rajah was sure he had hit the bull and I was equally sure he had missed. I had not heard the familiar "sough-zup" of a bullet striking flesh.

Eager to prove their patron right, the doctor and the secretary set off to look for bloodstains on the ground. While they were wandering about, a bull rhino came trotting out of the bush toward the doctor. The animal had evidently been disturbed by the stampeding buffalo and was looking for a quieter spot. If the doctor had stood still, all would have been well, but instead he screamed and raced for the startled secretary, apparently hoping the rhino would take off in pursuit of the other man. The secretary quickly realized what was happening and made for the nearest tree. He flattened himself against the stem like a poster and yelled "Go away! Go away!" to the frantic doctor.

The rhino had stopped for a moment when the doctor began to run. Then he started after him, making rooting motions in the air with his horn. The doctor put up a fine sprint, for his heart was in it, but the rhino easily overtook him. The doctor was in line with the rhino so I could not shoot but I soon saw that the beast was not making a serious charge. There is always some degree of safety in a rhino's coming unexpectedly on a man instead of vice versa for the beast is not unduly alarmed. The doctor ran through the thorn trees screaming "Help!" while the rhino galloped behind, encouraging his victim to fresh efforts by an occasional jab of his horn. As the doctor became so weak he could only stagger, the rhino slowed down to a trot, still keeping behind him. I became so interested in this performance that I forgot all about shooting the bull and watched with curiosity while the rhino chivvied the man through the scrub. At last, tiring of the sport, the rhino trotted off and the doctor returned to us, sweating and exhausted. His first earnest words were, "I have had much troubles."

Perhaps a hunter's most disagreeable task is to guide a man who behaves like a stoat in a hen house, killing for the very love of causing destruction. I have done my share of shooting but always with a purpose. Yet some men delight in killing simply for the pleasure of seeing death. Often a client would say to me, "Hunter, I am allowed three hundred animals on my license and as yet I have only shot two hundred. Are you sure I can get the rest in the next few days?" However, with most of them the mania soon passes. I have guided several Americans who came over hoping for a big bag, only to throw their rifles away after a few days and devote the rest of the trip to photography.

I remember particularly a story told me by Mr. Jack Holliday, an American whose encouragement was largely responsible for my writing this book. He and Roy Home, his guide, were on the track of a very fine bull elephant. Contrary to the opinion of many hunters, it is my belief that the size of an elephant's spoor does not indicate the size of his ivory. Often an elephant with a comparatively small footprint will carry better tusks than a giant. "Down-at-the-heel" footprints usually mean that the bull is old and, therefore, probably has big tusks. This bull's imprints showed he was a grand old chap and probably had magnificent ivory. After a long and very hard track, Jack and Roy found him standing by the bank of a stream. He must have heard some sound, for his great ears were spread to the uttermost to listen and his trunk raised to scent the wind. His tusks were two of the finest Roy had seen in many years of hunting. He made an unforgettable picture as he stood there in the forest, noble and unafraid, his ivory gleaming against the slate blue of his body. Jack slowly raised his rifle. He is an excellent shot and Roy stood waiting for the bull to drop. Instead, Holliday lowered his rifle and with a shake of his head said, "I can't do it, he's too fine to kill." They turned and left the bull standing there, watching them with his wise, old eyes.

Very few sportsmen will pass up a fine trophy for sentiment after spending weeks of hard work to get the animal. Yet I have seen it happen. I took out a young Yale student who was very keen to get a bongo, one of the finest and rarest of the forest antelope. Now almost the only way to get a bongo is to run the animal down with dogs. My client and I had a long, hard trek to a native village deep in the forest and I told the headman that we needed dogs for a bongo hunt. He willingly supplied me with a scratch pack of a dozen village dogs, shabby little brutes but keen on a trail. We started out and after several false starts we heard the dogs barking and the villagers shouting. Tearing our way through the thick undergrowth, we found the dogs had bayed a fine bongo in a little stream. The buck was standing up to his knees in the water with one foot raised, challenging his tormentors to come any closer. Around him was the baying pack, flanked by the yelling natives.

"There's your trophy," I said pointing.

My client raised his gun and then lowered it again. "I can't shoot that poor beast. He hasn't a chance with all those dogs and people around him. It isn't sporting."

Back we went without our trophy to the intense irritation, I may add, of the natives, who had been counting on a fine dinner of bongo steaks.

An amusing and harmless type of fool is the self-proclaimed expert on African game. I attended a dinner in Nairobi where one such individual was giving us a long discourse on game animals. Later, someone handed him a collection of game pictures, among them a photograph of a male hyena. The man nodded intelligently,

"Ah, yes, a very fine bull hyena," he assured the group. As the hyena is a doglike animal this was like speaking of a "bull fox terrier" but I thought it better to keep my own counsel.

I was with another man who took great pride in his shooting. He had the best of firearms and talked knowingly about muzzle velocity, calibers, and ammunition. One day we happened on a herd of warthogs and the pigs broke across the plain at full gallop, their tails carried straight up in the air as is the custom of the beasts. My client threw up his magazine rifle and opened fire on the pigs. I watched with great interest while his bullets went high, wide and every other way except among the porkers. After the barrage had finished and I was thinking what a good thing it was that in the wilds of the African bush you seldom heard of accidents from traveling bullets, my client turned to me and said solemnly, "Hunter, I hope you didn't disapprove of this slaughter but I like blotting out these swine because they spread disease." I assured him I had no objections. Privately, I only wished I would never be any closer to death than those warthogs were.

Some clients may be headaches but they are also a pleasure to be with. I remember a young English girl called Fay, barely out of her teens, whose greatest joy was to be on safari. Much snow has fallen on the summit of Kilimanjaro since I took this girl hunting, but I can picture her before me now, dressed in a semi-cowboy fashion, a silk bandana loosely tied around her dark hair, ends tucked into a shirt blouse, while a fancy-headed pigskin belt was wound around her slim waist to hold her cartridges. Fay was a true open-air girl: a fine fisherman, an excellent shot and a splendid rider. Her horses and dogs adored her. Vim and dash surrounded her like light around a lamp. No matter what came up, Fay was game for it.

When we started off on safari, I hired a number of donkeys from the local natives as pack animals. The donkeys hated the smell of an European. Hours were wasted and tempers frayed getting the nervous brutes loaded but at last it was accomplished. In no very good mood, I ordered the safari to start. The donkeys refused to budge. Fay quickly solved that problem. From some hidden recess of her luggage she produced an Australian stock whip with a short, thick handle and coils made of pleated kangaroo hide. The weapon looked absurdly heavy in Fay's small hand and I had no idea she could use it. The next thing I knew, she had cracked the ten-foot lash with a report like an elephant rifle across the donkeys' backs. The donkeys scattered like beads, bucking and kicking. In an instant their loads were under their bellies. Before the boys could grab their heads, all our kit was scattered across the veldt. Four hours of hard work was destroyed in ten seconds. I turned on Fay in a rage but she was sitting on the ground screaming with laughter. Between her howls of mirth she managed to gasp out, "Hunter, what are you looking so glum about?" Dullness was not her failing.

The donkeys did not prove a success so I engaged an oxcart to carry our supplies. This cart was a heavy vehicle and moved slowly, the yelling native driver cracking his giraffe-thonged whip constantly and the ponderous oxen throwing their weight into the yoke as the driver called them each by name. Traveling by oxcart was far too slow a means of progress for the lively Fay. "We'll never get there at this rate," she told me. "You and I will go ahead in my car." As there were no roads where we were headed, I doubted if a car could make the journey, but Fay had an old Studebaker that she assured me could go anywhere. We loaded up the old car with the more important camping supplies. I perched on top of the load and off we went with Fay at the wheel.

In a few minutes, I decided I had made a mistake in not staying with the oxcart. Fay's Studebaker seemed to have the properties of a modern jeep and Fay always drove at high speed no matter what the country. We tore through thorn bushes, the branches flicking me from either side. We rushed through streams at such a rate we had no chance of getting stuck in the mud and reached the other side by sheer momentum. On the open plains, Fay really let the car out. We were tearing along at a terrific speed when the car hit an old antbear hole. Up went the load with me on top of it. When the load came down the car had shot from under and was speeding off across the plains leaving a wake of churned-up grass and dry leaves. I made a perfect landing on top of the load just where nature intended with my pipe still clutched between my teeth.

Fay had covered a good two miles before discovering my absence and then only because some more kit bounced off. Back she came at full tilt and found me still sitting on the load, smoking my pipe. She drew up with a scream of brakes, leaped out of the car and stood regarding me, arms akimbo. "Hunter, what kind of a game are you playing?" she demanded severely.

Fay was a magnificent shot. Elephant and lion were her particular game. She favored a d/b .360 No. 2 rifle made by William Evans of London, and as, in my opinion, this gun was too light for elephants, I made a point of taking her hunting in open bush where we could see the bulls a fair distance off. A good shot can easily drop an elephant with a light rifle if the animal is in the open and the hunter can aim carefully at the bull's earhole. In thick bush where the bull may charge you at close quarters, it is a different matter. Then you need a heavy gun that will stop the animal with a frontal brain shot.

Fay had unlimited energy and could hunt all day and play all night. I was not so gifted. One evening we returned to camp after tramping through the bush since dawn, and after a quick meal, I went to bed. Fay did the same, but with her superabundance of spirits she could not sleep. We were sharing the same small tent, for our boys had not come yet with the slow-moving oxcart that held our other tents and the bulk of the equipment. After tossing about for a few minutes, Fay swung her feet out of the cot and called, "Hunter, I'm bored. Get up and talk to me." I pretended to be asleep for I was tired and had no wish for an all-night session of drinking and talking with the lively girl. Fay called to me again. Then I heard her mutter, "I'll wake him up." The next moment a knapsack full of cartridges hit me on the side of the head while

Fay shouted, "Don't be so stuffy! Get up and amuse me." Knowing when I was beaten I got up.

I fear that as an all-night companion I was less satisfactory than as hunter, for on our next safari, Fay brought along a handsome young man she had picked up in Nairobi. I could not imagine what a girl like Fay could see in the chap for he was a very poor shot, but from what she told me I gathered he had other qualities not immediately apparent. This seemed an ideal arrangement for Fay could hunt with me during the day and spend the evenings with her escort. Unfortunately, Fay was an impulsive girl and insisted that her friend share her enthusiasm for hunting. The man did not like to use a heavy-caliber gun because the kick hurt his shoulder so he borrowed a .275 of Fay's while she took her trusty .360. We were after lions, so these fairly light rifles were usable, but I took along my .475 in case we should meet an elephant or rhino.

We were going single file along a game trail that led through the heart of some tall grass. Suddenly we saw ahead of us a lone bull buffalo grazing. Now the African buffalo is a very formidable animal. When he charges with lowered head the only mark for a hunter is his thick forehead, protected by the wide boss of the horns. Nothing but a heavy-caliber rifle will stop the charge.

I was quite willing to withdraw and leave this bull to his grazing but Fay would have none of it. She was determined that her sweetheart should return to Nairobi saying he had shot a buffalo. "Hit him in the shoulder, dear," she whispered. "If he doesn't drop, I'll nail him for you."

The young man nervously raised his rifle and fired. He hit the bull high. Instantly, the buffalo wheeled and charged us at terrible speed. We could see nothing but the wide horns rushing at us along the narrow path. With admirable coolness, Fay raised her rifle and put two shots into the beast's forehead. She might as well have been throwing spitballs. When Fay saw the animal was still coming, she dropped her rifle and threw herself into her lover's arms.

With the two of them locked together in a close embrace on the narrow trail, I couldn't get around the idiots to shoot. The bull was

almost on us. I could see the white foam on his black chest and
the ridges on his great horns. If the two thousand pounds of
animal hit us, we would be knocked flat and trampled into the
ground. When the horns seemed only a couple of yards away, I
managed to force the barrel of my rifle between the two sweethearts
and fired. The bull came crashing down, throwing foam and blood
over Fay's trousers. The shock of the fall was so great that I believe
both Fay and her friend thought the bull had hit them. After a few
seconds, Fay opened her eyes and saw the bull lying dead at her
feet.

"Darling, Hunter shot him!" she cried happily. "But you mustn't
feel badly because you didn't get him. We'll start out right now and
find you another."

"Thank you very much," said the young man, wiping the sweat
off his forehead with a shaking hand. "I only want to know one thing
—how long will it take to get me back to Nairobi?"

Poor, gay little Fay. When all other thrills failed to satisfy her
she took to drugs. What finally happened to her, I have no idea.
She was a girl of free morals, no doubt, but she was an excellent
shot and a good companion. You can't expect to find everything in
a woman.

I believe that most sportsmen's reluctance to use a heavy-caliber
gun is responsible for the majority of hunting accidents. I admit
this is a pet subject with me and I have had many an argument
over it. I grant that if you hit an elephant, rhino, or buffalo in the
correct spot, you can kill him with a light-caliber bullet. But if you
are stopping a charge you must have a bullet with sufficient hitting
force to knock the animal off his feet. Many a hunter has been
killed by a "dead" buffalo or rhino that he has hit in a vital place;
the impetus of the charge was sufficient to carry the animal onto the
man with fatal results.

Unfortunately, very few sportsmen care to endure the punishment
of a heavy gun's kick. After a few shots at target practice, the
sportsman begins to wince instinctively as he squeezes the trigger.
Of course, this ruins his shooting and he turns to a lighter gun.

The man forgets that in the excitement of a hunt he will not feel the kick.

I realize a sportsman has several problems when it comes to selecting his battery. Most men like to use their own weapon yet few own the heavy guns necessary for African big game. If the man rents a gun while in Africa, he cannot later show it to his friends as "the gun that shot that big bull." Also, many sportsmen have read accounts written by the old-time hunters who often used very light-caliber weapons. But in those days the game was so tame that a man could pick his shot, and the early hunters seldom bothered to venture into dense brush after a trophy.

Sportsmen's insistence on using light guns has given rise to a very miserable custom among some white hunters. When his client shoots the white hunter fires at the same moment with his heavy gun. The hunter cares not a jot whether his client hits the beast or simply fires into the air. The animal drops and the client can have the glory. The men I have guided like the McMartins, Commander Glen-Kidston or Major Bruce would have sent me packing back to Nairobi with a flea in my ear if I had tried any such tricks with them. Yet I understand the modern white hunter's motives. It is a law of the bush that you cannot leave an injured animal to die, so if your client wounds a dangerous beast, then the hunter must go into cover to get the animal. The client cannot go himself for the danger to him would be too great and also the hunter can do the job far better if he is alone.

I remember I was once hunting with a certain Continental prince and princess near Kasigau in the Voi area of Kenya. We saw a buffalo bull coming toward us and we lay down so he would come closer. He trotted up to within fifty yards or so. The princess was using a small-bore rifle and she was determined to kill the bull without any assistance. She fired, hitting him in the chest. With a heavy or even medium-caliber rifle this would have been a fatal shot, but the wounded bull was able to swing away and reach a dense thicket of thornless bush.

We checked the spoor. The tracks were spotted with minute blood drops. Part of a hunter's work is to be able to identify the different types of blood resulting from various wounds. Lung blood is light-colored and usually means a long hunt. Blood from the kidneys is very dark and means the animal is mortally wounded. Blood from the body and limbs is medium in color and generally means a superficial wound. This blood spoor was of the last type. So here was a wounded beast sound in limb and wind that would fight it out in cover of its own choosing—an unpleasant prospect.

The princess still insisted on following the wounded animal with her popgun. When I objected, her royal blood boiled and she gave me a fine tongue-lashing. These people who have never been crossed in their lives are apt to be difficult. I still refused to allow her to commit suicide. The prince, a clear-thinking fellow, finally interfered and told me to go ahead and finish off the animal.

Taking my Walingulu tracker, I entered the bush. The Walingulu tribe are, in my opinion, the best trackers in Kenya and I had every confidence in the man. The ground was sandy soil and we could move quietly through the brush. It was very quiet and I knew that probably meant the bull was waiting motionless in ambush for us. Such knowledge serves to keep your mind alert.

We came to a spot where the blood spoor was very heavy. The bull had stopped there for several minutes. He had heard the princess screaming at me and had paused to listen. When the argument stopped and we began trailing, he had moved on.

Suddenly we smelled the pungent odor of the bull. We both stopped. He must be only a few yards away. The Walingulu stood with his nostrils flaring, like a pointer trying to locate a covey of partridges. Then he pointed into the bush. I could see nothing. Thinking the bull was still a little distance off I motioned the man to toss something in the direction of the animal. He picked up a stone and flung it straight into the bush ahead of us. I heard the stone smack against the bull's horn. The animal was standing there in full view but his black hide blended so perfectly with the shadows that I hadn't seen him.

Instantly the bull charged. I had no time to aim. I flung my

.500 d/b express to my shoulder and fired the rifle as though it were a shotgun. The bullet hit the buffalo below the left eye, killing him in his stride. If I had been using a lighter rifle, the animal would certainly have killed us before he died.

The most remarkable task a client ever asked me to perform was to crawl down a hole after a wounded warthog. I was guiding the Earl of Carnarvon when he shot and wounded a big boar warthog. The animal took refuge in a hole. When a warthog enters a hole, he always turns and backs in so as to have his tusks pointed in the direction of a possible pursuer. The earl wanted the animal badly but I could think of no way to get at him. We had no digging tools and there was no way of smoking the pig out.

I asked my scouts if they would go down the hole after the boar. They explained that they were all of the Islam faith and were forbidden to touch a pig, otherwise they would have been delighted. There was nothing for it but do the task myself. I peeled off my coat and after telling the boys to drag me out by the legs when I began to kick, I started down the burrow.

The hole was a fairly tight fit for my waistline and the stinking breath of the pig nearly stifled me. With my body blocking the entrance the hole was pitch dark. I wriggled along, feeling ahead with my right hand, until I touched the boar's snout. Then I grabbed him by the tusk. The boar promptly tried to jab my hand against the top of the burrow but I hung on, kicking madly. I was close to fainting from the lack of air and the heavy odor of the pig. The boys pulled me out and I dragged the smelly beast with me.

When I stood up, wiping my face, the earl said, "Splendid, Hunter. I don't want the boar as a trophy. I just want his hide for saddle leather. Are you sure you didn't damage it getting him out of that hole?"

I can only hope the earl got enough pleasure from his saddle to justify the agony I went through extracting that boar from his burrow.

6

Lion Hunting in Masailand

One spring about the middle of the twenties, I was called into the office of Captain A. T. A. Ritchie, O.B.E., M.C., head of the Kenya Game Department. Captain Ritchie laid before me one of the most remarkable offers ever made to a professional hunter.

To understand the reasons behind his offer, you must first know the unusual conditions prevailing in part of the colony at that time.

In the center of Kenya lies a great tableland—the home of a warlike tribe of herdsmen named the Masai. The Masai are a nation of spearmen. They scorn the bow and arrows as the tools of cowards who are afraid to close with their enemies. The young warriors of the tribe, called the moran, subsist mainly on a diet of fresh blood and milk. This they consider the only proper food for fighting men. The neighboring tribes lived in terror of the Masai for none of them could stand against a Masai war party. For sport, the moran amuse themselves by killing lions with their spears—a feat I would have considered well-nigh impossible. In the old days, the Masai had lived almost completely on other tribes, much as any predatory animal lives on its weaker neighbors.

Now it is a strange fact that although the true hunting animals that insist on killing their own prey, such as hawks and wild dogs, have no natural enemies they seldom increase in numbers. They live at such a high pitch that they use themselves up very quickly. Also, in spite of their strength and ferocity, they are strangely delicate while their prey is apt to be much more hardy. This is also true of humans. When the British government stopped the raiding, the tribes near the Masai increased so in population that they became a major problem. But the Masai, with their whole way of life changed, were threatened with extinction. They were forced to raise more cattle as a means of livelihood. Partly as a result of the overcrowding caused by the increased herds, a terrible epidemic of rinderpest swept the district. The cattle died by the thousands until only a minor number of breeding stock remained.

Lions readily became scavengers, and with the plains littered by the carcasses of cattle, these big cats increased greatly in numbers. Weakling cubs that would soon have died under normal conditions grew to maturity and thus in a surprisingly short space of time the Masai country was overrun with lions. When the epidemic had run its course and there were no more dead cows lying about, the lions turned on the live cattle. The Masai sallied out with spear and shield to defend the precious remnants of their breeding stock but for every lion killed, one or two of the young moran were mauled. A wound made by a lion almost invariably causes blood poisoning, for the claws of the animals are coated with a rotting film from their prey. Thus even a superficial scratch often means death to a native. So many of the warriors were injured fatally in these lion hunts that the elders of the tribe feared the Masai were losing all their best men. In the old days, the Masai would have corrected this state of affairs by raiding other tribes for more women and cattle. But under present conditions they had no solution except to appeal to the government for help.

The District Commissioner of the Masai Reserve was a young chap named R. Pailthorpe. He went out to reduce the number of lions, using a magazine rifle. To my mind, a magazine rifle is not the ideal weapon for close-up work in the thick bush. After a shot, it takes a second or so for the next cartridge to enter the breech. This delay can be fatal. Although I use a magazine rifle for shooting from a hide or for hunting in the open, I prefer a double-barreled rifle for dense cover. The double barrel gives you two shots and you can fire them almost simultaneously. If your first shot misses, you can fire again instantly. In case of a charge, this is an important consideration.

The majority of lions lie up in thick bush and if you wish to wipe out the lions in a district you must go into the cover after them. Mr. Pailthorpe had previously shot lions only for sport—in the open. Now he went into the bush and fired at a lioness. The lioness charged before he could get another cartridge in the breech, and knocked him down and started mauling him. He would surely have been killed had not one of his native policemen fired and killed the animal on top of him. As it was, Pailthorpe was badly injured and taken to the hospital.

"After Pailthorpe's experience, I don't think it wise to allow this work to be handled by ordinary sportsmen," Captain Ritchie told me. "This is a task for an experienced hunter. After considerable discussion, the game department decided that you are the man best qualified for the task. We want the trouble-giving lions killed in the next three months to bring the lion population within control. You will be allowed to keep the hides as your pay."

The skins of first-class, black-maned lions were then bringing twenty pounds each and even lioness hides were worth three pounds. Although the risks were great, this would mean a large sum of money for Hilda and me. We had four children by this time and it is surprising how much children cost to raise, even in Kenya.

That evening I talked the matter over with Hilda. To kill ten or even twenty lions in brush country could be done by an experienced hunter without too great risk. But to kill a hundred in the short space of time mentioned would almost certainly mean a serious mauling sooner or later. Hilda, who is a very shrewd person, came up with an excellent idea.

"Do you remember Captain Hurst's pack of hounds that you used to hunt lions in Ngorongoro? They were a great help to you. Why don't you use dogs in this work?"

Here was an inspiration, but Captain Hurst's kangaroo hounds had long ago been sold by his brother and I had no idea where to get a similar pack. After trying vainly to purchase some suitable

hounds, I finally went in despair to the dog pound at Nairobi.
There was a motley collection of twenty-two dogs, all awaiting
their doom as worthless strays. They were all sizes, shapes and
breeds. At least with me they would have a chance for their lives,
so I purchased the whole collection at ten shillings apiece and took
them home. Hilda's face fell when she saw my pack of lion dogs
and it fell far worse in the next few days, for none of the creatures
was housebroken. They barked by day and howled by night. They
fought with each other and with our houseboys. When things grew
dull, they went out and attacked the sedate dogs of my neighbors.
But in a week, I had the collection—I can hardly call it a pack—
under some sort of discipline and was ready to set out for the Masai
Reserve.

The government had provided me with six oxen, for dragging bait
to different spots in the reserve. With these valuable but slow-
moving creatures, a few native porters and my dogs, I set out for
Masai land.

We followed the main highway to Konza about eighty miles
southeast of Nairobi and then turned almost due west. After a
day's trek, we began to leave behind the forested country and come
into the open plains. The thatched huts of the Kikuyu, an agricultural people who were long the favorite prey of the Masai, grew
fewer. The cultivated shambas disappeared and ahead of us lay the
open grassland, dotted with game. Here was perfect grazing country
and here, for untold ages, the Masai had lived, pasturing their
cattle beside the herds of zebra, and wildebeest. The air was clear
and cool, a pleasant thing to breathe, and not a house or a road to
mar the sweep of the great rolling country. We went on and on,
farther and farther into the wilds of the reserve. Except for Hilda,
I would have little cared if I never returned to Nairobi, for here
was Africa as God made it before the white man arrived and began
to deface the country with villages and farms. At night we camped
wherever we happened to stop and when the sun rose over the
hills, we went on again following no guide but our own wills.

One evening after we had penetrated deep into the reserve, I heard lions grunting around the camp. From the deep-drawn quality of the sounds, I knew them to be males. At dawn the next morning, I saw my first Masai, two young moran who were out lion hunting and had seen my camp. Completely self-possessed, they came strolling up to my tent and stood leaning on their long spears as they studied me. They were different from any natives I had yet met— tall, slender men with very delicate features more finely cut than those of a white man. There is even a theory that the Masai are the descendants of the ancient Egyptians who traveled south on some great migration in the distant past. These young warriors had their faces painted red with ocher and outlined with white chalk made from powdered bones. Each man wore only one piece of clothing, a blanket thrown carelessly around his body and fastened at the shoulder.

I told the moran that I had come to kill the lions. The warriors seemed rather amused at this idea and said I would have trouble killing lions with nothing but a gun. A spear was the proper weapon to use on a lion. The Masai have a great contempt for firearms, dating back to the old days when a Masai war party had little trouble defeating Arab slave traders armed only with muzzle-loading muskets.

Apparently to call my bluff, one of the young men told me that he knew of two lions not far from camp. His friend chimed in, saying these animals were particularly fine specimens and he would be delighted to see me have a go at them. Now I had not intended making my first hunt before such a critical audience. The dogs were completely untrained and I had no idea in what kind of country these lions might be. But as the two young men were regarding me with amused contempt, I felt duty bound to do my best. I told them to lead on, calling to one of my porters to uncouple the dogs.

The Masai led me to a drift, the dry bottom of a ravine that in the rainy season turns to a roaring torrent. The floor of the drift was covered with sand and the Masai easily picked up the lions' spoor and began tracking. The dogs trotted along, examining the strange scent doubtfully. We rounded a bend in the winding course of the

drift and saw before us two lions lying stretched out on the sand
like big cats. They both rose and stood glowering at us. When
the dogs saw what they had been trailing, they took one horrified
look and most of the pack fled, yelping in panic. None of them had
ever seen a lion before or even imagined that such a creature ex-
isted. But four dogs of Airedale strain bravely stood their ground.

Neither the Masai nor I could spare any thought for the dogs. The
two moran stood with their spears upraised waiting for the charge.
A noble sight. I took quick aim for the chest of the largest cat
and fired. He reared at the impact of the bullet, grunted and fell
heavily on his side. His companion promptly bolted into some
heavy bush on the left bank of the drift. Instantly my four Airedales charged in and began to worry the dead lion. I let them pull at
the mane to their hearts' content, and when the rest of the pack
gingerly returned, I encouraged them to do the same. There were
two other dogs of remote collie ancestry that also seemed to show
pluck and I hoped with these six animals to build up a true
pack of lion dogs.

When the dogs had wearied of worrying the dead lion, I went on
with them toward the bush where the second cat had taken refuge.
As we approached, I heard the lion give a low, harsh growl of
warning. The Airedales and collies promptly charged the bush, barking in fury, while the rest circled the cover, giving tongue but not
caring to approach. One of the Masai tossed a stone into the cover.
The lion charged out a few feet, making a feint at one of the
furious Airedales, and then dodged back before I could get in a shot.

The dogs were now growing bolder. I could tell where the lion
was from the movements of the upper twigs in the cover. The
braver dogs were crawling through the bush to drive him out, keeping up a furious yelling. I knew it would not be long now before
the lion charged and steadied myself to meet the attack.

Suddenly the bushes swayed violently and the lion burst out and
came for me at uncanny speed. He was bunched up almost in a
ball, his ears flattened back and his back arched. He seemed to fly
through the air across the sandy bottom. One of my gallant Airedales met the charge full on and tried to seize the monster by the

throat. The lion knocked him over as a child might knock over a toy. Without even pausing in his charge he rushed toward me, ignoring the rest of the pack that were snapping at his flanks.

When he was within ten yards, I fired. The bullet hit him fairly between the eyes. He dropped without a quiver. In the cool morning air, a tiny curl of smoke rose from the bullet hole.

The two Masai went into a war dance of delight. The tense excitement of the charge and the thrill of seeing two fine-maned lions lying before us was too much for them. Still holding their spears, the men bent forward, thrusting out their behinds. Then they suddenly straightened up, throwing out their chests at the same time. As their ecstasy increased this curious jerky motion speeded up in tempo until they were going like pistons. This was a curious sort of emotional seizure, common among the Masai, and now known among whites who live with this remarkable people as "the shakes." I had never seen anything like it and could not understand how men who had calmly prepared to meet the charge of an infuriated lion with nothing but their spears should behave like hysterical women.

My own satisfaction at the death of the lions was largely spoiled by finding that the fine Airedale that had tried to stop the charge was lying with a broken back. The cowardly curs that had done nothing but bark were now bravely mauling the dead animal as though they had behaved nobly, while this great dog was lying uncomplaining in his death agony. I could do nothing for him but put him out of his pain. It is death for a dog to try to close with a lion. No dog that was ever whelped can come out of a lion's grip alive. The dogs must keep out of a lion's way, forcing him to break cover by snapping and barking at him, but never taking a hold unless the lion is distracted by mauling one of their comrades or their master. Captain Hurst's hounds understood this perfectly and all of them carried the marks of old scars they must have received while learning their lesson. My poor Airedale had died before he could learn the trick. I could only hope the rest would profit by his death.

I drew the dead lion and allowed the dogs to eat some of the flesh to encourage them in future hunts. The pack had little liking for the strange diet but at last they all pitched in, snapping off mouthfuls and growling at each other. I had my porters skin out the beasts and we started back for camp.

News seems to travel through Africa with the speed of radio. When we returned to camp, there was a crowd of young warriors there waiting to greet me. I can only suppose they heard the noise of the shots and hurried to the spot. There was wild jubilation and my first two friends informed me that the crowd had come to take me to a spot where lions were thicker than grass. They expected me to start off at once but I told them I could not break camp until the next day.

I spent the afternoon targeting my rifles as my two shots at the lions that morning had not gone exactly where I wanted them. I took the dogs with me and closely watched their reaction to the rifle fire. Only one of them was really gun shy and I gave him to an old Masai, who seemed pleased with the gift.

At daybreak the next morning we started off, the Masai trotting ahead with their spears and balancing their huge buffalo-hide shields on their shoulders. These shields are bulky affairs weighing fifty odd pounds, and yet the moran carry them like feathers. They are painted with elaborate designs in black, red and white, the patterns serving somewhat the same purpose as the heraldic devices of our forefathers. By glancing at another man's shield, a Masai can tell what section of the country he comes from, to what moran club he belongs, his rank and position in a war party, his age grade, his name and what honors he has won in battle or lion spearing.

By noon we had reached the foothills of the Embarasha Mountains. The mountains threw out great spurs into the valley, each spur covered with fine, short grass dotted with tiny wild flowers. The slopes of the spurs were not precipitous but they made a steep climb. The moran bounded up them like springbok but with our heavy-footed oxen we had to zigzag back and forth up the grades. When we reached the top of a spur we would follow along it for a mile or two until it dropped away into the next valley. That meant another climb—this time down. Then we followed the valley to the next rise.

Late in the afternoon while we were toiling through some open brush, the moran began to give their curious yodeling calls, which were answered from just ahead. We came through the bush onto the banks of a muddy stream where a group of old men and women were watering a herd of the long-horned native cattle. These animals resemble the Brahman cattle, having humps on their backs. They were covered with a network of complicated brands, which, to a Masai, told the animal's entire pedigree.

The old people clustered eagerly around us while the young Masai, with many whoops and much spear waving, told how I had killed two fine lions within a few minutes of each other. I could see the old people literally beam at the news and the children with them danced around, going into a miniature version of the "shakes" in their excitement. It seemed I had come to the right spot, for only a few days before lions had killed six head of their precious cattle as well as two herdsmen who had tried to defend the animals.

The enthusiastic crowd conducted me to their village. I expected to see a large cluster of thatched huts like the villages of the Kikuyu but I was almost on top of the place before I realized it was a village at all. It looked like nothing but an unusually thick mass of brush. The "village" was surrounded by a boma of thorn bushes, piled high as a man's head, and the huts within were no higher than my chest. They were made of cow dung, plastered like clay over a wattle frame. The dung had been baked as hard as brick by the hot sun and was quite odorless. To enter the huts, I had to bend nearly double. Unlike most native homes, each hut was divided into small rooms by wattle partitions. There were no windows except thin slits in the wall and the interiors were dark but cool and comfortable.

As the Masai were subject to occasional retaliatory raids from other natives, they constructed their homes in this manner to escape notice. The buildings seemed crude, but they were easy to heat during the night and pleasantly cool in the day.

After we had rested and the women had brought us milk in orange-colored, goosenecked gourds, I went out to see the bodies of the cattle that had been killed. The Masai had removed most of the meat. This was unfortunate, for a lion's own kill makes a perfect bait as he will almost invariably return to the carcass to feed. I explained this to the Masai and one of the old men told me that there was a dead heifer still in the bush some fifty yards away that they had not disturbed. I inspected the dead animal and found that, although the stomach had been partly eaten by the lions, there was still plenty of flesh left. The bodies of the two herdsmen killed by the lions had also been left out in the bush but these had already been devoured by lions and hyenas. The Masai make no attempt to bury their dead, leaving the job to the scavengers that roam the plains.

I should add that these lions were not man-eaters in the true sense of the word. They had killed the herdsmen because the men had attempted to drive them away. It is a curious fact that a man can usually drive a lion off its kill if the quarry is wild game, but when a lion kills domestic stock, he will fight to the death rather than abandon his prey to its rightful owners.

I trailed the lions and found they had entered a thick patch of sansevieria. They were evidently waiting in the undergrowth for night to fall so they could return to their kills. The Masai told me that when they drove their cattle into the kraal in the evening, they shouted to urge the herd along. The lions recognized these shouts and came out soon after, knowing the coast would be clear.

I asked the men if they could drive their cattle to the kraal earlier this evening while I waited in ambush beside the dead heifer. The old men were greatly amused at this idea and remarked it should work—the same system had always worked when they were fighting the Nandi. The Nandi were another warlike people who occasionally attacked the Masai. If the Masai knew that a Nandi war party was in the neighborhood, they would drive their cattle to the kraal with additionally loud shouts and the Nandi, thinking that the Masai had now retired to their village for the night, would stage a raid—only to fall into an ambush of warriors.

I took up my stand in some thick bush near the dead cow and waited for evening. Just as the sun was setting, I heard the high-pitched, unmusical cries of the herdsmen as they drove the cattle in from pasture. While I was still listening to the fading sounds, I suddenly saw three maned lions sitting dog fashion on their haunches with their ears cocked as they also listened to the faint yells. When the cries died away, the lions rose and trotted toward me in single file. I felt every nerve in my body grow tense as I waited for them to come within gunshot. They stopped at the spot where they had killed a bull and sniffed around, but the animal had been removed. As each lion finished smelling, he raised his head with a curious expression on his face that resembled a snarl but was really a contortion of the features to enable him to smell to better advantage.

They were still just out of range. While I was waiting, a vulture came sweeping down and lit on the ground a few feet away from me. He had evidently seen my form in the bush and thought I was something to eat. I kept absolutely still for I knew if I frightened the vulture, the lions would take alarm.

The lions also saw the vulture and thinking he had found food came trotting toward me. Their heads were up and they sniffed the air like pointers trying to identify what the bird had seen. I held my fire until they were within thirty yards. Then the vulture which had been studying me with his little black eyes suddenly took alarm and with a whisk of his great wings leaped into the air. Instantly the lions stopped, looking after the alarmed vulture, and then turned to examine me more carefully.

I was still in a prone position and I had to raise myself slightly to fire. It seemed to take years while I gradually lifted my body enough to bring the rifle into position. Still keeping my eyes on the lions, I turned over the safety catch with my thumb and aimed at the leader. At the shot he dropped as though poleaxed. The others leaped back but did not run. Wild animals that have never heard firearms before apparently think the noise is thunder, for often they are not particularly alarmed by it. I fired at the next lion and hit him in the shoulder. He spun around in a circle, roaring with rage, and the third lion instantly sprang on him and they began to fight. This uninjured beast seemed to be in a maniacal rage, tail lashing, hair bristling, and mouth gaping open as he tried to crush the skull of his comrade.

I fired again and hit this animal in the shoulder. He reared like a bucking horse, and while he was still on his hind legs I fired again into his neck. He dropped without a quiver. The second lion was now also dead, whether from the effects of my bullet or the mauling he had taken from his friend I cannot say.

In the distance I could hear the whoops and yells of the Masai who had heard my shots. They came pouring through the bush and would have been overjoyed to find one of their enemies dead. But when they found all three animals lying stretched out in front of me, the whole community went mad with delight. We returned to the village in triumph. A sheep was killed in my honor, its spitted ribs were roasted over a fire and tasted better to me than the best sirloin. The women brought out native beer called "pombe" in an earthen pot. Each man grasped the bowl in his two hands, took a swig and then passed it on. As the liquor took effect the men gathered in a close-knit group and started a strange kind of dance that consisted simply in leaping up and down in the air. I watched, drinking my beer and chewing on my sheep rib while the dogs lay around me under the star-covered sky. Near us the cattle were lowing and from afar off I could hear the calls of more lions as they moved through the brush on their night's hunting. Truly this was my country and my kind of people.

When the time came to retire, I was ushered into the largest of the huts and shown a big bed in one of the compartments. It was made of soft rushes and covered with bullock skins, the hair worn off with continuous use. The chief's two buxom young wives entered with me and obviously intended to share the bed. I wondered where the chief would spend the night as there was clearly only room in the bed for three people. However, it turned out he was staying with some friends so as not to interfere with any plans I might have for the evening.

I noticed the younger girl place four gourds of milk in a rack behind my skin pillow. I did not quite catch the full meaning of this act, but I afterward found it was to serve as a restorative, in case I became exhausted with my night's work. The girls, clad in Eve's attire, except for a thin string of beads around their waistlines, remained at the end of the hut. They lay quietly and said nothing for, according to ancient custom, the male has to make the advances. But I was tired after my long trek and soon fell into a heavy sleep.

In the next few days I was besieged by Masai runners who had come for miles to beg me to kill their lions. Each runner vied with the others in making wild claims for his particular district. One man assured me that near his village the lions were more numerous than leaves on the trees. Another said that in his valley a man could hardly walk fifty yards without seeing several of the beasts. It seemed that no matter where I went I was sure to find plenty of lions. I started out with my oxen and dogs for the next village, where lions had killed several cows in the last week and badly mauled an old man. A group of spear-carrying moran went with me, as they still did not like to see a man risking his life hunting lions with no protection but a gun.

When we reached the village where the latest stock killings had taken place, the natives showed me what was left of the kills. Lions, vultures, and hyenas had been at work on the carcasses so there was little meat upon them. I was interested to see that lions kill domestic stock exactly as they do wild game—that is, by leaping on the animal's back and turning his head with a quick twist of the forepaw, thus dislocating the neck. Blood immediately collects in the rupture and the lion bites through the break and laps the blood.

There was not enough flesh on the bones to tempt the lions back, so I set out with moran and the dogs to spoor them. There were so many lion tracks in the vicinity that it was difficult to follow these particular cats, yet, if we did not settle on one group of tracks, we would be spending all our time going around in circles. The tracks we were following were the freshest, although it is not always easy to tell the age of a track. Old pug marks made in the lee of a bunch of grass and sheltered from the wind will often seem fresher than new tracks made in the open and full of drifted sand. Generally, old marks are covered by the tracks of small animals that have run over them, but the only sure way to tell that you are on a fresh spoor is to find some of the lion's droppings. A good tracker can tell at once from the condition of the droppings how long it is since the animal passed.

The moran were excellent at spooring. Often they would lift the branches of some low bush with their spears to show me marks that I would have missed. I noticed they did not go from pug mark to pug mark but seemed to follow the trail ten or fifteen feet ahead of them. They knew the habits of lions so perfectly they could roughly tell where the animals were likely to go. When at fault, they would stop and cast around, much like a pack of hounds that have lost the scent, examining every sandy spot nearby that might bare the impression of a pug mark until they had picked up the trail again.

After several hours of spooring, we tracked down the lions into a small belt of bush, the kind of dense cover that is the hunter's nightmare. There was no way of getting in to the lions, and yet I knew that unless they were destroyed they would be back in a few days killing more cattle and maybe the herdsmen as well. Here was the place where the dogs must prove their worth. I sent the pack into the cover.

The Masai and I waited outside. The moran leaned on their shields, the tips of their long spears resting on the ground in front of them. I stood with my rifle ready, waiting for the charge I knew must come. Suddenly all hell broke loose. I could hear the excited screaming of the dogs and the savage growling of the lions. The dogs were slowly retreating from the angry beasts, trying to lure them into the open. The Masai took a firm grip on the handles of the shields and raised their spears. I stood ready for the first lion to break cover.

The dogs began to appear, backing out of the bushes and barking furiously. Most of the pack formed a half circle outside the undergrowth, while the braver Airedales and the two collies remained in the bushes, trying to chivvy the lions into the open.

Without an instant's warning, one of the lions charged out of the bush and went for the dogs. They opened out to let him through but he managed to knock over one of the pack with a swing of his paw. The motion was so swift I could hardly follow it. I simply saw the dog go down. At once the rest of the pack charged in, snapping at the lion's rear to distract him from their friend. The lion whirled on them, cuffing left and right, as fast as an expert boxer could use his fists. I fired. The lion gave one great bound into the air. The second he hit the ground, he was covered by the dogs. Before I could call them off, a second lion bolted out some distance from us. Instantly the Masai were after him with upraised spears, giving their wild, yodeling whoops. The lion went bounding across the plain in great leaps that must have easily been twenty feet long, with the dogs and Masai on his tail. For a while the lion kept ahead, but eventually the dogs caught up to him. I was panting in the rear and by the time I came up, the dogs had formed a circle around the lion to hold him. The Masai had also formed a circle and were beginning to close in with their spears.

I shouted to the fools to stop. They hesitated and I raised my rifle, trying to get in a shot without killing one of the hysterical dogs. The lion saw me. Suddenly he charged. He leaped right over the dogs to get at me. I waited until he was clear of the pack and then fired. My first shot sent him down in a whirl of sand and dust. In an instant he was on his feet again but now he was motionless and a perfect target. My second shot hit him in the chest and he died instantly.

In the next few weeks I killed over fifty lions with the dogs. After seeing a number of their friends killed, the pack became more cautious and kept well away from the lions' paws. I never saw a lion attempt to bite one of the dogs. They always used their claws, striking at their tormentors with those lightning-quick blows. Apparently they didn't consider dogs worthy of a bite. When the dogs fastened on a lion to pull him off one of their friends, they grabbed him by the mane rather than the hide. I suppose the mane offered a better grip.

In the bush, the advantage was all with the lions. I began to lose so many dogs that I did not dare to use the pack except to pick up a special animal that was a confirmed cattle killer. Most of the time I left the pack in camp and continued to hunt as best I could.

One evening while I was out alone, I became lost in the tangle of spurs and ravines that laced the foothills. I tried to backtrack myself but before I reached camp, night came on and I could no longer follow my trail. A storm had been brewing during the late afternoon and now it broke over the distant ridges. For a while I could guide myself by the flashes of lightning, for I knew the approximate position of the storm in relation to the mountains. But by midnight the storm had blown away and I could only go on blindly through the darkness. Then I heard the distant tinkle of cowbells in a kraal—a lovely sound to me at that moment. I headed toward the noise, shouting as I went. In a few minutes my shouts were answered. A light appeared and I saw ahead a small Masai cow-dung hut with the usual thorn-bush kraal nearby. The Masai couple took me in and promptly started a fire in the tiny hut. The man was in his early forties, too old to be considered a moran, and so from the Masai point of view, already started on the downhill grade that would finally lead to his being left out for the lions. He had heard about my exploits as a lion killer and eagerly asked me questions about my gun, myself, and how many animals I had killed. I found his name was Kirakangano and that his father had been killed by a rhino years before. Kirakangano had developed a hatred for dangerous wild animals and had devoted his life to hunting them. He told me stories of lion and buffalo spearings in which he had taken part that sounded incredible, yet I knew that the Masai never lie. Most Masai take great pride in their cattle or in the number of their wives, but Kirakangano had no interest in anything but tracking big game through the tangled intricacies of the bush and then meeting the charge of some infuriated beast with his shield and spear. Here was a man who liked hunting as I did.

I had learned something of the language by this time, and I asked Kirakangano if he would like to come with me as a guide and helper. Without a word he rose, took up his spear and shield, and asked when we were leaving. This was a little sudden and I asked him what would happen to his wife and cattle. He shrugged. "My wife will take care of the cows and I have a good friend who will look after my wife." I inquired if he had no objection to having another man live with his wife. He seemed mildly surprised. "Why should I? She'll still be the same woman when I come back, won't she?" Thus the whole matter was satisfactorily settled. The wife offered no objections, which did not surprise me for I suspected that Kirakangano must have made a very indifferent husband.

Kirakangano became my right hand—the second barrel to my rifle, so to speak. A magnificent tracker and absolutely fearless, I relied on him as I did on myself. Such men are all too rare. Several times I have had the terrible experience of firing both barrels of my rifle at a charging beast to no avail and then turning to snatch my second rifle from the hands of my gunbearer only to find the man has run. But Kirakangano never let me down. Not only was he absolutely trustworthy but he was a marvelous bushcraftsman and could think in the same manner that an animal thinks, thus often foreseeing the quarry's next move and preparing for it.

With Kirakangano as leader, I formed small groups of spearmen to make organized drives down gullies that lay between the mountain ridges. These gullies were full of thick brush and here the lions would lie up during the day. I stayed at one end of the gully and the moran drove the lions down to me, shouting and waving their spears and shields as they forced their way through the brush. By lying on the top of the ridge so the lions passed below me, I kept out of their sight and also above the level of scent. From one such ambush, I shot seven lions in quick succession. As one lion after another dropped to my shots, the others would whirl around snarling to see where the firing was coming from. But it never seemed to occur to them to look upward.

Although Kirakangano was invaluable to me, the man cost me one of the finest lions I have ever seen. It happened like this.

The natives in a village had complained that a lion was killing their stock, so Kirakangano and I set out to investigate. It was evening before we arrived at the village. After listening to the herdsmen's accounts, I decided to shoot a zebra and leave the animal out for bait to lure the lion in. Kirakangano and I went out to look for a zebra herd. We found one just at dusk and fired at a fine stallion. I hit the animal too far back and in the fading light we were unable to follow him up. Next morning, we took up the trail, confident that we would soon locate the carcass by the circling vultures.

While we were skirting some bush, the Masai stopped and pointed with his spear. I saw a fine-maned lion in possession of the zebra, slowly dragging him off toward the shade of an acacia tree where he could eat at his leisure. The lion would straddle the zebra, lift him by the neck, and walk clumsily with him a few paces. Then he would stop to rest, panting like a huge dog.

As the zebra must have weighed seven or eight hundred pounds, I was greatly impressed by the strength the old fellow displayed. We cut through the brush toward the acacia tree, Kirakangano going ahead to show me the easiest way. There we waited for the lion to come closer. He was a magnificent beast, his mane covering the whole forepart of his body and even hiding his ears. Such fine manes are rare on wild lions, as most of them tear out the hair going through brush. I could see Kirakangano fidgeting beside me as the lion came closer.

Suddenly the Masai gave a whoop and charged the lion with his spear. The big cat stared at him in astonishment for a moment and then dropped the zebra and ran. Kirakangano ran parallel to him, feinting for a thrust, but the lion was too fast for him and disappeared in some bush. When I reprimanded the Masai for attacking, he innocently replied, "Ah, but he was such a big one."

I did not entirely stop using the dogs during these hunts. If a wounded lion managed to escape into the bush, I sent the dogs in to locate him. Otherwise, I knew he would be pulled down by hyenas—a dreadful fate. Lions hate and despise these scavengers. A lion will not let hyenas approach his kill while he is feeding, though they seem quite fond of the little, doglike jackals and often drop them tidbits much as man might throw a scrap of his meal to a pet dog. The hyenas seem to resent the lions' haughty superiority, and when the noble animals are wounded or too old to defend themselves, the hyenas close in to revenge themselves. No lion dies a natural death. In the end, he is always destroyed by hyenas. It seems to me that hyenas would rather feast on lion than any other meat.

The Masai complained particularly about a group of lions that lived in a swamp where it was impossible to reach them. One member of this pride was a lioness with three cubs. She had seriously mauled a native who tried to defend his herd from the pride. As this group were confirmed cattle killers, I felt it necessary to destroy them, especially the lioness, as by all reports she was becoming increasingly more aggressive. As I could not get into the swamp, I decided to bait them out.

I had had my troubles in baiting lions on the reserve. The Masai had a custom of putting the elderly members of their tribe out in the bush for hyenas to eat when the old folk reached the point of death and became too enfeebled to move about.*

* I remember one occasion when with Major David Sheldrick, a professional big game hunter and now a warden of the great Tsavo National Park, I sat up all night by a fine zebra, hoping to get a lion or two. No luck attended us, although during the night we heard lions grunting and the giggling sounds hyenas make when on something they like particularly. Our bait was not touched. I had thought it represented what lions and hyenas were most attracted by. I had something to learn. Masai natives laid our failure to an elderly Masai lady who had died the previous evening. It was she upon whom the *liwaru* and *majeannies* (lions and hyenas) had been feeding. Maybe that dear departed in the flush of her youth had been a graceful, dainty damsel for whom the Masai vied. To me the hard way of life among primitive people seems stickily grim. Beasts of the wild preferred an old Masai woman to a fat juicy zebra.

To bait out the swamp dwellers I shot a hartebeest some distance away to make sure that the noise of shooting would not disturb the lions. Then I had my oxen drag the carcass around the entire swamp. No matter where the lions left their refuge, they would cross the blood trail and probably follow it. I left the carcass of the hartebeest under the acacia tree and had my boys build a hide in the branches. These tree hides are called "machans" by hunters and are widely used for shooting the larger cats over a bait. Personally, I do not care for them, preferring to shoot from a boma built on the ground, because when shooting down from a height you are very apt to shoot over your quarry. However, there were a great number of elephants in this district that might very well blunder into a boma during the night, so I decided on the machan. I considered myself perfectly safe and did not foresee that I would be closer to death within the next two nights than at any other time on the entire trip.

The first night's vigil was a failure. The lions came, but as I raised myself to shoot, I disturbed a bird that had roosted in the upper branches of the acacia. The bird broke out of the foliage with a great noise and frightened the lions. There was nothing to do but take up my position in the machan the following evening.

As darkness set in, a heavy rain began to fall. I sat in misery, soaked to the skin, while mosquitoes wafted by a breeze from the swamp buzzed around me constantly. I could not even slap at the pests for fear of alarming the lions. But the shower also served a useful purpose, for the smell of rain always inspires lions with confidence. I could hear them giving tongue to their hunting grunts and semi-roars in the bush around me. About three o'clock in the morning, I knew they were very near. I could hear their long-drawn sighs, a sound that cannot be confused with any other African noise. I was feeling cramped, having lain all night in an uncomfortable position, and I moved slightly to get my rifle into place. Instantly I heard the lions go bounding off. Although a lion is absolutely noiseless when stalking, he makes a surprising amount of noise when he runs, his big pads thumping distinctly as he leaps along the ground. I knew they had not gone far and were probably standing nearby in the brush, watching and listening. I settled myself to wait.

Luck plays a large part in hunting. The night before, I had missed my chance because of a bird. Now a tree hyrax began to call from the hollow of a tree near my machan. The hyrax gave the lions confidence, as they knew he would not be calling if he suspected danger. Slowly they approached the bait, using the greatest caution and stopping frequently to look around. I lay on my stomach in the machan with the rifle snugged to my shoulder so I could fire without any disturbing movement.

There were two lions, both males. Holding my electric torch alongside my gun barrel, I aimed for the right-hand one and fired, knowing it would be easier to swing the rifle at the left beast from my prone position. The lion dropped. His comrade stood there watching him.

I fired at the other lion. Down he flopped and I gave him another bullet to make sure. Still no sign of the lioness. I crawled down from my machan and pulled the two dead lions under the tree, covering them with my raincoat to keep the hides from being ruined by hyenas.

I fell asleep on my perch with some branches over me for weight if not for warmth. I was awakened by the sound of something feeding at the bait. There was the lioness with her three cubs beside her. Making as little sound as I could, I raised my rifle and shot her through the head. She dropped across the bait and the cubs bolted off into the darkness. I had now accomplished my task. I climbed down from the machan and grabbing the lioness by the tail, I started to drag her over beside the other two lions.

I had put down my electric torch so I could use both hands to drag the carcass over to the trees. Suddenly I saw a form in the darkness ahead of me. For a moment I thought it was one of the cubs. Then I saw this object was far too big to be a cub. I stopped to stare at it. I was face to face with a big male lion, probably the mate of the lioness I had just killed.

I had left my rifle in the machan. For an instant the lion and I

stood looking at each other. That lion seemed as big as a bull. He
never uttered a sound. He just stood and watched me. I could see
his great shaggy mane and black muzzle not fifteen feet away. If I
started to run he might charge. But flesh and blood could not stand
the strain. I made a bolt for the tree. There were no branches but
I went up the trunk like a squirrel. When I reached the machan,
I was covered with sweat—not from the exertion of the climb but
from fear. In my fright, I nearly knocked the rifle out of the machan
as I climbed over the side. I still could see nothing for I had left
my electric torch below.

After a few minutes, I could hear the lion move over to the bait
and begin to eat noisily. After listening for some time, I could judge
his position. I aimed as carefully as I could and fired. There was no
sound after the report of the shot had died away but I could faintly
see him lying beside the bait. He had died instantly. Much as I
wanted to inspect his mane, I stayed in the machan the rest of the
night and not all the black-maned lions in Africa could have
tempted me down.

I kept dozing off and waking with the most vivid of horrible
dreams, imagining myself being torn apart by the peaceful beasts
lying beneath me. When morning came, I went down to examine
my lions. The last lion had a fine oaten-colored mane and I considered it one of the best trophies of the whole trip.

Kirakangano and I set out at dawn the next morning to look for
the lioness' cubs. We found all three of them hiding under some
tufts of dried grass. They looked like woolly teddy bears but
snarled and spit at us with a vengeance. We carried them back to
camp and I fed them by sticking their noses into a bowl of milk. The
cubs did not know how to lap as they were used to getting their
meals direct from their mother, but they licked their milky noses and
got a taste of the warm fluid. For a long time after that they got
their substance by sticking their noses or paws into the bowl and
then licking the milk off their fur. But they eventually learned how
to drink and became very tame. I kept them tied to the foot of my
camp cot and a great nuisance I found them, fighting and squalling

most of the night. Yet they were plucky little chaps and always ready for a fight or a frolic. Once they got loose during the day and had a fine fight with my only pillow. When I returned to camp, my tent looked as though a blizzard of white feathers had struck the place. Later, I gave them to a friend of mine who liberated them in a district where they could live without doing harm to native stock.

I have often heard it said that wild animals have an instinctive dread of fire. This old saying has been repeated so often that most people accept it as a fact. I was no exception and took it for granted that lions would never approach a campfire. An incident that occurred one night while I was on the Masai Reserve taught me differently.

I had shot a zebra for bait that afternoon, and had the oxen drag the animal to my camp. I usually let a carcass "ripen" for twenty-four hours or more before putting it out. I told the boys to leave the zebra near our campfire for I was confident that no animals would come close to the blaze.

Kirakangano went off to spend the night at a nearby Masai kraal, taking the dogs and oxen with him. We never left these animals in camp if we could avoid it. The oxen scented the odor of prowling lions and would stampede if they were not in a kraal and we had lost two dogs to leopards, which will go to any lengths to obtain dog meat, their favorite food. After Kirakangano had left, my porters curled up around the fire in their blankets and fell asleep. I sat in my camp chair watching the fire and smoking my pipe, my thoughts far away among the sand spits of Lochar and scenes of my youth.

Suddenly I realized that I was looking into the faces of nine lions that had come out of the shadows and were standing facing me. I did not dare to move. My rifle was in my tent where I had left a Dietz lantern burning. I could only sit motionless and watch them. The lions studied me carefully. Then they walked around my sleeping boys to the other side of the campfire and attacked the dead zebra. They fell on the carcass with growls and snarls, ripping off great strips of hide as though the thick zebra skins were so much paper.

I faded out of the camp chair and inched for the tent flap, my flesh tingling with every move. The lions stopped eating to glare at me. I felt dwarfed by the great beasts. In a couple of bounds they could have been on top of me. Meanwhile my boys lay soundly sleeping only a few feet from them. I wanted to make a dash for the tent but was afraid that any sudden movement might bring on a charge. I waited until the lions had returned to their feeding, then moved foot by foot until I was opposite the tent flap. Quickly I stepped inside and grabbed my rifle. The touch of the cold steel had never felt so welcome.

Now I was in another dilemma. If I fired, my porters would leap to their feet and be between me and the lions. The trek chain which had been used for dragging the zebra to camp was still around his neck and as the lions fought over the carcass, they banged the chain up and down, making a terrible din. I was afraid this noise would awaken the porters and when they saw the lions they would panic. To have terror-stricken natives bolting about amid nine lions was not a pleasant prospect. I decided to take the chance and shoot. I aimed at the chest of the largest lion and fired, hitting him squarely. He died without a murmur. At the report, the other lions drew back a few feet and then sprang again on the carcass. The natives continued to sleep. For a moment I wondered if they were all dead.

I began firing steadily into the pride. The back blast of my rifle put out the Dietz lantern behind me and I aimed by the light of the fire. Four lions went down, the last one hit rather low in the chest. He leaped up and began to bound about stiff-legged as though on springs. I hastily jammed another cartridge into the chamber of my rifle and finished him. The rest of the pride dropped back into the fringe of darkness. I reloaded singly as there was no time to do otherwise. Stepping forward to get a better aim, I fired at a big lioness. She gave her tail an upward flick as the bullet hit her and then turned and vanished into the darkness. The rest followed her.

It seems incredible but my porters were still fast asleep. Neither the noise made by the lions nor my shots had disturbed them in the least. I had many times noted this almost trancelike sleep of natives but never before had I seen such a remarkable example of it.

I built up the fire and then went around kicking the soles of the porters' feet. One of them woke, stretched, and sat up. He yawned, and then saw the four dead lions lying within a few feet of him. The man gave a frantic yell and leaped straight up into the air. Screaming like a lunatic he bolted into the tent, followed sheeplike by the rest of the porters who had no idea what the trouble was about. They sat in the tent shivering until I explained what had happened. In a few minutes they were all asleep again, lying on the floor of my tent. Insomnia was not their failing.

Kirakangano returned with the dogs next morning and we at once started out on the trail of the wounded lioness. We left the porters singing their cheerfully indecent songs and skinning out the lions. They carefully collected the already smelling fat from the covering of the stomach, heart and kidneys, as the natives believe this fat can be used to prearrange the sex of a child. If the man eats a tablespoon of lion's fat before sexual intercourse, the child will be a boy. Half a tablespoon produces a girl. Natives care little about the hide of a lion, but prize this fat highly.

We hit the blood spoor a hundred yards from camp. The lioness was badly wounded. She had lain down several times, the rest of the pride stopping to wait for her. For a while the trail led through open bush, perfect hunting country for you could see twenty yards ahead of you. We pressed on eagerly, hoping to come upon the lioness in this easy cover. But the spoor made a circuit toward a thick, nasty tangle of brush. Here was real trouble.

It was deathly quiet in the thicket. Not so much as the chirp of a bird could be heard. I knew we must be close to the wounded lioness and at any moment she might burst out of the cover on top of us.

The dogs were growing increasingly more restless. My Airedales were whining with excitement and at last I told them to go ahead. They sprang forward. Almost at once a din of savage snarls and growls broke out directly in front of us. The other dogs dashed past me, going in single file through the dense cover. I could hear the familiar sound of a fight raging through the bush, the deep-throated growls and harsh grunts of the lion mixed with the yelling cries of the dogs.

Kirakangano and I forced our way through the bushes to reach them. We had hardly taken a dozen steps when we came on a rounded lair in the high grass streaked with dried blood. Here the lioness had been resting. Beside the lair two of my brave Airedales were lying dead, their mouths and eyes still open. They had burst in on her and taken the brunt of her attack. Kirakangano and I owed our lives to the dogs, for the lioness was so cunningly concealed we would never have seen her in time.

The other dogs were still fighting with her and we could hear them racing through the brush, stopping to bark frantically when she turned at bay. We hurried toward the sound. The dogs were driving the lioness from the thicket into open bush. We followed. The Masai was carrying his spear at the ready, the long shaft beautifully balanced between thumb and forefinger. His every muscle was tense and quivering.

One of the collies came limping back to me, horribly torn. I saw nothing could be done for the poor brute and shot him quickly for he was in great pain. At the sound of my shot, the wounded lioness suddenly leaped up from a tuft of dead grass a few feet away. At the same instant, a second lioness broke from the cover on my right and charged us.

There was no time to think. Both the cats were nearly on us, each coming from a different direction. I fired at the second lioness as she seemed more determined. The bullet hit her half an inch over the left eye. At the same moment, I saw Kirakangano plunge his spear into the body of the wounded animal beside us. She turned fiercely, grabbing the spear shaft with her teeth, and tried to pull it out of her body. Kirakangano started to draw his double-bladed knife from his belt, but before he could get the knife free I finished her with a shot in the neck.

Kirakangano and I silently shook hands. Without him, one or the other of the two lionesses would surely have gotten us. Of all the natives I have known in Africa, this man was undoubtedly the bravest and the coolest head in a tight spot.

My time on the Masai Reserve was beginning to run out. I had up to now shot seventy lions and still the tribe had cause for complaint. Captain Ritchie wished me to eliminate the damage doers, so I decided to try shooting from a thorn boma at night. This is hardly a sporting way of hunting, but I had come to the reserve not for sport but on business and so I went ahead with my plans for a night shoot.

I hitched a yoke of oxen to a zebra that I had shot and had them drag the bait several miles across the plains, finally leaving the carcass on the upwind side of a likely cover. If there were any lions in the thicket, the wind would carry the scent of the zebra to them. At the same time, other lions wandering across the plains at night would come upon the dragged trail and follow it like hounds until they reached the bait. Thus I was fairly sure of getting some visitors.

My porters cut brush wood and thorn branches making a horse-shoe-shaped boma near the bait where I intended to spend the night with Kirakangano. We made sure the zebra was well staked down so the lions could not carry it away. I took particular care to have my boys cover the top of the boma with double layers of thorn bush so no light could come through. I have often seen lions run from a bait when I made a slight motion in the boma, and for a long time I could not understand how they knew I was inside. Later, I discovered that the cats could see moving shadows cast by starlight filtering through the top of the hide.

When all was ready, Kirakangano and I took up our positions in the boma. I gave him an electric torch and showed him how to flash a light on the bait when the time came to shoot so I could see to aim. Kirakangano was fascinated by the torch and kept switching it on and off until I told him to stop. I had two rifles loaded beside me and cartridges in my pockets and belt and on the ground near me. No matter where I reached, I could not fail to grab a handful.

As it grew dusk, several hyenas slunk up to the bait, followed by two jackals. The jackals sat anxiously feasting their eyes on the zebra while the hyenas slunk back and forth to make sure all was clear. Finally one dashed in and grabbed the exposed entrails, dashing off with them and giving vent to wailing guffaws. The others now came closer. They began to pull at the bait. Then I saw them rush off while the jackals approached confidently. That meant lions were coming in. I laid my rifle in position and waited.

In a few minutes I heard the low, hollow, deep and unmistakable breathing of lions behind the boma. They circled us and suddenly sprang on the zebra. I whispered to Kirakangano to switch on the light. To my astonishment, I heard him whisper "Taballo!" Masai for "Wait!" I glanced over at him and saw the man was paralyzed with fear. The unaccustomed experience of shooting lions at night from a boma had completely unnerved him, yet in daylight this man would walk up to an infuriated lion with nothing but his spear.

I grabbed the torch from his hand and flashed it through a small opening overlooking the bait. What a sight! There were at least twenty lions and lionesses a few yards in front of us, some standing by the carcass, others lying down and licking the bait. Two fine, black-maned lions stood staring at the light, the essence of defiance, their manes and chests covered with blood and filth from the stomach contents of the zebra—for they had already begun to feed. By this time Kirakangano was literally shivering with terror, but I knew he would gain confidence as soon as the shooting began. Wedging the torch between two thorn branches so it shone on the scene I slipped my rifle barrel through a hole in the brush and fired at what seemed to be the larger of the two males. A chorus of grunts and savage growls went up from the pride. I fired again and yet again. The animals had retreated beyond the range of the torch so I stopped to reload. Kirakangano was beginning to recover from his funk and I gave him a piece of tobacco to chew on. Masai love the weed. The sting of the tobacco seemed to restore him some-what and the sight of the three dead lions was more than any Masai could regard indifferently. The pride had begun to return. Kirakangano grabbed the torch and began to shine it from one lion to another, moving so rapidly in his excitement I had scarcely time to aim. A lion dropped at every report of my gun. It was a stern measure but it had to be. The lions paid no attention to the shots. They would turn to sniff a dead friend fallen beside them and then go on with their feeding.

Ten lions now lay dead around the zebra. Then for some reason a fine black-maned lion came sneaking around our boma from the side. He stood there, giving vent to some bloodcurdling sounds. The ground seemed to quiver with the reverberation of his roars. This outburst of sound alarmed the rest of the pride and they slowly withdrew with the old male following them.

I had no intention of allowing these fine hides to be torn to pieces by scavenger hyenas. When I was sure the lions had de-parted, I told Kirakangano to hold the light on the scene while I went out and pulled the dead animals closer to the boma. The Masai had now lost all his fear and was very keen. I left the boma and started toward the dead lions. I had almost reached them when the light suddenly went out.

Calling to Kirakangano to turn the torch on, I took another few steps forward. Suddenly I stumbled over the supple, hot body of a lion and fell on top of him. I heard a muffled breathing beneath me and a low grunt. The lion was still alive. I flung myself clear and raced for the boma. I expected every second to feel the lion on my back but I reached the doorway and bolted inside. There was Kirakangano sitting with the pieces of the torch laid around him. He had become curious as to how the strange thing worked and had taken it apart while I was out in the darkness stumbling over wounded lions.

I spoke to him pretty roundly and he apologized. I reassembled the torch and put another bullet in the lion to make sure he was properly dead. Then we settled down to wait. During the night two more prides came to the bait. When dawn broke, I saw a sight I doubt if anyone has ever seen before or will ever see again. Eighteen lions lay dead before me. After the noise and turmoil of the night, the scene looked strangely peaceful. Nothing was moving except lion flies that were doing their creepy, jumpy antics between the hind legs of the males. Taking care that there were no wounded lions about, Kirakangano and I left the boma and went out to stand over the dead animals. I must own that I felt regrets. Yet I knew these animals must die or the Masai would suffer by their depredations. An artificial condition had created the surplus of lions and it could only be corrected by artificial means. Brave and skillful as the Masai were, they could not cope with the problem alone.

Today, the government has forbidden the great Masai spearing lion hunts there which were customary when I first came to the reserve. Too many of the young men were killed pitting shield and spear against fang and claw. As there are few people alive who ever saw one of these desperate encounters, I will describe in the next chapter how these battles took place.

7

Masai Spearmen: The Bravest of the Brave

I saw my first spear hunt when I was staying in a small Masai community not far from Lake Magadi. The night before, a lion had jumped the twelve-foot boma that surrounded the village, seized a cow, and leaped back over the barrier with the cow in his mouth. I know this feat sounds incredible, as the lion weighed no more than four hundred pounds and the cow probably weighed nearly twice that. Yet a male lion can perform this exploit with no more trouble than a fox has in carrying off a chicken.

A lion shows a special knack in getting partly under the carcass and shifting the weight onto his back while still holding the cow's throat in his mouth. When jumping the barricade, the lion's tail becomes absolutely rigid and seems to act as a balance. The Masai have assured me that a lion without a tail could not possibly perform this feat.

I was prepared to start out on the lion's trail the next morning, but the moran in this community told me somewhat contemptuously that my help was not needed. They would handle the situation themselves. At that time, I found it hard to believe that a group of men could kill an adult lion with spears. I asked if I could go along and bring my gun. Permission was politely granted me. That night I loaded my .416 Rigby magazine rifle, never doubting that it would fall to my lot to kill any lions that we might find.

We started off at daybreak. I followed the spearmen. There were ten of them. Magnificent-looking men, slender but finely muscled, not one under six feet. To give their limbs free play, each man removed his one garment, the long piece of cloth they wear draped over their shoulders, and wrapped it around his left arm. They carried their brightly-painted shields balanced on their shoulders. Their spears were in their right hands. The warriors wore their ostrich-plume headdresses as though going into battle and bracelets of fur around their ankles. Otherwise, they were completely naked.

We picked up the spoor of the lion and the moran began to track. The lion had gorged on the cow during the night and was lying up in some dense cover. They threw stones into the bushes at random until the savage growls of the lion showed he had been hit. When the moran had spotted the cat by his angry grunts and snarls, they began to throw stones in good earnest; then the bushes began to shake. Suddenly the lion burst out a hundred yards from us and went bounding away across the plains, his gorged belly swinging from side to side as he ran.

Instantly the Masai were after him, giving their wild cries as they sped through the tall, yellow grass. The lion, still heavy with his great meal, did not run far. He stopped and turned at bay. The spearmen spread out to encircle him. The lion stood in the middle of the ring, looking this way and that, snarling in a way to make one's blood run cold as the spearmen slowly closed in.

The lion allowed the men to come within forty yards. Then I could tell that he was preparing to charge. His head was held low, just above his outstretched forepaws. His hindquarters were slightly arched so he could bring his rear legs well forward and get the maximum spring behind his rush. He began to dig his claws into the ground, much as a sprinter digs in with his spiked shoes to make sure he does not slip when he makes his first jump.

I concentrated on the sinister inverted curve of the lion's tail. Just before he charges, a lion always twitches the tasseled tip of his tail three times in rapid succession. On the third twitch he comes for you at amazing speed, going so fast he seems only a small part of his real size.

The spearmen knew as well as I did that the lion was preparing to attack. By what seemed to be a single impulse, all their spear arms moved back together for the cast. The men were so tense with excitement that their taut shoulder muscles twitched slightly, making ripples of sunlight play along the spear blades. You could have driven a nail into any one of them without his feeling it.

Suddenly the tip of the lion's tail began to twitch. One! Two! Three! Then he charged for the ring of spearmen. At once half a dozen spears leaped through the air toward him. I saw one plunge into his shoulder and the next instant the spear head broke through the hide on his other side. The lion never paused in his stride. In his path stood one of the moran, a youngster on his first hunt. The boy never flinched. He braced himself to meet the charge, holding his shield in front of him and swaying back slightly so as to put the whole weight of his body into his spear thrust. The lion sprang for the boy. With one blow he knocked the young moran's shield out of his hand as though it were cardboard. Then he reared up, trying to sweep the boy toward him with his outstretched paws.

The boy drove his spear a good two feet into the lion's chest. The mortally wounded beast sprang on him, fixing his hind claws in the boy's belly to insure his grip while at the same time he seized the boy's shoulder in his jaws.

The young warrior went down under the weight of the great cat. Instantly all the other moran were around the dying lion. It was too close quarters for spears. The men used their double-edged simis, heavy knives about two feet long. Shouldering each other out of the way, they hacked like madmen at the lion's head. In a matter of seconds, they had sliced the head to pieces, starting with the muzzle and shearing off an inch or so at a time. I saw one man deliver a terrible blow that split the lion's skull open, but whether the animal was still alive at the moment I can hardly say.

I had been quite unable to use my gun during this battle. A man with a gun is a positive menace at such times. Once the frenzied warriors begin to circle the lion, a rifleman cannot fire without running a grave chance of hitting them.

I examined the wounded boy. His wounds were truly frightful yet he seemed completely indifferent to them. I sewed him up with a needle and thread. He paid no more attention to the process than if I were patting him on the back.

The hide of the lion was so perforated with spear thrusts and simi-slashes that it was worthless as a trophy. It was simply a cut and bloody mass of dirty yellow hair. The dignity and majesty of the noble beast had completely departed, leaving only a sorry remnant.

When we returned to the Masai manyatta or village, the wounded boy was urged to eat great quantities of raw beef and then given cattle blood as a purgative so he could gorge himself again. Some of the other moran had been clawed by the lion but they made no attempt to guard against infection, except to wash their wounds with water. Later I saw some Masai communities soak the root of a bush called the "olkilorite" in water, which gives it a permanganate of potash color. It seems to act as an antiseptic and promotes healing.

I hope the lad recovered. He certainly held top honors for the day, and the young girls were looking at him with such admiration that, if he lived, he would have no trouble picking out a suitable sweetheart.

The Masai believe that the bravest act a man can perform is to grab a lion by the tail and hold the animal so the other warriors can close in with their spears and simis. Any man who performs this feat four times is given the title of "melombuki" and ranks as a captain. It is also an unwritten law among them that any man who gains this title must be willing to fight anything living. I doubt if more than two out of a thousand Masai ever become melombuki, although the competition among the moran to gain this honor is very keen.

I have seen several of these "tail pullings" during Masai lion hunts and it is a wonder to me that the men attempting the feat ever come out alive. I remember one hunt in which fifty or more spearmen were involved. They had put up two lions and a lioness. The animals tried to reach some heavy scrub but the warriors cut them off. The lions retreated into a small clump of bush near a dry, sandy watercourse. When possible, a pursued lion nearly always makes for one of these dry stream beds with its canopies of over-hanging bush. In a matter of minutes, the moran had the thicket surrounded and began to move forward for the kill.

As the circle of yelling warriors closed in, the concealed lions began to growl. Then without any warning, the largest of the lions broke from the cover and made a rush for freedom. He was a fine sight as he dashed along the stream bottom, tail down and going all out at a gallop. He was headed straight for two moran, who raised their spears and prepared to meet his charge. But the big male had no desire to fight; he wished only to escape. He gave a mighty bound straight over the heads of the two spearmen, spin-ning one of them around sideways with a blow from his flank.

The other moran made tongue-clicking sounds of disapproval, partly because the two young men had allowed the lion to escape and partly because the lion had refused to fight. I have often noticed that the old lions with the finest manes are more reluctant to give battle than young males or females. The same is true of elephants. An old bull with fine ivory is shyer than a young bull or cow. I suppose they learn discretion with the years. It has also seemed to me that lions are able to tell young, inexperienced moran and will deliberately direct their attack at these youngsters. This may be nothing but my imagination yet the younger men are apt to be hesitant and uncertain in their actions and I believe the lions can detect it.

As the spearmen closed in around the thicket, they bunched to-gether, jostling each other in their desire to be first to spill blood. The remaining two lions were clearly visible in the bush, standing shoulder to shoulder and both giving grating roars. When the moran were within ten yards of the lions, spears began to fly. One of the spears struck the lioness in the loin and she came out with a scream of rage and pain. For an instant she stood up on her hind legs, pawing the air like the crest on a coat of arms. Then she

dropped to bite at the spear in her flank. At that moment, one of
the moran threw down his spear and, rushing forward, grabbed her
by the root of her tail. A moran never grabs a lion by the tasseled
end of the tail. A lion can make his tail as stiff as a gun barrel,
and a man would be swept aside by a single jerk.

At once the moran's comrades dashed in, slashing with their
simis. At moments like this, the spearmen work themselves up to
a pitch of blind frenzy. They seem to be mere automatic stabbers.
Their faces are expressionless. There is no teamwork; each man is
out to do the killing by himself. The lioness was digging her hind
feet into the ground to get purchase forward and the tail puller
was dragging her back. Suddenly the lioness went up on her hind
legs, striking left and right with her paws at the men around her.
Although I saw her blows go home, the men never flinched. They
told me afterward that they never feel any pain at the time of a
mauling—they are at too high a pitch of excitement. Apparently
neither does the lion. Both sides continue to fight until one drops
from loss of blood.

Slowly the lioness fell to the ground. Then all I could see were
the flashing blades of the simis as the men hacked away in their
blind fury. When it was over, the animal's head was cut into
shreds. There must have been a dozen spears in the body. It looked
like a bloody pincushion.

From the noise on the other side of the clump of bush, I knew
another group of spearmen were busy with the second lion. I saw
a warrior kneel and hold out his shield in a taunting fashion. The
next instant the lion had leaped on it, knocking the man flat. The
prone warrior tried vainly to get in a spear thrust while the lion
mauled his exposed shoulder. I shouted to the other men to keep
back and let me get in a shot, but nothing could be heard above the
wild, falsetto yells of the warriors and the deep grunts of the lion
as he lacerated the prostrate man. I saw two spears plunge into
the lion's body and then the moran fell on the raging beast with
their simis.

Before the lion was dead, he had seriously wounded one of the attacking moran besides ripping open the shoulder of the warrior lying under the shield. I did what I could for the injured men. They both had deep claw and fang incisions and were losing considerable blood. As I sewed up one man's injuries, he glanced down casually at the terrible cuts and made the same contemptuous clicking sound with his tongue that the moran had made when they saw the first lion escape. The warrior's attitude seemed to be "What a nuisance!" yet a white man in a similar situation would have been wild with pain.

Strangely enough, I have never heard of any bones being broken by the lion's teeth. The wounds are all flesh wounds. Apparently the lion's fang teeth are wide enough apart to close around the bones. Yet when a lion grabs a man by the shoulder, his fangs often meet in his victim's body. If you pour disinfectant into one wound, it will run out the other.

The spearmen have assured me that a lion's most dangerous weapon is neither his teeth nor his claws proper but what might be called his dewclaws. On the inside of each lion's forelegs is an extra claw about two inches long. These claws roughly correspond to a man's thumbs. They are curved and very sharp. The dewclaws are usually kept folded against the lion's legs and are difficult to see, but the lion can extend them at will so they stand out almost at right angles. These two claws are keen as brush hooks and very strong. A lion slashes with them and can disembowel a man with one blow of these terrible hooks.

The Masai spears are made by native smiths from bits of iron ore picked up in the streams. The smiths do not understand the art of tempering the metal so the spears are soft. A man can easily bend the blade over his knee. But the moran are able to throw their weapons with such skill that the spear will sometimes pass completely through an animal. If the spear strikes a bone, it will bend almost at right angles. The owner never straightens the blade until he returns to the village. The bent spear is proof positive that he was in at the kill, and so is highly prized.

While I was in the reserve, I also saw the Masai spear leopards.

I consider this an even greater feat than killing lions. Although a leopard does not weigh more than two hundred pounds, he is far quicker and more aggressive than a lion. Leopards are cunning beasts and will lie quietly until you are almost on top of them. Then they will suddenly charge with the deadliest speed and determination. Also, leopards lie up in caves and other dark recesses, while lions prefer the open bush. A man crawling among boulders after a leopard is in an unenviable position.

I accompanied three spearmen who were after a leopard that had been killing their goats. Unlike the noble lions, a leopard will kill for the sheer lust of killing. This cat had left several dead goats behind him, never even bothering to eat their flesh. After considerable tracking, the moran finally marked the animal down in a narrow belt of high grass. If the cat had been a lion, a few stones would have brought him out charging or at least forced him to growl and show his hiding place. But a leopard is a wily brute and, although we threw a bushel of stones into the grass, he gave no sign. Unfortunately, I did not have my dogs with me so there was nothing for it but to drive the animal out.

With only three spearmen, I was able to use my gun without fear of hitting one of the men. I told the moran to spread out on either side of me and keep well back. I knew when the leopard came, he would come fast. I was sure that the men would not have time to use their spears, and I would have scarcely time for a quick snap shot at the cat as he sprang. I was underrating the moran, but I still did not realize their marvelous skill with their long, delicate blades.

We moved slowly through the waist-high grass, much as though beating for pheasants. The moran kept a few paces behind me, their shields held before them and their spears raised for the cast. We moved forward a foot at a time, stopping constantly to look around for the big cat. The strip of grass was not long, but this slow progress was nerve-racking, especially as we were all at a high point of tension.

Suddenly the leopard exploded out of the grass a yard or so in front of me and to my right. He made a great bound for me. Before I could get my rifle up, the moran on my right had transfixed the beast with his spear. The leopard had scarcely left the ground before the thin blade was through him. The spear hit the leopard between the neck and shoulders, pinning him to the ground. He lay there squirming and snarling, unable to free himself. Immediately the moran drew his simi and leaped forward to finish him off. I had great difficulty restraining him until I had time to put a bullet into the skewered animal and save a good skin from being slashed to ribbons.

When a moran is about to throw his spear, he takes up a position just like a shooting stance with his left foot slightly advanced for balance. When he throws, the whole weight of his body goes into the cast. The spear seems to shiver as it flies through the air. Most of the spears have a narrow ridge on either side of the blade and I believe this may cause the spear to rotate slightly in flight, somewhat like a rifle bullet. A moran is absolutely accurate with his spear up to twenty yards, even when throwing at a moving target.

At the end of three months, I started back to Nairobi with two oxcarts full of lion hides. In ninety days, I had shot eighty-eight lions and ten leopards—a record which I believe has never been approached and, I sincerely hope, will never be approached again. The natives had filled a hundred-weight drum with lion fat. I had a box full of lion "floating bones." These curved bones vary in size up to four inches and are found in the last shoulder muscle tissue. They are not attached to any other bones in the lion's body and apparently act as regulators, preventing shoulder rack when the lions make their great bounds. They are much in demand among the East Indians, who set them in gold and make ornaments out of them.

Only twenty of the lions I killed had really prime manes. The rest were either lionesses or had manes ruined by the thick brush. If I had been shooting only to get good trophies, I could have obtained more first-rate hides, but I was more interested in destroying cattle killers. Often these beasts had poor manes, for they were old or diseased, which may well be why they had turned to killing cows instead of their natural prey.

When the Masai heard I was leaving, they were greatly distressed. The elders of the tribe assembled and, after much jabbering, came to me with a proposition. They wanted to buy me from the Game Department. After due consideration, they had settled on five hundred cows as the price. As a good wife costs only three cows, I felt highly flattered.

8

Life and "Death" of a
White Hunter

The years immediately following my introduction to the Masai were big years for me. Nairobi was the heart of the big-game country and nearly every sportsman who came to Africa to shoot big game outfitted in Nairobi. I was seldom idle. I regarded the Masai Reserve as my own private shooting territory. The Masai were my friends and I was sure of a warm welcome in any of their kraals. I could guarantee any client I took there some of the best shooting in Africa and I profited by it. Today, the reserve with its great herds of game and magnificent lions is a prime tourist attraction. It has been cut up by roads and the best camping spots are all well marked. But in those days, few white hunters were acquainted with the district.

Hilda and I bought a big, old house outside Nairobi called "Clairmont." It was a lovely place with beautiful old trees scattered about the grounds and a river running at the bottom of the garden, which we dammed and made into a fine pool. The fish warden gave us some talapia fish spawn for our pool so I could have fishing right at my back door. In the evenings, we would often see wild game wandering through our garden. In Clairmont, I was able to gather together all my trophies. I had a great pair of elephant tusks that weighed 153 pounds each on either side of the living-room door, Masai shields and spears over the fireplace, and a collection of outstandingly fine heads and horns on the wall. Glass-fronted gun cabinets held my guns. Most important of all, I had room for my library of books on Africa and hunting. I think I may say that this was one of the finest collections of Africana to be found in Kenya and I was constantly adding to it. Dealers from all over the world sent me their catalogues. Often in the evening, Hilda and I would sit by the fire, she with her knitting and I with one of my books. I read the stories of the great hunters and explorers of the past— Selous, Speke, Sir Samuel Baker, Stanley, Livingstone, and many another. I liked to feel that in a modest way I was following in the footsteps of these great men.

We had six children—four boys and two girls. As the children came, Hilda found it increasingly hard to go out on safari with me. Of course, she had never been able to go when I had a client. But often I would round up some of my boys and old Kirakangano and we would go out for the sheer love of being in the bush. This was the best part of hunting—not having to worry whether you got a trophy in a limited time or trying to fill up your shooting license by senseless killing of game day after day. We would simply travel about opening fresh country, sometimes discovering new fertile places to take clients but more often finding nothing more rewarding than the pleasure of knowing that we were probably the first white persons to see that particular valley or range of hills.

Hilda never really cared much about shooting, and this has always somewhat astonished me. She is a slender little person and no doubt the kick of a heavy rifle is too much for her, but she showed signs of being an excellent wing shot with a light shotgun. However, her heart was never in it and I would not wish her to be any different. Several lady sportsmen that I have guided were magnificent shots, but I would hardly have liked to be married to them. I recall one woman I took out during the buffalo rutting season who was so fascinated by the big bulls in the act of breeding that she never fired a shot and would do nothing but sit on a hill and admire the great creatures. That woman should have been a man. However, I did miss Hilda's companionship. Before the children arrived, we had been much together—making plans for the future, discussing the details of my next safari, or arranging for a trip "into the blue" with as much enthusiasm as youngsters planning a picnic. Now Hilda was constantly worrying over the children. I had no idea that raising children was such a problem. It seemed to me that my parents raised me with very little trouble. My life and Hilda's life began to fall into two separate ruts—she worked at home with the children while I stayed on safari with clients. We seldom saw each other. I realized that Hilda's first duty lay with the children but a man can become very tired of clients.

However, I had my own solution for that. When I grew too tired of guiding, I would go off on my own—generally ivory hunting. In those days, there was little or no restriction on the numbers of elephants shot in the outlying districts and I made good use of this fact. Hunting elephants was a paying business. At that time ivory was selling for twenty-four shillings a pound—say an average of 150 pounds for a pair of good tusks. An experienced hunter could drop an elephant with nearly every shot, and a .450 No. 2 cartridge cost only one and sixpence. I was enough of a Scotsman to like a bargain like that.

I remember once returning to Nairobi after I had been gone for a long spell, ivory hunting. I had had a good season and brought back hundreds of tusks—just how many I no longer recall. My safari boys had loaded the tusks helter skelter onto the train with me and we had said good-by. When I arrived at the railroad station in Nairobi, the problem arose of how to transport the ivory to my home. In those days, there were no taxis, only rickshaws drawn by natives. I hired every rickshaw at the station, loaded them with ivory, and put myself at the head of the procession with my two largest tusks roped on either side of my rickshaw. Off we started down the main street. There was no traffic in those days. Cars were virtually unknown. As we went along, people came out of their houses to stare. Others stood on the pavement, counting the tusks and computing their weight. I doubt if any of them had ever seen such a display of ivory before. It was a proud moment.

Then I saw Hilda and Doreen, our little five-year-old girl, coming toward me in another rickshaw. I had a full beard that came down to my waist and Hilda did not recognize me. I sat grinning at them and suddenly little Doreen cried, "Mummy, that's daddy!"

Hilda glanced at me and tried to hush the child. "No, dear, every man you see with trophies isn't daddy. You've forgotten how he looks. This man has a beard."

"I don't care," cried Doreen. "It is daddy, I know! I know!" I burst out laughing. Hilda stared at me a moment and then was out of her rickshaw crying, "Oh, John, John!"

One way and another, I was doing well as a white hunter. Counting the sale of ivory and the occasional gifts made me by some wealthy client, such as an expensive rifle or some de luxe camping equipment, I was making as much as the governor of the colony. When some dignitary came to hunt in Kenya, I was often called upon to guide him. Once when I was out in the bush with a young American couple, I received an urgent message by runner from Nairobi. It read, "The Prince of Wales is arriving for a hunting tour. You have been selected as the white hunter best qualified to guide him. Return to Nairobi at once."

I showed the note to my clients. The young American exploded. "Who's the Prince of Wales?" he shouted. "My money's as good as his. You agreed to guide us. Are you going back on your word?"

I felt the young chap was in the right and sent a message to Nairobi that I could not break my agreement. So the great honor of guiding the prince fell to someone else, another fine hunter who did a very capable job of it. But I could not help but be amused by the indignant cry of the democratic young Yankee: "Who's the Prince of Wales?"

Although I could not accept the offer, I was naturally flattered that I should have been considered for the position. It meant that I had reached the top of my profession in the opinion of men who knew big-game hunting. When we were first married, Hilda and I thought that if I ever became a recognized white hunter all our troubles would be over. We would have security, for by Kenya standards, the salary of a white hunter was fabulous. I had now achieved my youthful ambition, but other problems were appearing that I had never foreseen.

Our children were growing up. One evening I found that the front door had been carefully left on the catch and our oldest boy Gordon was not in bed. I knew well where the lad had gone. I remembered my own youth and had no doubt the young rascal was out with net or snare in the brush. I was a bit disappointed that the boy had not come to me for advice, but doubtless he wanted to learn the art by himself.

Late that night, I heard him come home. I met him on the stairs, hoping to see his catch. Imagine my feelings when I found the boy in evening clothes. He had gone into Nairobi to attend some dance. I took the lad heartily to task for wasting his time over such nonsense and was still fuming next morning at breakfast. To my surprise, Hilda sympathized with the boy. "After all, John, everyone can't be a hunter," she told me.

"Do you want the boy to grow up to be a tradesman or a farmer?" I burst out.

"I want him to follow his own bent," Hilda said. "When you criticize him for behaving like normal boys, you are being as unfair to him as your parents were to you."

Although I have deep respect for Hilda's opinions, I must say I considered this a ridiculous statement. For a boy to want to spend his time in the woods with a good dog and a gun is a natural healthy desire. To dress up and go prancing around a floor with some young girl is sheer stupidity.

But I did not despair of the boys. Often a man cannot appreciate the art of hunting until he has actually been in the field and had some experience. Gordon showed great promise as a hunter and I spent hours drawing diagrams of the big game animals and showing him exactly where to place his shots. When I considered him ready, we went out after elephant together. We came on a herd and there was a fine bull standing in perfect position for an ear shot. Instead of shooting, Gordon whispered to me, "Father, where will I hit him?" Wasted were all my hours of instruction. I simply pointed to my ear. Gordon fired and the bull dropped—dead while he was still falling. I felt that one lesson in the field did more to show the boy something of elephant hunting than all the talking in the world. I had no doubt that as the others grew up, they too would learn from practical experience, rather than from my example.

Despite what I have said about clients, I want to make it plain that I was never one of those white hunters who affects to despise them. Clients were my bread-and-butter. Some of my clients were as good as the best and some were bad, but I did what I could to please them all. At times it was not easy. There were Americans, Europeans, British, and Orientals—each with his own customs and desires. The relationship between a white hunter and his clients is a peculiar one. He is paid by them and so becomes their employee, subject to their orders. Yet he is responsible to both the safari outfitter and the game department for the clients' conduct and also for their safety. If his clients wish to do something that the hunter considers unwise, he must stop them. If the client refuses to be stopped, the hunter is then in a difficult position. I have known of a few cases where white hunters became so indignant at their clients' constant refusal to observe the laws of common sense that they took the whole outfit back to Nairobi and canceled the safari. Such affairs are most miserable but fortunately occur very seldom. I am happy to say no such disaster ever happened to me.

Quarrels between the white hunter and his client are not always the client's fault. A white hunter is only a human being and he is under a constant strain. He combines the responsibilities of a ship's captain with the duties of the mayor of a small and constantly moving town. He presides over two or three dozen native boys, ranging from the kitchen *toto* who cleans the dishes, to the head tracker and gunbearer on whom his life may someday depend. He must preserve discipline among the boys and yet keep them happy. If anything goes wrong, he alone is held accountable. He cannot shift responsibility onto the shoulders of an inefficient head boy or a nervous gunbearer. He is supposed to know the capabilities of everybody in his outfit before starting out.

The white hunter must oversee the putting up and taking down of the tents. He must see that all the thousand and one items of equipment are correctly loaded and unloaded. If one of the lorries breaks down, he must be able to repair it. When someone gets sick, the white hunter must be able to doctor him. Yet he must never forget that his main duty is not merely to supervise the safari. He is hired as a hunter and must be able to produce game.

To do this successfully, he must know many different sections of the country and know each one intimately. Most clients want a representative bag—elephant, rhino, buffalo, lion and the larger antelopes. Not all these animals live in the same locality. After the client has shot his lion, the white hunter must then take him some two or three hundred miles to a completely different section after rhino or buffalo. Then into another section after elephant. The hunter must know all the twisting network of trails that cover each of these districts. He must know which roads are passable in wet weather, which drifts can be forded and where the fords lie, where the best camp sites are, which sites are likely to have water near them and at what time of year. Above all, he must know how the grass will be growing in the various parts of the country at different seasons. Grass is of the greatest importance in hunting. If the grass is high, little can be seen since the tall growth conceals the animals. Also, the game animals migrate from one region to another as they follow the grass and the carnivorous beasts follow them.

Food is an ever-present problem. No safari can carry enough food for all the native boys and the clients. The white hunter must shoot meat "for the pot." It is by no means always easy in Africa to knock over a suitable meat animal. Suppose the client wishes to go after rhino or elephant. These animals live in bush where there are comparatively few antelope. After going a few days without meat, the native boys grow restless and quarrelsome. Yet the client may not wish to spend a day or more going into plain country after meat for them. After all, the man is paying forty pounds or better a day for his safari and he does not want to waste time. He has a point. Yet the boys grow sullen on a diet of maize.

Even in good hunting areas, the white hunter must try to vary the safari's diet as much as possible. Clients grow tired of Tommy steaks, kongoni cutlets, impala roasts, and tinned foods. The hunter must try to knock over a spur fowl or grouse. Possibly he may catch a few trout for a change. All these little details go toward making the client feel that he is getting his money's worth and having a good time.

There are many small details that are vital to the success of a safari which are easy to overlook. The skinning out of the trophies is even more important than securing them. If the skinners leave even a square inch of flesh on the hide, it will rot and leave a hole in the skin. Even an expert taxidermist cannot repair the damage. On the other hand, if the skinners shave a hide too closely, they will cut it, leaving an ugly rip. Also, if the hunter does not make sure that the right kind of salt is taken to preserve the hide, or if the salt is not rubbed in correctly, the trophy will spoil. Then the client, who has spent much time and money to secure that trophy, will be understandably furious. Again, it is the white hunter who takes the blame.

In addition, the white hunter must have a working knowledge of several native languages, know how to drive a heavy lorry over plains full of holes and stumps, understand something of photography, know half a dozen card games, and never under any circumstances lose his temper. This last item is of great importance and yet very hard to follow. Some clients do not come to Africa primarily to hunt but rather to escape from some haunting dread that they hope to shake off in the bush. To be isolated with such people for weeks is often a trying experience.

I especially remember one man, an American millionaire who had spent most of his life in European watering places. He was the only son of a widowed mother and, although now middle-aged, he had never married. He was the saddest man I have ever seen and had taken up big-game hunting in the despondent hope that it might take him out of himself. The man was incredibly rich. Special liquors were flown into our camp by private plane. All his food had to be cooked in rare wines. We took along a bountiful supply of his personal beer, which had been double brewed to his taste. The man was always writing letters to women he knew in Europe, mainly actresses on whom he had lavished fabulous gifts. These endless letters were always sent as cablegrams, for he considered ordinary mail too slow. We had a portable radio with us and the letters were radioed into the Nairobi post office. If the ladies did not answer him in the next day or so, he would sit alone in his tent and cry like a child. Yet I would be very much surprised to learn that there was anything improper in his relations with these women. The man impressed me as impotent. He was desperately trying to buy friendship or at least something that would get him out of the pitiful round of his existence.

I had a nerve-shattering experience with this chap that I will never forget. One morning he told me, "No hunting today, John. We're going for a drive." I took along a light .275 in case we wished to pick up some meat for the boys. While we were driving along, a rhino ran past. My client picked up the .275 and shot him through the belly before I could stop him.

The wounded rhino bolted away into the scrub. I took the .275 and followed, hoping for a heart shot that would finish the poor brute off. While I was trying to track the animal, he suddenly charged me. I put four bullets into him with the .275. They never fazed him. I would certainly have been killed if my client had not come up with a .404 he had found somewhere in our safari car and managed to drop the animal. A few minutes after this episode, he was weeping again because some actress he knew in Paris hadn't written him that week.

As I have said, experiences like this tell on a man. After a few such safaris, I was always glad to accept a request to do control work for the game department. It occasionally happened that an elephant herd would start raiding native shambas. Once the beasts got in the habit, they would come back again and again until they had wiped out the entire cultivated area. When natives reported a herd of persistently raiding elephants the game department would assign a professional hunter to wipe out the nuisance. My usual arrangement with the department was that I could keep the ivory in return for my work.

I remember one such hunt especially—and so, I believe, will Hilda. I had been asked to deal with some marauding elephants in the vicinity of Mt. Jomvu, in the extreme southeastern corner of Kenya. I had my old tracker and gunbearer, Saseeta, with me. When it comes to dealing with elephants, I consider that Saseeta stands alone among all Kenya bearers. He is not only an excellent tracker but steady to a degree. He is also remarkably quick at changing rifles and loading. When one is shooting elephants with a double-barreled gun which permits only two shots, this is an important consideration. I doubt if even a trained English loader at a pheasant drive could give Saseeta any points on rapid loading. My old Masai friend, Kirakangano, had never been able to master this knack. Also at this time he was back in the reserve, checking on his cattle and keeping his wife pregnant.

Saseeta and I traveled by train to Kwale and then went on by foot to Jomvu. At Jomvu, I was near my well-beloved Marenge Forest. There is no place in Kenya that I prefer to this great wilderness with its huge trees. Unlike the semi-barren bush country, the Marenge is full of life. Monkeys and squirrels leap through the branches over your head. Hornbills with double-decker beaks, leap up before you with their heavy, swishing flight. The little plantain eaters in rich mauve and deep crimson jig-hop from one branch to another until they reach the shelter of the foliage that forms the roof of the forest. Elephant shrews, strange little beasts with tiny, upright trunks, rustle about over the fallen leaves. I caught one and kept him as a pet. He tamed very easily and learned to come to me for grasshoppers.

There were also more sinister animals. I was about to step over a fallen log, covered with moss and draped with delicate little forest ferns, when Saseeta gave my jumper a quick tug and pointed. A smoky-green snake lay coiled on an overhanging branch. Its head was raised and it was studying me coldly, waiting until I took another step. It was a cobra. I killed the creature with my rifle.

Porcupine quills lay upon the game trails. We came on two of these quill pigs eating the tusk of a dead elephant. There must have been some quality in the ivory that attracted them. They had reduced what had once been a ninety-pound tusk to a mere five-pound nub. Undoubtedly, porcupines are one of the reasons why so little ivory is ever picked up in the forest. Old-time hunters, wondering at this lack of "found" ivory, explained it by inventing the myth of an "elephant graveyard," a mysterious, hidden spot where all elephants go when they know that they are about to die. Actually, there is no such place. I have often found the skeletons of dead elephants in the jungle. But the bones do not last long, being soon destroyed by boring beetles and the occasional brush fires that quickly reduce dry bones to ashes.

I enjoyed being able to wander about hatless even at noon in the shadow of the great trees. After the burning heat of the bush country, it was a rare treat.

When we arrived at the native village where the raiding herd had been doing damage, the inhabitants swarmed out to greet me as their savior. They showed me the ruins of their little cultivated patched, tiny fields hacked out of the forest by the most primitive of tools. One man wept as he led me about his maize field, the result of long hours of tedious work by himself and his family, now trodden into a mass of broken stalks and unripened cobs. It is really astonishing the amount of damage an elephant can do in a few hours, but when you consider that each of the beast's soles measures up to two feet across and that they are constantly in motion, you have some idea of the area that a herd of elephants can trample down in a night's feeding. Of course, they are also constantly gathering in the green stalks with their trunks.

The efforts that the natives had made to keep the herd away were pitiful in the extreme. Little sticks hung with charms and pottery jars full of magic roots had been placed at the corners of the fields.

The natives told me that they had also tried to keep off the beasts by building fires and beating on drums but the elephants had paid no more attention to them than they would to a horde of baboons.

My boys pitched our tents under a group of palms. As soon as the natives saw we were going to stay, all their fears left them. In their simple creed, the white man has magic. He cannot fail. This utter confidence may flatter some men. It tends to depress me. I can recall too many failures in my hunting. I was tortured by the doubt that I might disappoint these hopeful people.

Saseeta and I started out at dawn the next morning on the trail of the herd. On the way we passed what had once been a flourishing coconut plantation. Its owners had fled, unable to cope with the elephants. Only three towering palms survived. The rest lay twisted and trampled. Their wide, fanlike leaves were yellow. We waded through the remains of a sweet potato patch, smothered now in a tangle of vines.

Bands of monkeys dashed through the branches over our heads. Many of them were Colibi, their long black-haired coats handsomely marked with bright white strips as vivid as the pattern of a skunk. These monkeys were once in great demand for their hides and many a dainty miss in Paris tripped along the boulevards in her coat of monkey skins. Fortunately for the monkeys, this fad has now largely passed. Among the higher branches, white-colored monkeys scuttled about like squirrels. The great trees were so high that these little beasts seemed merely specks. As so often, I regretted that I was not able to sit down and simply watch the animal life around me. But a hunter is on a time schedule and must keep moving.

We came on some elephant droppings with two red squirrels picking bits of undigested corn kernels from the mass. Saseeta touched the droppings. They were still warm. The herd must be just ahead. Then we heard them. They were making all sorts of noises, gurgling and sighing with an occasional shrill scream from the cows. As we got closer, I could see bush tops swaying as the herd moved about. Saseeta was beside me, constantly testing the wind with his fungus powder puff.

A group of brown, earth-colored masses loomed up among the trees. We crept to within thirty yards of them. It was a small segment of the main herd, composed of cows and two young bulls. I could see no vulnerable shots. Then one of the cows raised her head. I instantly dropped her. The rest of the herd milled about for a minute in panic. I was able to get two more before they broke.

All around us there was crashing in the undergrowth as the terrified herd dashed off. Saseeta and I started off on the spoor of the two young bulls.

The local natives had gone along with us as scouts. Now they were more of a nuisance than a help. They had spread out through the forest and I could see how the two bulls had shied away whenever they encountered the taint of human scent. An elephant has such an acute sense of smell that he does not have to cross a man's trail to wind it. He can pick up the odor many feet away. Before we had gone more than a few yards, there was a sudden crashing in the bush and both bulls rushed toward us. They were not charging. They had simply lost track of our position and were trying to escape.

They went by us in single file, one following the other. As they passed, I fired right and left barrels at them, aiming for the shoulder of each. Neither dropped. They crashed on through the heavy foliage, making it bend and break. We followed. The bush was so thick I had trouble seeing, but at last I made out a great brownish object that looked much like a vast anthill. I tried to circle the bush to get a fair shot, but the cover was so dense no man could get through it.

I went back to Saseeta. The elephant had not moved. I could not tell which was rump and which was head, but the part farthest off seemed to slant sharply, so I decided the closer part was the shoulder. I had to stand on tiptoe to fire. After the shot, there was absolutely no reaction. Not a sound escaped the elephant, although I knew I must have hit him.

When hunting big game with a double-barrel rifle, I always like to reload a barrel after firing so I am sure of having two shots in case of a charge. This, of course, if I have time. I opened the breech of my rifle to put in another shell. To do this, I had to glance down. Suddenly I heard Saseeta cry out. When I looked up, the elephant was on me.

I had heard nothing. The bull had charged through the thick cover apparently without making a sound. There was no time to aim. I flung the breech shut and fired blindly at the great beast towering over me. I hit him between the eyes. He came down on his knees, his tusks plowing up the ground. He was just eight feet away. I stood there very much shaken, and then looked about for my gunbearer. He was unconcernedly picking up my discarded cartridge case to use as a snuff container. In Saseeta's simple code, I was invulnerable. Nothing could hurt the white man with his potent medicine. I wish I had similar confidence in myself.

On investigation, we found the other elephant lying dead near the spot where the first bull had been standing.

Saseeta told me that as soon as I opened the breech of my gun, the elephant had charged. The tiny mechanical sound had brought him on, although he had ignored the report of my gun and even the impact of my bullet hitting him. We examined his footprints in the bush. He must have literally skimmed over the ground. He had been on me in two great strides.

While I was looking at some curious ticks on the dead animal, all of different colors, I heard a noise coming toward us through the bush that sounded like an oncoming wave. For an instant I could not imagine what it was. Then I realized that the elephant herd had turned and was coming back toward us.

It was not a charge. I knew well what must have happened. Some of the local natives had managed to get in front of the animals and had given the herd their scent. The terrified beasts had turned and run back. In a few seconds they would be on top of us.

There was no use running. We had no time. Also, I hate to turn my back on an elephant. They have a wonderful knack of stealing up on you unaware with a sure collecting trunk. I was using a Gibbs

.505 and had every confidence in the 525 grain solid bullets. They are indeed a great stopper. So we waited.

I saw a group of five elephants break through the cover and halt momentarily by the dead body of the first bull. They rent the air with a series of piercing screams when they saw the corpse. Then the rest of the herd came crashing through the bush toward us. Shooting was fast and furious. I fired a left and right at two cows in the lead. I could see their heads literally rock from the impact of the heavy bullets. Elephants were piled up in front and on both sides of us. Saseeta and I were sprayed by gushes of trunk-blown blood from the beasts that had fallen near us but I could not get sufficient time to finish them off. My rifle barrels became so hot that my left hand was severely blistered but I hardly felt the pain at the time.

When the herd finally drew off, twelve elephants were left dead on the ground around us. After a time, we heard the local natives calling to us from the brush where they had hidden. They refused to come out until we assured them all danger was past.

I had to stay by the dead animals to make sure that the tusks were properly cut out. The news that fresh meat was available in almost unlimited amounts spread like magic through the bush telegraph. In a few hours, over six hundred natives had collected around the dead animals, some of them coming from twenty miles away. They ranged from children to decrepit old hags with wizened breasts and folds of skin hanging over their shrunken bellies. How these old people ever made the long trip through the dense bush I cannot imagine.

The elephants soon began to taint in the hot sun, but that made no difference to the natives. They poured over the animals. The place was blood-soaked and strewn with intestinal filth from the elephants' great stomachs, but the natives were completely indifferent to the stench. They worked like lunatics, cutting off great hunks of flesh and stowing the precious stuff in their fiber bags. When they were thirsty, they drank the water in the elephants' guts. The liquid looked clear.

I was primarily interested in the beasts' ivory, but I noticed that the young native girls were fascinated by the beasts' other end. They were greatly impressed by the size of the genital organs. When the girls saw I was watching them, they demurely looked away.

Several men crawled inside the dead beasts to get the hearts and kidneys. Fights developed inside the animals and we could hear shouts and curses, coupled with the sound of knives clashing together. To make matters worse, the natives on the outside of the elephants were stabbing into the carcasses to cut off gobs of flesh. Often their long knives would plunge through an animal's body and hit another native crawling about on the inside. I saw several natives come out of the elephants dripping with blood, but in their frenzy for meat, no one seemed to care.

Fearing that some of them would be killed, I asked the headmen to organize the butchery into some kind of a system. They lined up all the girls, every tenth one standing to make the count easier. Then the men cut out great piles of meat. Each woman was entitled to all she could carry. Some of the girls hid their meat in the bush and then tried to slip back into line for more. When detected, they showed no embarrassment, but laughed heartily and tried again a few minutes later.

I would have thought there was enough meat there to support all Kenya for weeks, but in an astonishingly short space of time, the elephants were nothing but bones. Through the stripped ribs I could see naked men working inside the beasts as though in cages trying to get some last pieces of flesh from the skeletons. By sunset even the entrails had been carried away. To every village for miles around ran a red trail through the bush, made by blood dripping down from the loads of raw meat carried by the women.

I started back with my boys and the ivory. We remained in camp for a day or two and then headed north toward the railway. On the way we were met by a small, solemn safari. It was composed of a Liwali chief from Vanga, two medical dressers, and the Indian postmaster. I asked them what had happened. Sadly, the chief told me, "A white man named John A. Hunter has been killed during an elephant stampede. We have come to collect what is left of him and send the pieces to Nairobi."

"You might at least offer the remains a drink," I suggested.

The astonished looks on the men's faces were most enjoyable. The postmaster seemed not only surprised but disappointed. He had come a long way to view the mangled remains of an elephant hunter. Now I had swindled him. I apologized to the man and he took it in good part. At least, I appreciated their good intentions. I was glad to know that if anything did happen to me, I could count on a proper funeral.

It is amazing how quickly rumors spread in the African bush. Some of the natives who had panicked during the stampede had promptly rushed to the nearest village and spread the word that I had been killed. The news had reached a small railway station and been carried to Nairobi. I found that Loretto Convent near Nairobi (where my daughters were educated) had publicly announced that the sad tidings were indeed true and offered prayers for my family.

I left behind my porters with the ivory and hurried on to Mombasa. I was there when Hilda stepped off the train. Thank heaven she was not in black crepe. I had often asked her not to dress in mourning if I were killed on one of my hunts. She had remembered. For a second we stood there staring at each other before she ran to me. Although I have always liked being off alone in the bush with my boys, still it is pleasant to know that there is someone who cares whether or not you ever come out again.

9

The Hidden Isle of Fumve

After my return from Jomvu, Hilda and I decided to take a second honeymoon together. We left the children—our youngest son was then six—in a boarding school where we knew they would be well cared for while we were away. Fortunately we had an excellent domestic staff. One of the great advantages of living in Africa is that servants are no problem. All our domestics were bush natives that Hilda had trained herself. Neither of us cared to trust the town natives. Constant association with rich tourists and the unrest ever present in a town the size of Nairobi had become, had made them somewhat difficult. But we could trust our own staff to look after our home as we could trust ourselves.

We knew of a perfect place for our holiday. Some time before, Captain Charles Pitman, Game Warden of Uganda, had recommended making a collection of birds and small mammals on Fumve Island, a tiny spot in Lake Victoria. Fumve had seldom been visited. The only inhabitants are a tribe of eleven natives who came to the island some years ago and, finding it a perfect place, decided to settle there. There is a rare species of antelope, known as the Situtunga, that lives on the island and a museum was eager to secure some specimens.

Hilda was wise enough to know that I would become restless after a week or so on the island without some shooting. I become uneasy after a time without any excuse to take a gun in my hands. The little collecting that I was to do would answer the purpose.

Also, it would give me a good excuse to use my dear old Purdey shotgun that I had brought from Scotland and had sadly neglected of late. Simply taking the Purdey out of its case always meant the beginning of a holiday to me.

We traveled northwest from Nairobi by car and took a steamer from Entebbe. As we would be completely marooned on the island for several weeks, we took along everything we were likely to need, from needles to rifles. No steamer makes regular stops at Fumve so we would be entirely cut off from the rest of the world during our stay.

Our ship was the S.S. *Percy Anderson.* She made fortnightly visits to the main Sese Islands to pick up a cargo of groundnuts and bananas. By special arrangement with the Uganda Marine Department, the ship would stop at Fumve after making her regular run and drop us off. She would come back again in two months to pick us up.

Our little steamer went from one tiny island to another, stopping for a few hours at each port of call to take on a cargo. Much of the cargo seemed to consist of a species of red-tailed parrots with gray plumage. I was told that these birds are the best talkers in the world and sell easily in Mombasa markets for five pounds each, a very lucrative trade for the natives, who catch them by the dozen when the parrots come to nest on the islands. I believe that a good talking "African gray" will bring up to $600 in the United States. There is an old legend that natives used to feed the birds ground glass before selling them so the parrots would die in a few months, thus keeping up the demand. Whether or not there is anything to this story I cannot say.

Coasting along the lake shore in the steamer was indeed a pleasant way to spend one's time. The country was new and fascinating to me. We drifted past great beds of emerald green papyrus that were almost small forests, for the plants grew to be twenty feet in height. These vast beds were intersected by little waterways that led deep into the swamps, so narrow that they could only be negotiated by canoe. Masses of water-lily pads covered the water, marked here and there by lovely purple blooms. Bird life was all around us. We saw hundreds of cormorants and the long-necked snake birds sitting in low trees or perched on bits of brush with their wings stretched out to catch the warm sun. Flocks of the sacred ibis waded through the shallows and pelicans flapped slowly over the smooth water. Ducks, coots, and grebes were everywhere. Occasionally we would pass fish eagles with their white heads and breasts sitting on top of high trees, resting quietly until hunger moved them to start their day's fishing.

The sunsets stained the heavens with the most fantastic hues and the falling dusk seemed to blend with the placid lapping water of the lake. At such times a man realizes the great companionship of his wife and finds himself falling in love with her all over again.

Late one evening, our Indian captain brought the ship into anchorage at Fumve. A treacherous reef of jagged rocks guards the harbor and I was somewhat perturbed to hear our captain arguing with a native member of the crew over the correct channel. I had no wish to have to swim the last half mile, especially as the lake is full of crocodile. The ship's only lights were two ancient Dietz oil lanterns, but I hastily got two more from our safari kit and by their combined light we managed to make the harbor.

The little colony of natives on Fumve had seen our lights and built a fire on the beach to guide us. A canoe came alongside, full of astonished natives who could not imagine what a ship was doing in their secluded harbor. When they heard that we were planning to spend two months with them, they were even more surprised. They had never heard of a white man going anywhere except to get record trophies or for commercial reasons. They could not believe we were simply coming for a rest.

We pitched a tent under the shade of the trees and set up housekeeping. For a week we did nothing all day long and enjoyed every moment of it. In the morning we were awakened by the shrieking and whistling of the thousands of red-tailed parrots that nested on the island. When our native boys heard us stirring, they would pad noiselessly into our tent with cups of hot morning tea. After bathing, we would breakfast. During the morning, we wandered around the island watching the birds and small beasts. There were few large animals on Fumve except the Situtunga antelopes, but we did see herds of hippos sporting and splashing in the reed beds. Sometimes we saw a group of these great water pigs lying on a sandbar, sunning themselves. They seldom went far from water except on cloudy days or at night when they would come ashore to feed.

Hippos are more powerful than most people suppose. A big bull hippo is a dangerous adversary for even a rhino. I once came on a spot where a hippo and a rhino had met on the banks of a lake— both being fully matured bulls. The animals had killed each other. The hippo had evidently come ashore to feed on the lush grass. He had met the rhino coming down to drink. Neither animal would give way. A terrible battle must have followed. The rhino's back was severed by the hippo's terrific span of bite. The hippo was badly holed in several places by the rhino's horn. The animals lay within a few feet of each other, both killed in a completely unnecessary duel. But doubtless a point of honor was involved.

Among the reeds, flocks of pigmy geese lived quiet undisturbed lives and showed no fear of us. These clean-cut, dapper little fowl have always been favorites of mine. We also saw great flocks of teal and spur-winged geese. Flocks of several thousand birds were not unusual.

The waters around Fumve were full of crocodile. The outlines of their heads in the water looked like countless pieces of driftwood. They ranged from monsters eighteen feet long to youngsters no bigger than a monitor lizard, and varied in color from blackish brown to a yellowish green. I believe that a crocodile is the only wild animal that makes absolutely no distinction between man and his ordinary prey. When shooting crocs for their hides, I have often found native ornaments inside of them, in addition to the hooves of wild pigs, the horns of antelopes and a curious collection of small stones. Why these reptiles eat stones I have no idea unless they help the animal's digestion as do the pebbles swallowed by an ostrich.

The only time I left Hilda while we were on the island was to collect two specimens of the Situtunga antelope. These animals were once common along the lakeshore, but the natives have nearly exterminated them, stretching nets along the reed beds and driving the animals into them. A number of the delicate little beasts swam out to Fumve where they have increased greatly in numbers, having learned to graze only in open glades, beyond the reach of a thrown spear.

I went out with my bearer one morning carrying a light rifle. The forest was so thick that we were forced to leave blaze marks on the trees to make sure of finding our way back to camp. We found several of the open glades and could tell by the signs that the antelopes had been feeding there. But as it was still the middle of the day, the animals had not come out to graze. We waited until five o'clock and then tried again.

There, sure enough, was a Situtunga in the middle of one of the glades. He was about fifty yards away. Being overconfident of my powers as a stalker, I tried to get closer to him. I crawled to the place where he had been feeding, but he was gone. Suddenly he bolted out of the grass beside me and headed for the forest. I fired and overshot. A stupid miss. We tried again. In the next glade, I had better luck. We spied a young buck feeding, so deep in the grass that all I could see was his back and the whitish tips of his horns. I sat down and whistled. The buck stood up—an easy shot. He was our first trophy.

The buck stood about forty-four inches at the shoulder. His coat was long and silky, a dark brown in color. I was particularly interested in the hooves. A few generations ago when the Situtunga was primarily a marsh dweller, their hooves were enormously elongated—measuring well over six inches. These long hooves enabled the animal to run over marshy ground without sinking, much as snowshoes support a man in soft snow. But these animals had lived for so many generations on the island that their hooves were not much longer than those of an ordinary antelope. In a few more generations, the elongated hoof will doubtless disappear. An interesting example of how animals adapt themselves to changing conditions.

I shot only two of these interesting little animals. I had no wish to disturb them unduly in their island refuge.

I also collected over two hundred birds. Captain Pitman was most interested in this collection. Among them was the Superlative sunbird, the handsomest of this gorgeous species. I also collected several species of railbird that I had never seen before. I knew that Captain Pitman would be pleased.

The only incident that occurred during our peaceful stay on the island was a terrific thunderstorm that struck one night. Trees swayed around our tent in an alarming fashion. Branches crashed and fell. One great limb narrowly missed our tent, embedding itself like a spear in the ground close by. Continual flashes of lightning lit up the water on the turbulent lake. Parrots screeched as they were dislodged from their perches on the whipping branches. Although we suffered no damage, it was a wild night.

When our time was up, the S.S. *Percy Anderson* came for us. The natives were sorry to see us go and we were equally sorry to leave. I have never seen any place as perfect for a vacation as Fumve. There were almost no insects on the island, a pleasant change from many parts of Africa. We saw no signs of the dread tsetse fly whatever. Hilda and I left, promising each other that some day we would return for another vacation. Alas, we never have. Yet it is probably just as well. Perhaps another trip to that perfect place would have been disappointing, as over the years it has become enshrined in our memories as an ideal.

10

Buffalo Hunting

When Hilda and I returned from Fumve, there was a note awaiting me from Captain Ritchie of the Kenya Game Department. I went to see him at once. The department was confronted by another control problem. In the vicinity of Thomson's Falls, a community some hundred miles north of Nairobi, a herd of buffalo had been doing great damage. The animals were destroying shambas and had killed several natives. Captain Ritchie had come to the conclusion that this herd must be dealt with.

In ordering these animals killed, Captain Ritchie was also interested in the general welfare of all the Kenya buffalo. This particular herd had become a nuisance and Captain Ritchie, ever out to assist the farming community, wanted their numbers kept in check.

Many hunters believe that the buffalo is Africa's most dangerous animal. When a buffalo attacks, he charges with admirable ferocity and will not flinch away from a bullet as do rhinos and even elephants. A buffalo usually continues to charge until he is killed or he has killed the hunter. They are most cunning. Frequently a wounded buffalo will double back and wait beside his trail, hoping to ambush the hunter. Then, too, a buffalo will often attack without any provocation at all, so he may well be regarded as a difficult and uncertain quarry.

I decided to use a heavy rifle on this trip, a .500 double Jeffery. I consider the heaviest weapon a man can conveniently carry is none too powerful for buffalo. Knowing that some of the wounded animals would escape into the bush and have to be driven out, I de-

cided to use dogs. If this appears non-sporting, I can only say I
was performing a task assigned to me by the department and I was
not interested in personal glory.

The pound in Nairobi contained nothing but a small collection
of worthless curs. Still, I was in no position to pick and choose, so
I bought the lot. Later, I was able to add to this pack by buying a
few larger and more alert dogs from settlers. I still badly needed
a "head" dog, a leader of the pack, that would show his mates the
way by his courage and determination. Dogs easily follow a leader
and even one first-class dog can transform a group of curs into a
reasonably respectable pack. No leader was forthcoming so I prepared to leave Nairobi with my mixed bunch of mongrels.

A few days before I left, I received a call from a prominent official
asking me to get rid of his pet dog. This animal was considered to
be incurably vicious. He had attacked and bitten several natives
and was killing livestock near Nairobi. From the owner's descrip-
tion, I decided the dog was hopeless but at that moment anything
was grist that came to my mill. I went over to collect him.

At first look, I liked the dog. He was big-boned, tawny in color,
and about the size of an Alsatian. He had powerful jaws and clearly
knew how to use them. He seemed to be a general crossbreed with
a strong dash of bull terrier. I decided to call him Buff, an easy
word for the tongue. He took to the name and I felt that we were
going to get along well together. I believed him to be a keen, ad-
venturesome animal, never intended by nature to be a house pet.
He could not endure being confined in a city, and I knew that feeling well myself. If Buff had lost his temper and chewed up a few
bad characters, well, I was not the man to hold that against him.

Buff soon established himself as leader of my pack. There were
several that fought him, but they quickly learned discretion. Even
the bitches showed preference by transferring their affections to
him while the other dogs slunk about at a safe distance. Yet for all
his ferocity, Buff was a true dog and would lie at my feet by the
hour, looking up at me with his profound, wistful eyes, trying to
read my thoughts. Even before we left Nairobi, I was more attached

to Buff than I had ever been to any other dog. I could only hope he would prove himself in the buffalo hunts and learn to avoid the fierce animals' horns and sharp hooves.

Near Thomson's Falls, I began to realize why Buff's former owner had been so eager to part with him. I took the pack for a stroll one evening and on the way we passed a herd of sheep being driven by a native. The sight of the sheep was too much for Buff. He charged into the flock, cut out a fat-tailed ram, and in a matter of seconds the sheep was on its back with Buff's teeth buried deep in its throat. I tore him off and, removing my belt, gave the dog a beating that he never forgot. Buff took the punishment without a whimper, for which I liked him all the better. I paid the native for his sheep and we returned to camp, Buff cheerfully trotting by my heels all the way.

I had several Nderobo scouts attached to my control camp, a people one-quarter Masai and three-quarters bushman. They are a praiseworthy tribe, being reasonably good hunters, although they do some tilling. We had been at the village only a few hours when I heard a dreadful commotion outside my tent. Rushing out, I found that Buff had knocked down a native woman and was busy disrobing her. Her clothing was only a loin cloth, but he had torn this off and fastened his teeth in her flank. I grabbed Buff by the tail and, exerting all my strength, managed to pull him off. The woman fled for the nearest hut, red and white marks showing on her plump black posterior. I expected a fearful protest from the natives, but the woman's husband was rolling on the ground shouting with laughter and the other natives were equally amused. Several of them came up and congratulated me on having such a fine animal. They considered Buff's aggressiveness a good omen for a buffalo dog.

I talked to the Nderobo concerning the buffalo and heard many stories of the animals' vindictiveness. I quote two of these stories to give the reader some idea of the determination with which a buffalo will follow his victims.

One of the Nderobo walked with a limp and I inquired the cause. The man showed me that his heel was gone—bitten clean off at the ankle. He told me that a buffalo had done it. I could hardly believe his statement, but when he had finished his story, I concluded that the man was telling the truth.

He had been walking through the bush on his way to his shamba, when he heard a snort from the underbrush. He turned and bolted; the thunder of hooves behind told him that his pursuer was a buffalo. The man had a fair start but the buffalo rapidly gained on him. The sound of the hooves grew steadily louder. At the last instant, the man made a desperate jump and managed to grab the limb of a tree just as the buffalo rushed under him. The animal turned and coming back stood below the man, pawing the ground and snorting with fury. The native had pulled his feet up under him but the strain of holding them there grew too much. His right leg became cramped and for a moment he had to extend it. Immediately the waiting buffalo rushed up and nipped off the man's heel with his teeth as though it were a twig. Then, seemingly appeased by the taste of blood, he went away, leaving the half-fainting man still clinging to the tree limb.

After thinking this story over, I saw nothing incredible in it. There is no reason why a buffalo should not use his teeth. A horse can give a vicious bite. Indeed, an angry stallion will fight with his teeth quite as much as with his hooves. Later, I was to discover that a buffalo will indeed use his teeth to tear his victims—and very deadly weapons they are.

The injuries produced by an infuriated buffalo are often extremely grisly. One afternoon a native came to my camp and asked me to employ him as a game scout. While I was talking to him, I noticed large, smooth scars on the insides of his thighs. I asked him the cause. As innocently as a child, he casually let fall his loin cloth. To my horror, I saw the man had been completely castrated. At my astonished exclamation, the native said simply that he considered himself a very lucky man. If Mungu (God) had not been looking after him, he would now be dead.

I repeat his story as he told it to me. He had left his hut early one morning to visit his beehives. These hives are hollowed-out, wooden receptacles and natives hang them from the upper branches of trees throughout the bush. The boxes may become in succession the nesting site of birds, the home of snakes and the hive of a swarm of wild bees. If bees move in, the native collects the honey. Sugar of any kind is a rare commodity in the jungle and highly prized.

This native was walking through some high grass on his way to his beehives when he almost stepped on a resting buffalo bull. The bull leaped up and one of his great curved horns caught the man between the legs, tossing him into the air. The man fell straddle-legged over the withers of the maddened bull. In desperation he clutched the bull's ear with one hand and hung to his shoulder with the other. The grunting, infuriated beast broke into a heavy gallop, still ridden by the terrified native. The man did not dare to slip off, so he clung to the bull with all the power his life possessed. The buffalo carried him some sixty yards, and then, driven frantic by his burden, dashed under a heavy thorn bush, knocking the man to the ground.

The native was half stunned by the fall. Lying on his back, he saw the buffalo wheel and come back for him. The bull stopped a few feet away and then launched a terrific hook at the helpless man's belly. As the horn ripped into him, the man lost consciousness.

When he recovered his senses, the sun was sinking. His whole body was numb and seemed to be paralyzed. Forcing himself to think, he realized he was lying near a little stream. He managed to drag himself to the bank. One hand was broken, but with the other he was able to scoop up water and lift it to his mouth.

The man lay by the bank of that stream for two weeks. He kept alive by drinking water and eating what grass he could reach. He could do nothing for his wounds except to splash water on them. At night, he heard rhinos come down to drink and twice he heard the high-pitched screams of cow elephants near him. Often he heard hyenas wailing and laughing in the brush around him, but they never ventured close. Crocodiles would silently appear on the surface of the water and swim up to within a few feet of him. He was too weak to move and could only lie there watching them. After studying him for a few minutes, the reptiles would soundlessly submerge again.

The man was finally found by other honey seekers. He had long before been given up for dead by his village for after a man has been gone a few days in the bush, his relatives abandon all hope. His wounds had practically healed and he was soon as well as ever except for his terrible mutilation.

I asked the man why, after such an experience, he wanted to hunt buffalo. His eyes lighted up as he said, "Bwana, I will know that buffalo again by his horns. When I find him, I will cut off his makende (testicles) and eat them, just as surely as he galloped off with mine."

The buffalo herd I was after lived in the Marmanet Forest. The cover here is very dense, making hunting both difficult and dangerous. I do not consider a buffalo a formidable animal in the open, but in underbrush he can be very deadly indeed. I was glad I had my dogs with Buff at their head.

I let the pack rest a few days after their trip from Nairobi, then I started out early one morning with my pack and the game scouts. There were buffalo signs throughout the forest and the dogs showed little hesitation in following the tracks. My former pack in the Masai Reserve had been most reluctant to trail lion—the odor of the big cats seemed to daunt them—but apparently dogs are not fearful of buffalo scent. In a few minutes we could hear the buffaloes crashing through the bush with the dogs yelling on their heels. Followed by my native scouts, I kept as close to the pack as I could. Suddenly there came a shrill yelp and I saw one of the dogs go flying up above the bush as a buffalo tossed him. I could not see where he landed. Not wishing to lose dogs unnecessarily, I tried to call them back but in the hubbub of barking I could hardly hear my own voice.

When we came up with the pack, I found they were holding five buffalo bulls at bay. The bulls stood in a ring with their tails together and their horns pointing outward to keep off the dogs. Suddenly Buff rushed straight for the bunch and grabbed one of the bulls by the nose. The bull plunged forward and tried to dash the dog against the bole of a tree. Buff was not to be squashed so easily and slewed his hindquarters around at the last instant. A bullet from my gun put an end to the bull's struggles.

From then on, Buff always used the same tactics. After the pack had bayed a buffalo cow or bull, Buff would charge in and grab the animal by the nose. When attacked by dogs, buffaloes naturally hold their heads close to the ground to give their horns full play and this habit gave plucky Buff ample opportunity for his favorite hold. Apparently all cattle have tender noses. I remember how in Scotland farmers would put a ring through the nose of a dangerous bull, and as long as the man held the ring, the bull was comparatively helpless. Once Buff got his grip, the buffalo was seldom able to shake him off. Buff took a good stance with all four legs spread wide apart and a buffalo could not get sufficient purchase with his head held down to toss him.

A big buffalo bull is a grand creature, weighing up to 2,000 pounds, with great sweeping ink-black horns as thick as a man's leg at the boss and tapering to points as fine as daggers. When a bull charges with lowered head, he presents his thick skull to you, reinforced by the heavy boss. Under such conditions, only the heaviest-caliber rifle can bring him down. In hunting buffalo, I prefer to shoot for the chest, neck, shoulder or under the eye, but in case of a charge, you have little choice and must fire where you can.

The dogs were more effective in buffalo hunting than my other pack had been with lions. Dogs can keep out of a buffalo's way more easily than they can avoid a lion's rush. As with my former pack, some of the dogs had more courage than discretion. Instead of dodging an infuriated buffalo's charge, they would stand their ground. A buffalo is so quick in dealing a swipe with either horns or hooves that unless a dog takes good care to leap clear, he will be instantly killed.

Several of the dogs were tossed on different occasions. As a dog went up in the air, the buffalo would watch to see where he was coming down and then make for the spot, hoping to catch the dog while he was still dazed from the fall. The pack would rush in to help their friend, nipping at the buffalo's hocks as I have seen dogs do with domestic cattle, and try to turn him. If they could hold the beast even a moment I was generally able to get in a shot.

The buffalo herds often grazed in the open along the edges of swamps, frequently accompanied by egrets, which flutter about the big, dun-colored beasts like bits of white paper. The egrets sometimes ride on the buffaloes' backs and I believe they pick ticks off the animals. Occasionally a hunter can locate buffalo in tall grass by the egrets flying above them. It is a fine sight to come upon a herd of these magnificent beasts, proudly bearing aloft their great ebony horns and walking through a pasture of rich, green grass while the snowy white birds balance on their backs or walk with stately strides beside them.

Even when we encountered a herd of buffalo in the open, I had great trouble getting close enough to them for a shot. Their excellent eyesight and hearing made it hard to approach them. Often I had to whistle on the dogs. The pack would chase the buffalo into the cover and then out again while I fired at the animals almost as though at target practice.

In cover, it was a different matter. A hunted buffalo is wise enough to stand motionless in deep bush until the man is almost up to him before starting his charge. Even shooting nearby will not make him move until he is certain of getting his enemy. Here dogs are invaluable. The dogs can often smell the waiting buffalo and give the alarm. If not, they are fairly certain to come on him while they are trotting ahead of the hunter. I have no hesitation in saying that the dogs saved my life a dozen times during these hunts.

Buff was invaluable. He was that rare combination, seldom found among either dogs or humans, of great courage mingled with intelligent discretion. He knew enough to avoid a buffalo's rush and yet had absolutely no fear of the animal. Only when some unusual situation arose was the gallant dog in any real danger.

On one occasion, the pack had taken off after a very large buffalo bull. To keep the dogs from closing with him, the bull had taken up his stand in the center of a stream. This is a common trick among hunted animals when pursued by dogs. The dogs lined up on the river bank, making a great din with their barking, but not caring to swim out to the bull. Not so Buff. When he came up, the plucky dog took a great leap into the water and sure enough, managed to grab the surprised bull by the nose. For a moment the old buffalo stood there astonished by such audacity but he quickly recovered from his surprise and countered by pushing Buff under water. Buff would have drowned in a few minutes had I not been able to end the unequal struggle with a bullet. When Buff swam back to shore, coughing and spitting up water, I discovered that he had taken such a fierce grip on the tough gristle of the bull's nose that the tips of his front teeth were broken off. This will give some idea of Buff's strength and determination.

Up to date, this was Buff's seventeenth kill, all the buffalo having been gripped and held until I dispatched them.

In the next scrap with a buffalo herd, Buff did not get off scot-free. The pack had surrounded a herd and were holding them together by barking and making quick, heel-nipping rushes. Buff tore in and grabbed a large buffalo cow by her nose. He was holding her but her half-grown calf came to her help and butted the dog in the side with its short, stubby horns. Buff gasped, but refused to release his grip. He would have been killed if my scouts had not shot the two buffalo.

After this misadventure, I retired Buff from hunting until his wounds healed. I had shot over two hundred buffalo and the task of wiping out the herds was almost completed. Buff moped in his enforced security, watching wistfully while the rest of the pack trotted out after me for the day's hunt. One of my scouts went daily to a nearby kraal to get milk for the pack, and I told him to take Buff along on these walks. I felt the exercise would keep Buff from getting stiff while he was recuperating and also give him something to do.

On one of these trips, a warthog crossed Buff's path. This was a familiarity he could not stand. In spite of the shouts of the scout,

Buff started all out after him. The hog went down a hole, first turning around and backing in so he would have his tusks toward the entrance in true warthog style. Buff was about to go down the hole after him when the hog suddenly charged out. I firmly believe that if Buff had not broken off the points of his teeth, he would have succeeded in holding the animal. Instead, he lost his grip on the pig's sweaty hide. Instantly, the boar made a quick lunge with his tusks and caught Buff in the chest, ripping the brave dog open and killing him instantly. The scout shot the boar but the damage was done. When I returned from my day's hunt, there was the body of my noble Buff, killed at a time when I thought nothing could happen to him.

I have never owned another dog like Buff, before or since. The rest of the hunt was poisoned for me because of the loss of this great animal. I hoped some of Buff's puppies would take after him, but none of them were fit to run in the same pack with their father. You get too fond of a dog. Not until after his death do you realize how much he meant to you. I sometimes wonder if the pleasure in owning a dog is worth the misery caused by his death.

Because of their strength and ferocity, buffalo have always been a favorite quarry of mine. I have hunted them not only in Kenya, but also in Uganda and the Congo. Although I am far from underestimating the powers of this great animal, yet I think the dangers of buffalo hunting may have been somewhat overestimated. I have heard many a story of the danger of "buffalo stampedes." According to these accounts, a herd of buffalo will charge a man and trample him to death. Although I have shot over 350 buffalo, I never saw a herd charge as a group, unless they were in a ravine where they could not spread out, and even then the animals were trying to escape rather than making a proper charge. In my experience, a charge is always delivered by an individual animal, usually a beast that has been cut off from the rest of the herd. A solitary buffalo can be most aggressive, but as a member of a herd he is often no more savage than many breeds of domestic cattle.

Some years after this hunt, I was sent a second time to the

Thomson's Falls area to control marauding buffalo. I had been in the district only a few days when a native named Abeya arrived at my camp to apply for a position as a game scout. He was of the Turkana tribe. The Turkanas are a very wild, primitive people, mainly distinguished by a sort of bracelet they wear made of a single curved knife, ground to razor sharpness. The Turkanas are very expert with the use of this bracelet and can cut a man's throat with one twist of the wrist. When I first met Abeya he was clothed in little more than his own skin. His hair was plastered with cow dung and seen from behind his head resembled a baked bun. Abeya had spent much of his life in prison for poaching game with his bow and poisoned arrows. Even though he was a savage-looking specimen I considered him a likable chap for he was unquestionably a keen hunter. Abeya was joining the game scouts because he had a passion to own a rifle. This in itself was a laudable ambition, but I knew that natives have a strong tendency to regard a rifle as a fetish that can do no wrong rather than as a useful tool. I agreed to take Abeya as a game scout but insisted that he first thoroughly understand the mechanism of a rifle before using the weapon on big game.

Abeya's poaching experience made him an expert scout. He quickly learned how to handle his rifle and became a more than passable shot. But nothing I said to the man could convince him that a rifle did not make him invulnerable. However, as he was one of my best men, I finally sent him out buffalo hunting with two other scouts.

A few days later, the two scouts returned to say that Abeya had refused to hunt with them. "We Turkanas always hunt alone," he told them proudly. This was a direct violation of my orders for I believe that no one man can hunt in safety. Two men are always necessary—one to follow the spoor and the other to watch in case of a charge. I determined to take Abeya very severely to task when he returned.

Abeya did not return. I was away up country on a five-day hunt and when I came back Abeya's wife was waiting for me. She was a recent purchase, clad mostly in layers of dirty white beads. She said that Abeya had not turned up and she feared the worst. I instantly organized a searching party and we started out to comb the vastness of the Marmanet Forest for the missing man.

Among the Marmanet's forested slopes are strips of open table-land. By a large tree on one of these open areas we found what was left of Abeya. The body had been eaten by hyenas and vultures but we were able to identify him by the skull. From all the signs, Abeya had been murdered by another native. Several of his ribs were broken, as though by blows from a club. There was also a long, oblique cut across two bones that resembled a spear thrust. His rifle and ammunition were gone. Certainly no animal would have carried off the man's equipment. I reported the circumstances to Inspector Jay of the local police.

At that time there were a number of bush outlaws in the district who had attacked and robbed several native communities. For a rifle and ammunition to fall into the hands of these "bad hats" was a very serious state of affairs. The inspector came up to inspect Abeya's body. The scout had dug out a little hollow under the tree where he could lie in wait for passing buffalo, but there were no signs of a struggle and no buffalo spoor around the spot. There seemed to be little doubt that Abeya had met with foul play.

Yet to make absolutely certain, Inspector Jay decided to examine the brush for miles around to see if there were any other explanation. Police Askaris, the native constabulary, were brought up from Thomson's Falls and I joined the search with my scouts. Early one morning a large group of Askaris, scouts and local natives gathered under the tree where we had found poor Abeya's body. Dividing the crowd into small bands, we started out to comb the bush.

The search had been on for two hours or so when a native reported to me that he had found the body of a large buffalo. I accompanied the boy to his find. The ground around the carcass was completely covered with vicious safari ants, busily engaged in devouring it. The native had disturbed their trails when he found the buffalo, and the insects were on a rampage, ready to attack anything that approached within five yards of their meal.

I told the natives to cut a long pole and turn the body over. As they did so, I noticed a round hole in a rib bone. Making a dash through the biting ants, I pulled out the rib, and ran back again. I wanted to find out if an 8 mm. caliber bullet would fit the hole. That was the caliber of our scouts' rifles.

The bullet fitted perfectly. Knowing that a wounded buffalo will invariably run to a thicket and then turn around to face his assailant, I told the scouts to spread out and search in the direction the animal had been facing. A hundred yards away they came on a log covered with bloodstains. After examining the signs, I had no doubt that it was here the buffalo had caught and gored Abeya. A few feet from the log, I came on Abeya's missing rifle in the tall grass. There was an unfired cartridge partly in the chamber but not fully pressed home. A single empty cartridge case lay nearby.

Next I examined every foot of the ground between the log and the tree where we had found Abeya. Along the way, I picked up the balance of the scout's cartridges, scattered at intervals through the grass. I also found dried splotches of blood, mixed with the watery fluid that comes from a wounded animal shot through the stomach.

I pieced the scene together from the forest evidence. From his position under the tree, Abeya had fired at a passing buffalo, hitting him in the stomach. The wounded animal had run through the bush, leaving a blood trail. Abeya had followed him. The wounded bull, waiting in ambush, had suddenly charged while the scout's eyes were on the spoor. Abeya had fired but failed to stop the bull. Before he could get a second cartridge in the chamber, the buffalo was on him. He had dashed Abeya against the log, breaking his ribs, and then had died himself. Abeya, mortally injured, had managed to crawl back to his little hollow under the tree and there had died. On the way, the rest of his cartridges had trickled out of his pockets.

There only remained the spear thrust across his bones to be explained. I could tell by the nature of the injury that it had not been made by the bull's horns. On re-examining the log, I found a projecting knotted branch with a sharp point. This branch was covered with caked blood. The bull had thrown Abeya against the branch and it had gone through him as neatly as a short sword.

When I first came on the body, I would have been willing to swear that the scout had been murdered by other natives. Fortunately, due to the quiet common sense of Inspector Jay, the matter was carefully investigated and the mystery solved. Yet I still consider it one of the most remarkable combinations of circumstances I ever encountered in the bush.

I am far from underrating the buffalo as an antagonist, but I believe that deaths caused by this animal can generally be laid to two causes—either a man has become so intent on following the spoor of a wounded buffalo that he has forgotten to watch ahead or he has insisted on using a light-caliber gun that does not possess enough shocking power to stop a charge.

I have already mentioned my dislike of using light weapons against formidable game and the reader may think I am something of a fanatic on the subject. I can only say that the deepest personal loss I ever sustained in Africa came about because a sportsman insisted on using a light rifle to hunt big game. Two men lost their lives simply because this man did not want his shoulder bruised by the kick of a heavy gun.

This man was by rank a prince of royal blood; I do not care to identify him further. I was acting as his guide and with us was my dear friend and comrade Kirakangano. Even since we first met on the Masai Reserve, I had often called him in to help me on hunting trips. There was also another native who acted as gunbearer for the prince. This gunbearer was a conceited chap who considered himself a great bushcraftsman although he actually knew little about the business.

We had completed a highly successful lion hunt and on the day we were to leave the district, the prince sighted several buffalo bulls grazing near the edge of some cover. Nothing would do but he must have one of these animals as a trophy. The prince was using a .416, excellent for lion but only capable of dropping a buffalo if the animal is hit in some vital part. Followed by Kirakangano and the prince's gunbearer, his highness and I stalked the herd. By keeping a small bush between us and the bulls, we were able to get to within eighty yards of them. The prince took careful aim at a good bull and fired. The animal dropped, but at the report of the gun another much finer bull dashed past us. The prince fired again, and from the noise of the impact I knew this second animal was hit in the stomach. The wounded bull plunged into the bush and vanished.

I prepared to follow him with Kirakangano and dispatch him. But the prince insisted on coming with us. He claimed that unless he was able to finish off the buffalo, the trophy would have no interest for him. Unfortunately, I yielded to his wishes and we started into the cover.

We had scarcely gone fifteen yards when Kirakangano pointed the animal out to me, standing in a little clump of bush. I tried to point him out to the prince but he could not see him. While we were whispering and gesticulating the buffalo realized he was spotted. He turned and ran farther into the cover.

The animal now knew he was being trailed and was sure to be on his guard. We went on into the thick bush, Kirakangano doing the spooring while I walked beside him with my rifle at the ready. The prince came next, followed by his gunbearer carrying an extra rifle. I had my Jeffery .500 and Kirakangano, as usual, had nothing but his moran spear.

The cover was so thick that I could not see through the dense upper foliage. Several times we could smell the pungent, dairylike odor of the bull as he stopped to wait in ambush for us. Each time I lay down, hoping to catch a glimpse of his legs through the more open lower stalks, but he always saw me and dashed off again, uttering hoarse grunts of defeated anger.

This sort of hunting began to tell on the prince's nerves. Although

End of a marauder. This male rhino had been damaging native *shambas* near Makindu, Kenya.

Young Masai girl.

Wakamba girls.

On safari.

Male rhino seldom fight. Among themsleves, they are usually very docile animals. This remarkable picture is probably the only photograph of such a combat. These two bulls were quarreling over a female.

Masai, the bravest of the brave.

Wakumba bowman.

Leopard: "The most dangerous game."

Great herds of game still cover the plains of Kenya. Although there are several dozen different species of "meat" animals, the various types live peacefully together and mixed herds are common. Here a herd of zebra and impala graze within a few yards of each other.

Rhino on the plains below Mt. Kilimanjaro.

Photographers in a "light" safari car—especially designed for African travel—take pictures of a pair of lion. The lion pay little attention to the car, apparently thinking it is simply another animal.

The author returns from a recent ivory hunt.

Mr. and Mrs. Hunter.

Although they have poor eyesight, rhino have very acute scent and hearing. This animal has heard the photographer and is trying to decide what the strange object is that he is carrying.

Lion can climb low trees. To keep the bait from being eaten too quickly, the photographers have suspended it from a tree. This lioness is climbing the tree to pull down the bait.

A pair of rhino in their "lie-up" place, where they go to rest during the heat of the day. This is typical of the open bush country of Kenya. In other places, the thorn trees form an almost impenetrable thicket.

The same pair alarmed. Notice how their tails are carried curled up over their backs. This is a sure sign of fright. An angry rhino drops his tail when charging.

Elephant will often pull and tussle with small trees, apparently to test their strength.

An elephant herd crossing a small stream with the old bull in front. With much bigger ears and longer tusks, the African elephant is considerably larger than his Indian cousin.

Buffalo.

Elephant herd in forest. In the old days, elephant lived mainly in open country. Today, they are usually found in thick cover because of their fear of man. This has made hunting them far more difficult.

The Aberdare Forest. Through this forest John Hunter tracked the rogue elephant that had killed a native.

The python kills by constriction.

Natives cutting up a dead elephant. Many African tribes have such a passion for meat that they will gather by the hundreds around a dead elephant. Within a few hours, every vestige of the meat is gone.

Warthog. These pigs have tusks three and four times as large as those of European wild boar. John Hunter once had to crawl down a hole after one.

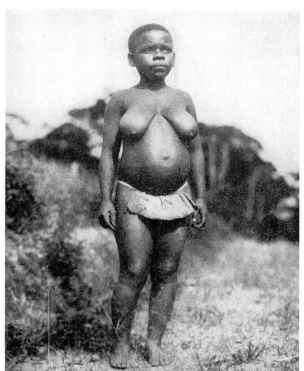

A pygmy woman of the Ituri Forest.

John Hunter with a pair of very fine elephant tusks, weighing 140 pounds each. Tusks like these are becoming increasingly rare.

Cars have replaced the foot safari.

Good ivory.

at first he had been all eagerness to finish off the animal, he now suddenly announced, "I have a strange foreboding that something is going to happen. Take me out of here."

I wished his highness had had his foreboding before he shot a buffalo bull through the stomach with a .416. However, there was nothing to do but take the man out. I left Kirakangano and the gun-bearer behind, warning them to wait there for me and to do no more spooring until I returned. I could see light through the bush on our right, showing that we were not far from the open plains. After taking the prince out of the cover, I left him there and started back to take up the hunt again.

I had scarcely gotten halfway to the two men when I heard a shot. For an instant there was silence. Then I heard the buffalo grunting. I knew what those quick, hard, savage grunts meant. They are the noises a buffalo makes when he is goring his victim. The bull was killing my natives. I tore through the tangle of wild briars and scrub like a lunatic. The vines wound themselves around me like lassos. I could hear the sodden thuds of the buffalo's horns as he pounded one of the men into the ground. I was now frantic, ripping up the clinging vines by the roots and plowing through the bushes by brute strength.

As I crashed through the last line of bush, I saw a terrible sight. The buffalo was down on his knees goring the motionless body of Kirakangano. The bull was so busy using his horns on the semi-conscious man that he did not notice me until I was less than five yards away. Then he leaped up. As he rose, I fired for the point of his shoulder. The force of the heavy bullet knocked him backward onto Kirakangano. The buffalo fell dead on its knees, hind legs spread-eagled. Kirakangano was lying diagonally behind the dead buffalo's forelegs, the whole weight of the great body across him.

I tried to drag the flabby, sweating mass off my dying friend. I could hardly move it. I lay on my back and braced my feet against the carcass, shoving until I scraped the skin off my shoulders. It was no use. Then I grabbed a sapling in both hands and with my feet locked around the buffalo's neck, I tried to pull myself and the body toward the tree. I even grabbed the sapling in my teeth for more purchase. I still could not shift the carcass off Kirakangano. The man was conscious and I could tell he was suffering badly, but he did not complain or even moan.

I shouted for the prince to come and help me. After an interminable time, he finally gingerly entered the bush. By pulling together on the buffalo's tail, we were finally able to drag the carcass off Kirakangano. The Masai had been badly crushed by the buffalo's horns and forefeet. Two of his fingers were broken where he had tried to grab the animal by the mouth.

I promptly gave him an injection of a quarter grain of morphine to relieve his pain. Within a few minutes he appeared eased. His first question was "Is the gunbearer dead? If not, let me kill him while I still have the strength."

The gunbearer had been the direct cause of the tragedy. The Masai explained that after I left him, the gunbearer had sneaked on ahead, in spite of my orders and Kirakangano's protests. The man came on the buffalo lying down and had fired. The bull leaped up with a roar and charged. The terrified gunbearer had run back toward Kirakangano, apparently hoping that the bull would take off after the Masai. Just as the man reached Kirakangano, the bull caught up with him. He gave the man such a blow from behind that the gunbearer cannoned into Kirakangano, knocking him down. Kirakangano had not even had a chance to use his spear before the buffalo was on top of him.

I went to look for the gunbearer. Six yards to the right of Kirakangano, I found the man's body. He was lying on his back, his tongue protruding. I raised the limp body from the ground. The neck was supple, broken in two places from the force of the buffalo's blow. The buffalo had hit him with turned skull, both curves of the horns connecting at the same time. The man was still alive. He muttered "Maji," the native word for water. I took my bottle and tried to pour a little down his throat. The water trickled out of the sides of his mouth. While I held him, I could feel his breathing stop. His hunting days were over.

When I told Kirakangano that the man was dead, the faint flicker of a smile passed over his face. Later, I found the Masai's spear embedded in the buffalo's shoulder. I thought Kirakangano must have gotten in at least one thrust but he told me that the buffalo had actually speared himself in the shoulder while kneeling down to gore him.

I went back to camp and had our porters bring a motorcar to the edge of the bush. With their help, we carried Kirakangano and the dead gunbearer to the car. The nearest doctor was a hundred miles away over appallingly rutted roads. The prince drove while I sat beside Kirakangano. Rain commenced to fall, making the going skiddy and difficult. About halfway, the car got stuck in a deep ravine. The prince tried to force it up the muddy bank, but the car kept slipping back again. I remembered getting knocked and bumped by the gunbearer's dead body while I was trying to hold Kirakangano in my arms to spare him some of the jolts. Every jar shrieked through my nerves in sympathy with him.

At last we got out of the ravine and went on. The dying Masai pointed out a warthog we passed that had unusually fine tusks. Even though he was dying, he was still a hunter at heart. He talked to me about his wife, his children, and his cattle, quietly remarking that he would never see them again. I tried to cheer him by saying we would soon be hunting together. Kirakangano smiled. He knew he was dying.

My friend passed away that night. A brave man, a great bushcraftsman, a true African. My only small consolation is that Kirakangano died as many Masai dream of dying—killed during the hunt by a noble wild beast. I am glad that at the end his spear was bloody, even though it was only an accident. I don't think Kirakangano would have wished to die with a clean spear.

11

The Ituri Forest

Most of my life in Africa has been spent in the open bush and great plains of the uplands—a district that has well been called "white man's country." But I have had my share of the jungle also, and although I would not care to live in those dark, mysterious depths, I must own to their fascination. The true jungle is a weird place, a land of perpetual twilight even at midday, and here live the tiny forest pygmies and the cannibal tribes together with strange beasts we never see on the open veldt. I was always glad to guide an expedition into the jungle country for the place possesses the same lure for me as does a haunted house. Yet I admit I was even gladder when the trip was over and I could return to Kenya.

At one time during the 1930's, I was chosen to guide an expedition into the great Ituri Forest, a vast district spreading across the northeastern part of the Belgian Congo. The expedition was sent out from London by the Kensington Museum under the direction of Dr. R. Ackroyd. At that time, very few expeditions had entered the Ituri and Dr. Ackroyd wished to take back to London a collection of animals and plants from the district.

The doctor and I met in Kampala, Uganda, about 180 miles east of the Congo frontier. I was most favorably impressed by the man. He was middle-aged, most pleasant in his manner, and obviously ready for anything. I was later to find that he was also a highly capable field naturalist. I told him that I had had some experience in the Congo, having guided sportsmen there after the

152

small, vicious red buffalo that live in the forests. But I knew little
of the Ituri. Dr. Ackroyd nodded.

"I foresaw that possibility and I have secured a highly capable
guide. You may have heard of Bezedenhout, the man who obtained
the first pictures of wild okapi. I have been able to get in touch
with him, and he has agreed to take us through the forest."

I met Bezedenhout later in the day. He was a thin, wiry man
with very fair hair and remarkably keen blue eyes. Like Fourrie,
my old friend of Serengeti days, he was a Dutchman. I gathered
that he had led a hard and not too respectable life, but after
talking to him for some time I was positive he knew the Ituri
well and could get us through. I asked him about his famous
okapi pictures. (An okapi is a curious animal, related to the giraffe,
but smaller and with a shorter neck.) Bezedenhout told me that
he had taken his pictures by crawling on hands and knees through
the jungle covered with the hide of a wild pig. He smiled a bit
as he spoke and I felt there was more to the story than that,
although I did not press him for details.

We traveled east across Uganda to the village of Mberemule on
the Semiliki River, the entrance to the Congo. Armed native
soldiers guarded both sides of the river and a Belgian prefect of
police checked our passports. When the man came to Bezedenhout's passport, he stopped and began to examine the paper carefully. I looked around for our guide, wondering if he had any
explanation for the prefect's strange conduct, but he had vanished
like a puff of smoke. The Belgian looked up and said, "This passport has been forged. I cannot approve it. Who is this man?"

Dr. Ackroyd described Bezedenhout and the prefect nearly
leaped from his seat. "That man is one of the worst ivory poachers
in Africa," he shouted. "On his last trip here, he persuaded our
own native troops to desert and go elephant poaching with him,
using their military rifles. He collected a fortune in ivory and had
his porters swim with it across the river into Uganda. We will
never allow him to enter the Congo again."

As the Semiliki river is forty yards wide, about eight feet deep, and infested with crocodiles. I could hardly credit the prefect's statement. Both Dr. Ackroyd and I pleaded with the man, promising that we would assume full responsibility for Bezedenhout's conduct while in Belgian territory. Dr. Ackroyd pointed out that it would be impossible for him to make his collection without Bezedenhout's services as a guide. Fortunately for us, the prefect was not an unreasonable man and realized the scientific importance of the trip. Finally he reluctantly agreed to allow Bezedenhout to enter the Congo with the strict understanding that he was to be under Dr. Ackroyd's supervision at all times and would leave the territory with us.

We crossed the river, Bezedenhout bowing politely to the prefect as we passed. Then we pushed on to Mboga, about fifteen miles further on. I asked Bezedenhout if the ivory-poaching story were true. He assured me it was. "The police were right on my heels when I reached the Semiliki," he told me. "The crocs were bad, but by shooting into the water I managed to keep a stretch of river clear long enough for the porters to make it."

I began to realize that Bezedenhout was a very resourceful and determined fellow.

At Mboga, we collected eighty porters for the trek. These men were very good. We paid them a franc (at that time, about a penny) a day and for that sum they would go from dawn until dusk, each man carrying a load of forty pounds on his head. After they had pitched camp, the more expert hunters in the group would scout round to bring us news of game. We had some trouble when the men discovered that Dr. Ackroyd had taken along several tins of methylated spirits for preserving specimens. They broke open the tins and went on a noble drunk. Two of them died from the effects. After that, the rest left the spirits strictly alone.

I had great difficulty in finding a reliable cook—the chosen man was an excellent cook but, unfortunately, it turned out that he was cannibal-minded. This led to certain complications which I will describe later.

When our expedition was organized, we left Mboga and headed westward toward the Great Ituri, about ten miles away. Near the river the country was mainly open grassland with vast patches of reeds. A clear flowing stream wandered through these meadows like an English brook. I saw several herds of elephant, the bulls carrying ivory of seventy to eighty pounds per tusk. A few years before, shooting had been unrestricted and thousands of these great animals had been killed for their ivory. Now shooting was forbidden without license. I was surprised to see how rapidly the elephants had lost all fear of man. They were scarcely perturbed by our presence.

By afternoon, our safari had reached the edge of the forest. I was surprised at the size of the great trees. Magnificent ferns grew in the moist shade. There were great patches of the maidenhair variety that one so often sees in pots at home, growing in huge clusters near mossy rocks. Even in the stony places, dwarf ferns were growing. Thousands of lovely orchids lived in the nooks and crannies of the vine-covered tree trunks. The flowers were in all varieties of pink and some were a delicate white. Long-haired, black-and-white Colibi monkeys swung from the trees and eyed us just as do our East African species.

We camped by a clear running stream that reminded me of a highland brook with its tiny terraced waterfalls. The next morning, under Bezedenhout's guidance, we plunged into the forest.

The middle Ituri Forest is remarkably free from undergrowth. There are no stinging nettles and prickly briars and one can walk almost as through a park among the boles of the great trees. Their upper branches are so thick that little light can filter through, thus discouraging the growth of lesser plants. We flushed a little flock of forest guinea fowl and they flew up to the lower branches of a great tree. They were so high that I could not reach them with a shotgun. I shot a couple with a light rifle and was very surprised to find them a species new to me, although they were about the same weight and size as our Kenya birds.

We were several days in the Ituri before we saw our first pygmies.

Yet we knew they were watching us at all times. If we backtracked for any cause, we would find the imprint of their tiny feet over our tracks and occasionally we would catch a glimpse of a shadow flitting through the dark woods that was neither bird nor animal. I supposed the little people were merely timid but Bezedenhout explained that they thought we were tax collectors. Under the colonial government natives are required to pay taxes like everyone else but collecting from these shadowy little forms must indeed be difficult. As they have no money, they pay their taxes in goats.

"I'll bring them in when I wish to," said Bezedenhout proudly. "I'm the only man in the world who can. I am king of the pygmy people." This was a remarkable boast, but I soon found that it was a true one.

One evening Bezedenhout went into the bush and returned with two of the little men, armed with miniature bows in keeping with their stature. I watched Bezedenhout chat with them in pygmy. Their hairy faces literally beamed as he recalled earlier visits. Within an hour, dozens of other pygmies came gliding in from the forest and joined the group. They shook hands with us and danced around in infinite glee because Bezedenhout, their God, had returned.

Except for Bezedenhout, we were the first white men many of them had ever seen. They crowded around us, stroking our hands and feeling the texture of our clothes. They kept up a continuous chatter of questions, some of the queries being very curious. I remember one old man asking me if white men could dream. I assured him they could and he seemed surprised. "I thought we were the only people who could do that," he remarked.

Like most primitive tribes, the pygmies are delighted to meet hunters who can provide them with meat. Several old men whose hunting days were past begged me to shoot monkeys for them, monkey being their favorite meat. The branches of the trees were so thickly intertwined that often a shot monkey did not fall but was caught in some cleft or tangle of twigs. The younger men were remarkably skillful at retrieving them, peering upward until they saw exactly where the dead animal had been caught and then scrambling up the great vines and creepers to the spot. Their own tiny bows could not shoot an arrow high enough to reach the monkeys though they occasionally stalked a band while the animals were feeding on the ground.

The pygmies are not agriculturalists but live entirely by hunting and trapping. Their arrows are poisoned with a substance made from the decayed bodies of insects. It is yellow as mustard and, although potent, it is not as deadly as some other native poisons I have seen. Most of their game is caught in traps. Some parts of the forest were a network of ground and tree traps. The tree traps are made of spears weighted with heavy logs and suspended point down from branches overhanging game trails. A vine is stretched across the trail and connected to the spear by a clever trigger device. If an animal passing along the trail touches the vine, he releases the spear and brings it crashing down on him. Ground traps are pits, covered with a light matting of twigs and leaves. In the bottom are sharpened stakes, generally poisoned. If an animal steps on the cover, he plunges through onto the stakes. Not only elephant and buffalo but even the wary okapi are killed by these devices. These traps are a constant menace to hunters following game trails so Bezedenhout had several of the pygmies act as our guides while we were in the forest.

The pygmies did not kill animals indiscriminately or for sport. They caught only what they needed for food or as a means of barter, looking on the forest as other natives would their cultivated fields. I had always thought of the okapi as the rarest and shyest of all African animals and I was astonished to see the pygmies eating this animal as casually as we would eat kongoni or Thomson's gazelle. I tried some but did not relish the flavor. Our porters ate it readily and did not seem able to distinguish between this scarcest of all meats and ordinary game.

The pygmies make their own spears and arrowheads. Each community has its native blacksmith who practices the art as handed down to him through untold generations. His bellows were made of antelope hide and his hammer was an iron knob. Even with these instruments, the work turned out was surprisingly good.

The pygmies live in little villages scattered here and there throughout the forest. Their beehive-shaped huts are made of brush and leaves. As a full-grown pygmy is only about four feet tall, the huts are correspondingly small. The true forest pygmies seldom leave the depths of the jungle except to trade with another tribe that inhabit the bush country fringing the Ituri. These bush people are somewhat larger than the true pygmies and exchange salt and bananas for the flesh and hides the tiny hunters bring them.

Bezedenhout told me that the pygmies have the highest moral standards he found among any people. "The pygmy women are the only women of any race, black or white, that I have never been able to seduce," he once remarked. That was indeed a tribute to the high standards of the little people, for Bezedenhout was a sultan among women. He was a strikingly handsome man and had an air of mystery about him that women found irresistible.

The pygmies will not sell their women to other tribes and the little women quite literally prefer death to the dishonor of their tiny persons, as the following story proves.

There were many elephants in the Ituri and the ivory was of a very fine, soft grade, making it unusually valuable. In the old days, ivory hunters from many parts came to Ituri. They were a motley lot, some as good as the best and others little better than outlaws. One man of this latter type, a blond Englishman who stood six feet four inches high, met a pygmy girl in the forest and tried to catch her. The girl fled with the man after her. It must have been a strange scene, the tiny woman running like a frightened duiker and the great amorous stranger hot behind. The girl kept her head and led the man to one of the many ground traps in the forest. The little woman, probably not weighing more than seventy-five pounds, was able to rush across the light covering but the heavy man plunged through to his death on the poisoned stakes below.

After we had established friendly relations with the pygmies, we enlisted their services as hunters so Dr. Ackroyd could begin his collecting. It always puzzled natives why white men came such long distances and endured so many hardships simply in order to collect specimens of snakes, mammals, birds and insects. But as natives eat anything along these lines, they generally know where the various specimens can be procured. The pygmies have a desperate craving for salt, as their forest diet is sadly deficient in this necessary substance, so by the gift of a few handfuls of salt we obtained all the co-operation one could ask. Sitting around the campfire in the evenings we explained our wants to these wee hunters and judging from their enthusiastic gestures, our collection was as good as in the camp already, ready for labeling.

I soon found that the pygmies were so eager to please that they would cheerfully promise to bring in any sort of an animal we might mention, even though they might never have seen or heard of the creatures before. I had a copy of Rowland Ward's *Records of Big Game* with illustrations of game animals the world over. I started to turn the pages of this book to show the pygmies what animals we wanted. The little men were most co-operative, even pointing to pictures of the American moose and the Scottish antlered deer, asking me if I'd care for one or two of those animals. The climax came when I happened to turn to a page showing an Arctic walrus. The smallest of the hunters pointed a finger at the pictures and said, "Ah, I know that animal well. He lives in the deepest parts of the forest and comes out only at night. He is very fierce and kills men with those great tusks of his in order to eat them, but if you wish, I'll trap one for you."

Explorers who have penetrated the Ituri Forest often come back with tales told them by the pygmies of amazing beasts, ranging from dinosaurs to man-eating bears, that inhabit the jungles. I suspect these animals are no more plentiful in the Ituri than are walrus. Yet until recent years explorers did not believe the pygmy stories of the okapi, although this strange animal is not uncommon in some districts. Trying to decide how much truth there is to natives' tales is indeed a delicate and difficult task.

Although no walrus turned up, the pygmy hunters did prove to be highly useful. We had a grass-roofed banda built to house the collection and Dr. Ackroyd was kept constantly busy. The specimens varied from okapi hides to flying squirrels. I was particularly interested in the otter skins, a very fine fur with an unusually spotted belly. The pygmies wear these skins as covering and no princess ever had a more beautiful fur cape. Most animals are skinned by slitting them down the belly, but the pygmies skinned otters by cutting them along the back to preserve the finely spotted underparts. We later caught several of these otter in spring traps near waterfalls where the animals come to catch fish in the evenings.

Many of the reptiles brought in were snakes. The little people carried the reptiles in grass baskets and arranged them in rows by the door of the banda. One of the commoner snakes resembled a puff adder in size and girth but was a handsome purplish color that made them look less repulsive. I released two of these horned vipers on the floor and teased them with a stick to see how fast they could strike. One of them refused to pay any attention to the stick, merely trying to escape. But as soon as I touched the other, he doubled back like a flicker of light and struck. The pygmies certainly must have shown great skill in catching these reptiles alive without injury to themselves.

Many spitting cobras were also brought in. They are far more dangerous than the vipers. When provoked, they rear up with spread hood like an ordinary cobra. But these strange and terrible creatures can actually throw their poison at you. The poison can do no great harm on your skin unless it happens to fall on an open cut, but the snake is wise enough to aim for your eyes. The venom frequently produces blindness and is always terribly painful. The snake throws his venom by tilting his head back and pointing the fangs at your face. Then he suddenly contracts the muscles of his poison glands. The yellow liquid comes flying out of the fangs in two thin jets. I regret to say the reptiles are excellent shots.

I conducted some experiments on these cobras with a glass held in front of my face and a long pole. I found the first squirt reached a distance of nine feet. If the snake is teased a second time, he can squirt five feet. The third squirt was only a trickle.

Once while I was in the jungle with the pygmies, I saw one of the leading hunters suddenly reel back with his hand clasped over his left eye. Almost at the same instant, the greenish-black form of a cobra went slithering away through the ferns. Immediately I knew what had happened. The light-footed hunter, walking bare-footed over the soft earth, had come upon a spitting cobra before the snake realized he was there. The alarmed cobra had instantly reared and fired his venom at the little man, hitting him in the left eye. A heavy-footed white man would probably have avoided the accident as the snake would have sensed his presence and slid away. I had no idea how to help the pygmy, but his friends were quicker than I and applied an extraordinary antidote. Two of them laid him flat on his back and held him down for he was in such dire suffering that he had lost all control of himself. His eye was entirely bloodshot and tears were pouring down his cheeks. Then to my horror, another of the pygmies urinated in the man's eye. After he had finished, the injured native rose and in silence we returned to camp. The next morning I was told that a similar treatment had been given the man during the night. In the course of three days, he had completely recovered the use of his eye. The pygmies assured me that without this remedy, their friend would surely have gone blind. I can only suppose that the ammonia and uric acid had some curative effect.

With the pygmies as guides, I made many trips through the forest. The Ituri is a lovely place. Great vines and creepers hang from the vast trees, making cover for flying squirrels that dive through the tangle in squishing leaps. Screeching parrots lever themselves up with their bills through the branches and the lovely little sunbirds flit through the perpetual twilight, catching tiny insects among the gorgeous orchids. Great butterflies float among the tree boles, often gathering by the dozen to drink the ooze on elephant droppings. A man could spend a lifetime studying the animal life in one square mile of this jungle and still hardly scratch the surface.

We did not depend entirely on the pygmies for our specimens and did much hunting ourselves. We found that small animals and birds could be bolted out of the tangle of branches by smoke bombs. We also put out spring traps for voles and other small rodents. In one of these traps, we caught a mamba, considered by some to be the most deadly of all African snakes. The mamba is a very slender snake, being hardly thicker than a man's thumb, and very quick. This mamba was some ten feet long. He had been hunting voles and got caught in the trap by mistake. In his struggle to free himself, he had torn up the ground in a great circle and finally happened to get caught by two more traps. They held him until he died.

The pygmies brought in a number of elephant tusks that they had taken from elephants killed in their traps or found dead in the forest of natural causes. All that they asked for them was a handful of coarse salt—a penny's worth of salt for a tusk weighing twenty pounds or more. I began to understand why the ivory hunters had done so well. They had the forest comb to draw upon.

I collected quite a pile of ivory but nothing out of the way in weight. When we left I had the tusks buried, thinking I would come back for them. But when I later asked for an export permit for ivory, I was told by the Belgian official that I must first get an ivory dealer's license which cost 25,000 francs and was not easy to obtain. He advised me to forget about the ivory and I did.

I had never hunted okapi and I wished to collect a trophy for Dr. Ackroyd, especially as the hides brought in by the pygmies were much cut up. The pygmies simply regard the okapi as another meat animal and give little care to skinning the beast. But Bezedenhout assured me that the okapi was so shy and wary that finding one was virtually impossible. "I don't believe any white man has ever shot an okapi," he told me. "The men who come back with skins get them from the pygmies. Even the pygmies seldom manage to stalk and kill okapi. They find the animals in their game traps."

I still hoped to bag some of the larger forest animals. While out with the pygmies, I noticed a natural salt lick and saw by the signs that many animals came there at night. I had the porters build a machan in a tree overlooking the spot and took up my position that

evening. Mosquitoes made the place a torture chamber. These
irritating pests have a sure knack of finding even a concealed man.
Their constant metallic hum was almost as bad as their bites.

When the moon rose, a herd of elephants came down to the lick.
I was not after elephant and had no interest in them. A lanky young
bull detached himself from the herd and wandered over to the tree
where I was perched. The elephant began to rub his shoulder
against the trunk, trying to dislodge some tick. The whole tree
shook with every movement of the great beast and my machan
began to work loose. I did not fancy landing on the animal's back
so I fired a shot into the air, hoping to frighten him off. The herd
had been wheezing and chuckling to each other, but at the sound
of my shot there was absolute silence. Even the frogs in a nearby
swamp momentarily stopped croaking. The herd did not panic as
I had expected, but stood there some time, frozen into attention.
Doubtless they had never heard a rifle shot before and were trying
to decide what the sound was. Then they suddenly turned and
drifted silently into the forest.

The mosquitoes continued to plague me until daylight. After that
experience, I decided to give up hunting in the Ituri and leave the
job to the pygmies.

The pygmies were always eager to help us on any hunting expedition because of their desperate craving for meat. This passionate
need for meat is typical of many tribes and may lead to cannibalism.
Although many African natives practiced cannibalism to some extent, it was usually a religious cannibalism, performed as part of a
rite and not done for food. I have been told that fifty years ago it
was not uncommon to see a slave tied up in a village while purchasers felt and pinched the man like housewives examining a side
of beef. If no one wanted to buy the whole article, the owner sold
various parts of the slave to different purchasers. Each buyer drew
a line with white bone ash around his part and then put his mark
on it. Sometimes the unfortunate slave would stand there for weeks
before the less desirable parts could be sold. Then he was butchered
and cut up.

While we were in the Congo, I saw a string of natives being led along by a white guard. They were secured together by iron neck-bands, each man separated from the rest by a three-foot length of chain. The guard told me that they were guilty of cannibalism.

I had never thought of my own porters as being cannibals, but one evening I received a surprise. I had been hunting wild pig for meat and returned without any luck. I found the cook had prepared a savory stew for some friends. Thinking the porters had also been hunting but with better success, I sat down and asked for a plate. The cook served me without comment. The stew was excellent and tasted much like pig but seemed a bit more salty. I passed my plate back for a second helping. Then one of the porters said nervously, "This meat is taboo for you." I asked what it was and he said "Makono." This is the native word for an arm. A party of natives had passed through the camp after I left and our boys, being short of meat, had traded them some salt for a human arm they were carrying as part of their provisions. I decided to do without my second plate of stew.

Nevertheless, with all their shortcomings, I liked the natives of the northern Congo well. They were a good-natured lot, easy to handle and, when left to their own devices, easy to feed. We were never in any danger from them. In my experience, wild tribes are seldom dangerous. The dangerous native is the town-raised man. I have also noticed that some wild animals raised in captivity are more to be feared than beasts you meet in the bush. The natives we met wished harm to nobody but tax collectors and spent much of their time trying to kill these officials by means of witchcraft. The witchcraft was not successful—otherwise very soon there would have been no more tax collectors.

When Dr. Ackroyd had finished his work, we left the Ituri. We traveled northeast to Kasenyi on the western shore of Lake Albert and there took a steamer across the lake to Butiaba on the east coast. Here the party split up. Dr. Ackroyd and I returning to Nairobi while Bezedenhout left on business of his own.

Bezedenhout was one of the most unusual men I have ever met in

Africa. Intelligent and ruthless, he might have achieved great heights of power if he had been so minded. But the man could not be happy if long away from his jungle and his pygmies. Bezedenhout told me that he had once guided a count and countess through parts of the Ituri and the countess had fallen in love with him. One evening she came to Bezedenhout and begged him to run away with her. "We can spend our winters on the Riviera and our summers touring the capitals of the world," she told him. "I have great wealth and you'll want for nothing."

Bezedenhout considered the proposition carefully but finally refused. "What would I do on the Riviera?" he asked me. "There's nothing to hunt." I could see the man's point.

For many years afterward I made a habit of asking hunters returning from the Congo if they had seen or heard of him, but apparently the man has vanished. If he is still alive, I am sure he is somewhere in the depths of the Great Ituri with his beloved pygmies.

12

The Great Makueni
Rhino Hunt

I devote this chapter to one hunt which will doubtless rank as the
greatest big game hunt that was ever undertaken by me—or for
that matter anyone else.

The work involved was carried out at the urgent request of the
Wakamba tribe to the Machakos District Commissioner, George
Brown. Its principal object was to make extra land available for
settlement. Under British protection the population of the Wakamba
tribe had increased at least sixfold, and even in the settled areas,
rhinos had simultaneously increased to an alarming extent, so much
so that the rhinos disputed the natives' existing huts and crops.
Natives were afraid to wander out after nightfall. The rhinos had
become a genuine menace.

Had Wakamba bowmen been let loose with arrows, the place
would have been a living hell—complete with numbers of wounded
rhinos at large.

The thorn bush where the rhinos had refuge was of the densest
and contact extremely difficult. Hunting them successfully in the
inhospitable undergrowth became a game of cunning. I learned
many tips from the rhinos. Ear work, I mean listening, was even
more important than footwork. A silent approach was necessary to
make the grand finale possible. Many times I was sorely taxed; the
wind and the birds (feathered spies) communicated my presence;
the results were frequently disappointing. Fortunately the rhinos,

like myself, seemed at times to get properly confused. A method was born within me by sheer luck. I used to get as close to a beast as circumstances would permit, then sway my shoulders from side to side without moving stance. Believe it or not, the rhinos, aware of my presence, would not stand for this, but would come for me boldly, charging at their best speed, and in this way played into my shot. This was indeed exciting work.

It was Captain Ritchie who sent me on this undertaking, but before doing so he had thought long and hard. An ardent naturalist, Captain Ritchie has done more than anyone else to conserve African game. But there was the added problem of tsetse fly control. There are two types of these flies in the Machakos district . . . pawlipides and longipennis. These insects are about the size of a large horsefly and their bite feels like the sudden stab of a red-hot needle. Fortunately, these flies were not infected with the deadly sleeping sickness that is so fatal to man. But they did transmit a virus that killed domestic animals, especially cattle. The wild game in the district was immune to their poison but even today scientists have still to discover a practical serum that will protect cattle from them.

So far, scientists know of only one way of eliminating the insects. Tsetse fly live in bush and when the bush is destroyed, the flies are deprived of a breeding place. But to destroy the bush, you must first destroy the rhino. Labor gangs cannot work in bush where there are rhino. For seven years, Captain Ritchie had tried every device possible to avoid a wholesale wiping out of the rhino near the native area. The Makueni area of the Machakos district is the greatest rhino country in Africa so this would be the biggest rhino hunt in history.

Although I had often guided clients who shot rhino and had done considerable rhino hunting myself, I realized that this would be a very different state of affairs. I cannot too greatly emphasize the vast difference between trophy hunting and having to go into bush after animals. Trophy hunting is virtually always conducted in semi-open land where you can see the animals from a distance and select a good specimen. If the animal turns and bolts back into cover, you let him go. No sportsman wants to hunt in brush for he will almost surely end up by having to kill beasts in self-defense and thus obtain poor trophies.

I had three native scouts to act as trackers—men who had spent most of their lives in jail for poaching. One of them was in his early forties. It took me only a few minutes to become convinced that he was an expert bushcraftsman and thoroughly understood the business of tracking down game. The second man was somewhat younger and particularly proud of his ability as a tree climber— a very valuable asset in bush country where it is often necessary to send a man up a tall tree to locate game. "It makes no difference to me whether a tree is thick with thorns or as smooth as a reed, bwana," this man proudly assured me. "I can climb it as easily as you can walk down a road. Baboons watch me with envy." The third man was little more than a boy, but very keen. Although he obviously did not have as much experience as the other two, I suspected that he would be more amenable to instruction.

All three men had volunteered for this hunt, even though they fully appreciated the danger. By native standards, they would be well paid, but money was not the inducement. For the first time in their lives, they would be trained to shoot and would assist me when necessary. I could see their eyes shine and happy smiles break across their dark faces whenever they mentioned this miracle. Like me, these men had devoted their lives to hunting. Home, family, financial rewards, and personal safety were all secondary considerations. To them, nothing life had to offer could equal the excitement of tracking some great animal through the bush.

As time went on I felt my heart sink as I listened to these boys talk eagerly of what they would do with their guns. They were intelligent men. I had no doubt that the two older scouts were greatly my superiors in bushcraft. But it is almost impossible for a native to learn how to use a rifle except after long months of painful experience. In the back of the native mind is always a belief that the wonderful loud noise of a rifle kills the quarry rather than the bullet. To them, a rifle is such a marvelous piece of equipment that they cannot believe this glorious object has to be guided before it can kill. These men were expert with bow and arrow, but I can only say that the fundamental psychological approach to the piece of machinery that we call a gun is completely different from the mental attitude of an archer. A native archer uses his bow as a musician uses his violin, shooting by the "feel" of the instrument. Handling a gun requires a different type of mind.

There was a road from Nairobi to Makueni so we made the first part of our trip by lorry. Arriving there, we left the lorry and started off into the bush.

The East African bush is unique. I have never seen anything like it in Scotland and I doubt if similar country occurs in any other part of the world. The bush is neither forest nor open plains. There are few tall trees. The growth is mainly low thorn trees, growing ten or fifteen feet high. Sometimes these thorn trees, or "thorn bushes" they might well be called, grow in great clumps of an acre or more in extent. More often they are scattered about and a man can walk easily between them. The soil is mixed sand and reddish earth. Generally this soil takes impressions easily and makes tracking fairly simple. But there are many patches of tough elephant grass where tracks do not show. In some places, the grass grows in tufts, leaving open stretches of sandy soil between. But often the hunter comes on stretches of bush where the grass grows knee high, making a heavy carpet under the thorn trees. Here a tracker is really put to it to follow a spoor.

In some districts, there is a special type of soil which, when exposed to the full force of the sun, becomes almost as hard as brick; an animal walking over it leaves almost no impression whatever. In fact, this type of soil is used in Kenya to make highways and it stands up nearly as well as bitumen. However, even this soil remains soft under the shade of the thorn bushes and it is here that an experienced tracker looks for spoor.

The district commissioner in Machakos had been receiving many complaints about raiding rhinos from a small Wakamba village in the bush, presided over by a chief named Mutuku. This was the place we headed for first.

The Wakamba are a very different people from the Masai although the edges of their territories touch. In height, they are somewhat shorter than the average European whereas the Masai are considerably taller. Although the Wakamba do not have the pronounced negroid features of some tribes, neither do they have the thin lips and nostrils of the Masai. Instead of being a nation of warriors, they are a nation of hunters. Traditionally, the men did the hunting while the women attended to the shambas. I noticed several of the men carrying bows with quivers of poisoned arrows slung over their shoulders. Being much interested in weapons of all sorts, I asked to examine these deadly instruments and several were promptly offered me.

The bows were beautifully finished and came to sharp points at the ends. I should judge that they pulled about seventy-five pounds. They are made from a tree called the mutuba and are a dark mahogany color. I was interested to see that there were no notches to hold the bow string. Instead, the Wakamba wrap strips of rawhide around the bow to keep the string from slipping.

The arrows were excellent, the most ingenious part being the special construction of the head. The head had a stem about as thick as a knitting needle and some six inches long. An inch or so of this stem was inserted in the hollow end of the reed shaft and held in place with tree gum. The poison was smeared on the remaining five inches of stem. No poison was put on the head itself—not enough could be put there to do any damage unless the archer was after comparatively small game. Because the poison, though terribly efficient when fresh, rapidly deteriorates if wet or if exposed to sunlight, the Wakamba carefully wrap the poison stems with bandages made of soft antelope hide. These bandages are left in place until the last possible moment.

My scouts and I spent several days with Chief Mutuku before starting out on the rhino hunt. I spent the time teaching my scouts how to assemble a rifle and learning something of the Wakamba language and customs. I liked the Wakamba. They are a frank, honest people. The women work hard. In addition to their labor in the shambas, they also cook the meals and carry the wood for the fires. It is amazing what loads these women can carry. As soon as a baby girl can toddle, she goes with her mother into the bush to collect wood. On the way home, the mother solemnly ties a few twigs on the child's back as her portion of the load. As the child grows older, the amount of the load is increased until she is carrying a pile of wood weighing well over 150 pounds.

In spite of their low standard of living, I never saw a trace of the "oldest profession" among the women—except, of course, when they become corrupted by civilization. When a young girl reaches puberty, her suitor pays an agreed-on marriage portion for her. To the girls, the payment of this portion serves the same purpose as does the marriage ceremony with us—it is the only "Open sesame" which can command her surrender. She then goes to live with her husband and works hard to raise enough money so he can afford a second wife to help her with the housework.

Now that Kirakangano was no longer with me, I needed a man to act as my major domo—to run my camp and attend to the innumerable small details necessary on a safari. My scouts would be out in the bush with me after game and also I doubted if any of them had the qualities needed for a first-class head boy. But I was fortunate in finding a Wakamba hunter named Mulumbe who was an older man and absolutely reliable. Mulumbe and I got along so well together that he is still with me, handling my domestic staff and acting as my personal gunbearer when I go hunting.

One night I was awakened by the sound of the village dogs barking furiously. I did not connect the sound with the presence of rhinos. Dogs are cowed by the odor of lions and I had supposed that the scent of rhinos would affect them in the same way. Later, I found that rhino scent merely infuriates dogs. When dawn came, Chief Mutuku told me that the rhinos had been at the shambas. He was right. The huge tracks of the beasts were everywhere. My scouts and I instantly set about trailing them into the bush.

At first the bush was quite respectable, but it soon turned into a tangled growth of thorn and saplings. Fortunately, it was the dry season and there was almost no foliage. The few leaves remaining were dry and yellow, a sharp contrast to the rhinos' grayish hides. As we pressed on, the only game we saw was the little dik-dik antelope that compares in size with a Scottish hare. The little animals bolted out of the scrub like rabbits, always making one's heart give a leap at the sudden noise.

We hit a patch of almost impenetrable thorny scrub. The only way through the stuff was to follow the twisting rhino trails. I sincerely hoped we would not suddenly meet a rhino on one of these narrow paths. The trails restricted our movements so we could not get upwind of the animals. A feeding rhino generally moves upwind and knowing this, a hunter can often come in at an angle and take him by surprise. Here we could do nothing but hope for the best.

I give those ex-poachers of mine full marks as expert trackers. Several times my eyes became dizzy with strain as I tried to follow the faint footprints of the rhinos on hard or stony ground, only to find that my scouts were following the spoor as though it were a well-marked road. One scout would go ahead, following the spoor while I covered him with my rifle. When he grew tired of tracking, he would fall back and another scout would take his place. Thus they avoid undue eyestrain.

Suddenly the scout who was tracking stopped and held up his head in the act of listening. For a few seconds I could hear nothing. Then I caught the faint crunching of the rhino's molars as he chewed some twigs. He was grazing in the bush on our left. We moved forward as quietly as possible. One of the scouts constantly tested the wind by picking up bits of hard soil between his fingers and crumbling it into a fine powder that drifted with the slightest breeze. Although the wind is of vital importance, I was particularly careful to make no unnecessary noise. I believe a rhino has the most acute hearing of any big game and can pick up the sound of a human tread at an astonishing distance. I was wearing American moccasins which I have found excellent for stalking. If you step on a twig with these shoes, you can feel it beginning to break and can stop yourself in time. My barefooted scouts moved even more quietly. They had the additional advantage of being naked except for a wisp of gun-cleaning cloth around their middles and the scrub made no sound rubbing against their bare skins. But how they stood the torture of the wait-a-bit thorns that left whitish scratches on their bare bodies I cannot imagine.

We stopped continually to listen to the sound of the rhino's chewing. As long as that noise continued, the rhino did not suspect our presence. Suddenly the sound stopped. Then one of my scouts pointed ahead. I could see the rhino standing motionless in the bush, his head raised and his ears twitching back and forth as they strove to pick up the slight sound that had disturbed him. A rhino's ears work independently of each other; he can incline one ear forward and at the same time twist the other one backward to pick up sounds from both front and rear.

I stood waiting for the animal to move into position for a shot. My scouts began to grow restless as natives often do when the quarry is in sight and there is still no shooting. There were several tick birds riding on the rhino's back and keeping their usual sharp lookout. Rhinos have poor eyesight, but these amazing little birds serve as eyes for them. The birds live on the ticks that get under the rhinos' great folds of skin and, to preserve their patron, act as sentinels for him. When my scouts began to fidget about, the birds spotted them. Promptly the little creatures took wing, uttering their warning *chur-chur* call, and flew toward us. The rhino was instantly on the alert. He swung around to face the direction of the birds' flight, both his ears flipping forward to catch the slightest sound. Then he began to trot past us, holding his tail straight up in the air. He had hardly gone ten yards when he sighted our motionless figures. He walked slowly toward us, resembling a great, horned tank with a brain in the engine. It is hard to know what goes on in an animal's mind at such moments. I believe a rhino might be compared to an irritable, shortsighted old colonel who suddenly finds a trespasser in his garden. His first impulse is to drive the stranger away. Then he realizes that the man may be dangerous so he hesitates. If he can do so with honor, he may withdraw. But if his stomach is bothering him or he is naturally cross-grained, he may decide to cause trouble.

The scouts were twitching with excitement. Their slight movements were enough to provoke a charge. Down went the old fellow's head and he plunged through the bush for us. At my shot, he went down on his knees. In a moment he was up again, and swung away from us. My second shot hit him in the shoulder and he went down for good.

The sound of my shots had scarcely died away when we could hear the sound of exultant shouting from our rear. Soon a long procession of scantily clad natives came winding along the game trail through the bush. They were carrying every conceivable kind of container, from woven straw baskets to fiber bags slung over their bare shoulders. All of them had some kind of home-made knives clutched in their hands. Partly because of the depredations made by the rhinos on their shambas, these natives were in a condition close to starvation. They swarmed around the rhino like ants and I had difficulty holding them off while the animal was skinned. Once that job was done the carcass was completely hidden by a squirming mass of black bodies. Knives were rising and falling in such numbers that I am sure the desperate people must have often seriously slashed each other. In the excitement, no one seemed to care. Brown-plumaged kites dipped and dived over the crowd, occasionally even grabbing a piece of meat from a native's hand and flying off with it. The birds moved so rapidly that the native frequently did not know what had happened and would stand staring at his empty hand, wondering where his meat had gone.

I had reserved the horns and hide for the government. Rhino hide is worth tenpence a pound and can be used to make table tops, kiboko whips, and chair seats. When well oiled, it takes on a soft, deep amber color that is most handsome. The horns are worth thirty shillings a pound or more—ten shillings more than the finest grade of ivory. These horns are sold for a curious purpose. Orientals consider them a powerful aphrodisiac and there is an unlimited demand for them in India and Arabia. No doubt any man who has a harem of thirty or more beautiful women occasionally feels the need for a little artificial stimulant.

Except for this one purpose, rhino horn is worthless. It is not true horn at all but simply solidified hair and cannot be carved like ivory for it crumbles under the knife.

When we returned to camp, I tried some of the horn myself to test its powers. I closely followed a recipe given me by an Indian trader: take about one square inch of rhino horn, file it into a powder form, put it into a muslin bag like a tea bag, and boil it in a cup of water until the water turns dark brown. I took several doses of the concoction but regret to report I felt no effects. Possibly I lacked faith. It is also possible that a man in the bush, surrounded by nothing but rhinos and native scouts, does not receive the proper inspiration to make the dose effective.

I shot twelve rhinos in this section, none of them presenting any serious difficulty. Then I was joined by Mr. Beverly, of the Agriculture Department, who arrived with a large gang of laborers to begin the work of clearing out the bush. Mr. Beverly and I had a long conference during which we mapped out our campaign.

"Before I can send my boys into the bush, I must be sure that all the rhino in the district ahead of them have been cleared out," Mr. Beverly explained to me. "If one or two men get gored, the rest will refuse to work—and you can hardly blame them. My idea is for you and your scouts to keep constantly ahead of us. When you send me word that a district is clear, we'll move forward into it."

This was a sound idea, although it meant that my scouts and I would be constantly in the densest cover and must be sure of getting every rhino. But that was what we were being paid for.

The next day my boys and I started out. As we vanished into the bush, I could hear behind us the sound of Mr. Beverly's gang as they attacked the bush around the native shambas with their pangas.

The country we were in soon changed from level flats to low foothills cut up by narrow valleys. In such places wind is a constant problem, first blowing steadily in one direction and then, as you go over a ridge, shifting to quite another angle due to down drafts and cross currents. Hunting under such conditions is a constant series of disappointments, for after an elaborate stalk, you suddenly find the breeze blowing from you to the animal. It might have been my imagination, but it seemed to me as though the ground in this section magnified every footfall. Much of the district is volcanic, and the hard, porous substance gave off a hollow "bonk" at every step as though we were walking over the roof of a great cave.

The first day in this country, the youngest of my scouts was nearly killed. The boy had learned the rudiments of handling a rifle and was eager to try out his new-found skill. He spotted a rhino sidling along a belt of bush and promptly headed for him. The rhino disappeared in the bush and the scout followed through a partly opened gap in the undergrowth made by the animal's passing. The wind was in the scout's favor, but the rhino must have heard his footsteps on the hard earth. Suddenly he spun around and charged.

The boy had enough presence of mind mind to leap into the air with his legs apart. This quick action saved him from being rammed in the crotch by the rhino's horns as the beast rushed under him. Rhinos have two horns, one behind the other. The boy cleared the first horn but touched the second. Immediately the rhino jabbed upward. The scout went up in the air, his unfired rifle whizzing off in another direction. When he hit the ground, he lay there half stunned. I rushed over to him, thinking he was dead, but except for some bruises and losing a certain amount of skin from between his legs, he was unhurt.

When I lifted him up, the boy said apologetically, "Bwana, I did not have time to shoot. That rhino came as fast as a train. He seemed to fill all space and was on me before I could even think of getting my rifle up."

I knew well how the youngster felt. In spite of their great bulk, rhinos can put up a surprising burst of speed. They can turn within their own length, even when going at full run, and their ability to wheel and twist would do credit to the best of polo ponies. They have an utter disregard for bush and can crash through the densest thorn tangles as though it were so much greenery.

Every animal in the bush gives way to a rhino. I have twice seen elephants decline an encounter with one of these bad-tempered beasts. In both cases the two animals were coming toward each other on a narrow trail. Both seemed aware of the other's presence at about the same instant. The rhino stood his ground and waited imperturbably while the elephant, after nervously scenting the air, left the trail and made a careful detour around the rhino.

I have no idea why these animals are so ill-natured although a client of mine once had an interesting theory. This man had an unfortunate brush with an infuriated cow rhino and, as the beast attacked him without any provocation, the man considered her conduct most unreasonable. Afterward I noticed him carefully examining all the rhino droppings we passed. At last he said solemnly to me, "Hunter, do you know why these beasts are so irritable? It's because they are always constipated." I never forgot this remark and indeed there may be something to it as rhinos swallow their food partly chewed, leaving large quantities of undigested matter in their droppings.

I found it impossible to move steadily through the bush with my scouts, systematically killing all rhino that might prove a menace to Mr. Beverly and his labor gangs. I was constantly receiving so many distress calls from different native villages where the inhabitants were being menaced by a particularly aggressive rhino that it would have been inhuman to ignore them. By good fortune, the progress of the labor gangs was necessarily slow, leaving me time to handle emergency calls. Yet even so I was forced to work out a system of "priority" and "top priority." Chief Mutuku had called me in several times to shoot rhino that were destroying his shambas. Some of the other native chiefs grew impatient, feeling that I was spending too much time in Mutuku's district. A chief named Machoka came to me with his retinue and implored my aid in killing a particularly vicious rhino that was attacking his people. I told the man in some irritation that I could not be everywhere at once and that as soon as I had finished with Mutuku's district, I would come to him. The chief left me very crestfallen, although he had my promise to come to his district within the next two days.

Later that same afternoon, I was astonished to see Machoka hurrying back to my camp with his followers. He had returned to his village and found that in his absence the rhino had killed a woman who was gathering firewood. The natives were saving the dead body to show me.

I need hardly say what my emotions were on receiving this terrible information. Under the circumstances, of course, Chief Machoka's plea promptly received "top priority." I told Chief Mutuku that his rhinos would have to wait and left at once with Machoka and his men.

We found the woman lying on the pebbly slope of a ridge with bits of firewood she had been gathering scattered around her. A well-worn path, patted smooth by generations of naked feet, ran down the slope. The woman had obviously been walking down this path when she met the rhino coming up. The rhino must have charged on sight, killing her on the first pass.

From the spoor, I saw the animal was a female. A few seconds later, I found the track of a calf beside her. The presence of the baby undoubtedly accounted for the mother's unusual ferocity. No one likes to kill a female animal with young and I went about the business with considerable distaste.

A professional trapper named Mr. Sauvage had asked if he could send two of his native boys with me in case we happened to obtain any baby rhino, as these little animals are in great demand by zoos. I now told these boys to be on the alert. Then with two of my scouts, I prepared to start off on the spoor of the cow.

From the ridge where the woman had been killed, we could look out over a great valley completely covered with high scrub. Into this valley the cow and her calf had vanished. From our elevation, the cover did not look particularly dense. Scores of the local natives had been rapidly collecting to witness the death of the animal that had killed the unfortunate woman and also, incidentally, to get some fresh rhino meat. These locals spread out along the ridge for hundreds of yards in each direction and, squatting down on their haunches, kept a careful lookout for some sign of the cow moving through the scrub below us. This was a better way of locating her than trying to track her through the bush, so I sat down with my scouts to wait.

Half an hour passed. Then an excited cry went up. Several fingers were pointing to a spot far out in the valley. For a few minutes I could see nothing. Then I caught a glimpse of a slate-colored object that might easily have been a slab of granite except that it gradually appeared and disappeared as the animal slowly drifted through the cover.

In a straight line the cow was not more than half a mile away. The wind was in our favor and I felt confident of coming up with her very quickly. Taking one scout with me and telling the other to remain on the ridge and keep his eye on the cow's movements I started down into the valley.

I soon found that our hilltop view of the valley had been cruelly deceptive and the bush was far worse than I had realized. Within a few yards we lost all sight of the ridge we had just left. We had covered about half the distance to the place where the rhino had been sighted when we came on the cow's lie-up place. The signs were unmistakable—the large footprints of the cow and the small ones of her calf. Rhinos have a special bed, usually located in the shadiest part of the bush, where they go to rest during the heat of the day. As it was nearly noon, I knew the animal would soon wander over to her lie-up. I decided to wait.

We had been waiting about half an hour when the scout pointed a finger in front of him and then bent the finger my way. He had heard the cow and she was headed our way. Several minutes went by before I saw the cow coming toward us with the calf trotting after her. I could see the native woman's dried blood still on the rhino's horn as the two animals moved toward their lie-up. Then the cow stopped for a moment and the baby ambled up and began nursing. The wind was steady but somehow the mother sensed our presence and became fidgety. She turned around with the baby still sucking and stood studying us with her little pig eyes. We could hear the natives' voices on the ridge and I knew the sound made her nervous. She was prepared either to charge or bolt. It was hard but it had to be. I shot her. She slumped heavily to earth without effort or pain and the youngster remained beside her. At the sound of the shot, I heard the native voices stop for a moment and then change to an excited babble as the crowd ran down the hill slope toward the brush to see the dead animal.

When the baby rhino heard the mob coming, he started butting his dead mother to make her get up. When he found that was useless, he bravely turned to face the natives. There is no doubt that a baby rhino has pluck. When the crowd began to form around the dead cow, the baby charged the natives time and again, evidently thinking that he was defending his mother. He was not much bigger than a large domestic pig; his front horn was just budding and there was a well defined circle behind it that showed where his second horn would some day grow. Although he could not hurt them, the natives ran from his attacks like rabbits. My scout and I tried to catch the youngster but he was hard to handle. I was beginning to fear we could not secure him without hurting him when the two native trappers came up.

Their method of catching the calf was efficient but pathetic. One man crawled along the dead cow's back and, reaching over her body, took hold of her teat and waved it enticingly. The baby, tired and hungry, could not resist the familiar organ that had long meant food and comfort to him. He came in to suckle. The native deftly grabbed him by the left ear and the other trapper sprang in and seized him by the right. The baby squealed like a young pig but was soon tied up.

We transported him back to camp by making a sling out of gunny sacks and carrying him between two long poles. Six natives were needed to support his weight. In camp, we tethered the baby under a large, shady tree and fed him goat's milk from a bottle. For the first two days he was very aggressive, promptly charging anyone who came near him. He gave the same threatening sounds as a full-grown rhino—a "pruff"-like noise made by his top lip vibrating while he blew out air. I am happy to say that on the third day he began to grow more gentle. He would suck our hands like a young calf and his buttings were playful, all part of a game like the pretend growls of a puppy. I often fed the little fellow myself and he soon got to know me and the two native trappers. He would follow us everywhere, but if strange natives came near him, down would go his little head to a tilting angle and with a series of angry "pruffs" he would charge like a good one.

We had been in the bush several weeks now and had shot seventy-five rhino. I decided to take the skins and horns back to Machakos. My trophies were carried by a long line of scantily clad girls to a spot where they could be picked up by lorry. The afternoon was hot but the girls did not mind. Each carried a horn in either hand, and as they trotted through the brush in single file, each girl would prod the bare behind of the damsel in front, perfectly imitating the snorting and puffing noises of an angry rhino as she did so. So we advanced to the accompaniment of peals of laughter while beads of sweat ran off their dark bodies. When we stopped for lunch by the banks of an arid sand stream, I heard fresh outbursts of titters and giggles. I peered over the bank and found the girls had discovered a new game. One girl would lie on her back while another grabbed her by the bare legs and towed her around the sand. A herd of elephants had been digging in the sand for water and mounds of their great droppings were all over the place. The point of the game was to tow a girl over to a pile of these droppings and pelt her with the sunbaked dollops of dung.

I delivered my cargo of hides and horns in Machakos, and was frankly glad to get away from the continual shooting for even a few days, as my old hunting nightmares were recurring and keeping me awake at nights. In those terrible dreams I was always facing the same animals I had shot the day before except that now the animals were winning. I was standing with a jammed gun or had missed with both barrels and the charging beast was on top of me. I would awake soaked with sweat from such encounters and dread going back to sleep for I knew the same dreams would come again.

My scouts were never bothered by these emotional hangovers. No matter what close shaves they had during the day, the natives could sleep like hibernating animals at night.

My boys had ample opportunity to test their nerve in the next few weeks, for the hunting we had gone through was as nothing compared to the troubles that now beset us. Before I fairly had a chance to unload my trophies, I started getting more desperate messages from the natives. Confident that the white man would protect them, the natives were constantly extending their shambas into fresh areas and were running foul of rhinos. But even allowing for this, the rhinos seemed to have suddenly become uncommonly aggressive and I could see no reason for it.

My scouts and I returned posthaste to the bush. Chief Machoka took me out to the shambas of his village so I could inspect the damage. There was no doubt he was fully justified in his complaints. He said many of his people had been chased by the beasts and it was only due to their remarkable agility that none had been killed.

Although evening was coming on, I set out at once with two of my scouts on the spoor. After a long walk, I was almost ready to give up—crawling through brush in a bent-over position is hard on the back. Then one of the scouts called my attention to gruff squeals that were coming from our right. We followed the sounds. By the side of a water hole were two rhinos in courtship, the first time I had ever witnessed this process.

The two animals stood smelling each other's snouts and emitting gurgling grunts. Apparently the bull was not rapid enough in his love-making to suit the cow. She lost her temper and began to butt his sides savagely. There was nothing playful in these attacks; she was goring her partner severely. The bull did not retaliate although the blows caused him to belch heavily.

I could not imagine the cow's motives, but after a few minutes of this rough treatment, the bull began to show signs of becoming more passionate. He swung around the cow and prepared to mount her.

While we were watching, one of the natives nudged me. Another animal was coming through the bush. It was a second bull, obviously attracted by the odor of a cow in season. This newcomer pranced clumsily around the couple which had not yet begun to mate, spurting around, charging at nothing, and evidently showing off to the cow how dazzling he was. From time to time he would start off into the bush and then return when he found the cow was not following him. One of the scouts said to me in his own language, "He hopes to cut out the other man and get the woman."

The cow made the first move. She started off toward the bush followed by the first bull—her chosen mate. The rejected bull stood looking after them. I raised my rifle but the scouts vigorously shook their heads. It went against the grain with them to kill the animals at such a time and I sympathized with their rude sense of chivalry, although I knew that it was better to shoot now rather than wait until the cow had a suckling calf running with her.

As so often happens in the bush, the decision was taken out of our hands. The rejected bull either saw or scented us standing there. Instantly he charged. I shot, and at the sound the other two rhino went wild. They tore around in circles, uttering their "pruff-pruff" war cries. Then they saw us and charged.

I had had time to reload my rifle. The cow was coming first, the top of her shoulders covered with frothy slaver. I fired and she fell heavily, raising a cloud of reddish dust. The bull veered off, plunging into the bush.

The unusual ferocity of the rhinos in the district was now explained. The animals had begun to mate and were nervous and aggressive. I found that their mating season ran from September to November. Pairing is wholly influenced by the smell of the cow coming into use. The scent of a cow could be picked up by bulls for miles around. Several of them would collect around her, not fighting with each other as many male animals do, but allowing her to make her selection. The cow would finally choose one bull and go off with him. The other suitors would accept her decision and depart to look for other cows. A cow would mate with only one bull in a season, and as long as she had need of him, the two animals stayed together.

If the couple becomes separated, the cow will give voice to a mating call to bring her lover back. In my experience, only a cow that has been mated will use this call, although other hunters believe that any cow needing a mate will give the cry. Wakamba poachers are very clever in imitating this sound. They often take up a safe position in a tree with their bows and poisoned arrows, giving the call time after time until a bull rhino is lured into shooting range.

During rutting season, bull rhinos become restless. Instead of feeding slowly through the scrub as they do at other times, they roam about on the search for cows and, being constantly on the alert, their sense of hearing seems far more acute. This greatly added to our troubles.

I had been working hard to train my three scouts how to handle a gun. They still showed a strong tendency to blaze away at any exposed part of a rhino they saw. One day I started off with two of my boys, the youngest scout and the "tree climber." I told them that I expected them to do all the shooting. I would simply go along and watch. For the last time I cautioned them to hold their fire until they were sure of a killing shot.

We went through the bush until we hit some fresh rhino spoor. Then my tree climber mounted a tall acacia and signaled by his piping, birdlike whistles that he had located four rhinos. When he descended, we started out. The two boys went first. One was armed with a double-barreled Jeffery while the other had a magazine rifle. I had warned the boys that in case something went wrong, they were to leave me room to shoot, but they confidently assured me that nothing could go wrong. They were well equipped to handle any situation.

The brush was open and we had little trouble moving quietly. The scouts were listening intently for sounds of rhino feeding, and knowing that the natives' senses were far more acute than mine, I had no doubt about this part of the hunt. We went forward rapidly and I knew we must soon be up to the feeding animals.

Suddenly some tick birds came from behind, making a wide circle over us and calling. The younger scout made a clicking sound with his tongue as if to say, "Those little devils!" A moment later we heard the distinctive noise of rhinos ahead—those sounds that tingle the blood. Your rifle then feels like a toy. The scouts crept forward and I followed more slowly to give them a chance to show what they could do.

The rhinos were feeding in a patch of bush. For the life of me, I could not tell head from tail. Then one of the animals began to move. I saw he was going to pass by an open spot in the bush about five yards in diameter. The older scout saw it too. He turned over the safety catch on his gun and at the metallic click, both beasts swung toward us. There was a long pause while the tick birds chur-churred around us and the rhinos stood motionless.

Then the rhino began to move again. As he crossed the open space, I saw he was a bull. The scout lifted his rifle and took careful aim. It seemed as though the man would never shoot. The bull gradually passed through the open space until his neck and shoulders were obscured. The scout had waited too long to make a killing shot. Ordinarily, I would now have stopped the boy, but I waited to see what he would do. Suddenly he fired. Instantly the bull spun around and charged. After him came the second animal, his cow. The scout fired his second barrel and missed. Now the younger scout who had been eagerly waiting for his chance, lifted his magazine rifle, took quick aim, and pulled the trigger. Nothing happened. The boy pulled again and again. There was no report.

With the charging animals only twenty yards away, the boy broke open his rifle and turned toward me, holding the open breech so I could see that the cartridge had not gone off and it wasn't his fault that the gun had misfired.

In another few seconds both scouts would have been gored.

Fortunately, the older man had enough presence of mind to throw himself face down on the ground, giving me a chance to fire over him. I pulled off two of the snappiest shots of my life, dropping both beasts with a quick left and right shot. The rhinos died with one's head across the other's neck.

When I came to examine the younger scout's rifle I found the cap of the cartridge still undented. He had not fully thrown over the bolt of the rifle when loading. When the boy realized his mistake, he began to cry. He was a brave fellow and a good scout, but too anxious to show me what he could do.

Our hunting was now delayed for several weeks because of the seasonal rains. During this period, we were fortunate enough to find an ideal camping spot. My tent was set up under a grove of branchy fig trees. The grass here was very fresh and green and there was a little stream nearby of clear water, the life line of any camp. Tell-tale feathers on the ground nearby showed that guinea fowl and francolin were not far distant. This was a particularly welcome sight to me for it meant a change of diet. As my food supplies dwindled, I had been discussing our meals with Mulumbe, my head boy, in much the same way the lady of a house would discuss matters with the cook. But the conversation became somewhat monotonous.

Myself: What soup do we have tonight, Mulumbe?

Mulumbe: Rhino soup, bwana.

Myself: What meat?

Mulumbe: Fillet of rhino, bwana.

Myself: What for tomorrow?

Mulumbe: Rhino heart, bwana.

Whatever part I ate, I still had visions of the charging animal that had died in defense of his heritage and this hardly aided digestion.

It was pleasant to lie in my tent and listen to the rain beating on the outside. It reminded me of the times in Scotland when I used to hear the storms from Solway Firth lashing the roof of my father's home.

When the rains stopped I found that they had altered the nature of the country considerably and not for the better. Insect life appeared as if the raindrops themselves had turned into flying ants and mosquitoes. Sausage-shaped beetles buzzed constantly around my lantern at night, falling heavily into the soup. Scorpions, centipedes and big hairy spiders were everywhere, driven out of their holes by the water.

The rains also made hunting more difficult. The scrub awoke into life, sending out green leaves that cut visibility to almost nothing. Great masses of giant stinging nettles sprang up, some of them an inch in diameter. Even elephants avoid these nettles and there are authentic cases of horses dying as a result of having rolled in a bed of the terrible plants. From a hunting point of view, the only advantage to the rains was that they made the ground softer, thus enabling a man to walk more quietly.

As a result of these handicaps, the work went more slowly. We had now killed 137 rhinos. As the animals became fewer, the survivors showed a tendency to be more alert. The local natives were very useful to us, going out to find rhino on their own and then sending runners back to my camp when they had spotted one.

When I felt we had virtually eliminated the rhino in that section, I told Chief Ndeeva, the head of a nearby village, that I was planning to return to Machakos. He was greatly distressed and sent scouting parties throughout the hills and valleys for miles around to find more troublesome rhino.

A day or so before our departure, two natives burst panting into my camp with the news that they had located three rhino a few miles off. They had wisely left another man in a tree near the spot so he could keep track of the animals. I left at once with one of my scouts. We found the lookout still in his tree, and he informed us that the rhinos had moved on into the brush but we could find their spoor by a large cactus he had marked down. The native was right and we picked up the spoor with no trouble.

The thorns were bad. That bugbear of the bush, the wait-a-bit, was ever present, its thorns in pairs like miniature pike bait hooks.

There was also plenty of low acacia with thorns facing back to back, like Stuart tackle. No matter how you tried to avoid them, you were caught from any angle. My scout who was following me had to keep pulling the barbs out of my shirt so I could go on. My ears smarted and burned from the constant jagging. Then we came to some very dense stuff through which ran a narrow rhino trail like a tunnel. We started through this opening bent nearly double.

We crawled along in single file. Then ahead of me I saw two earthy-colored shapes. The shadows cast by the leafy foliage made their outlines a mere jumble of light and shade. Try as I would I could not tell head from stern.

My scout pointed toward our left. He had seen the third rhino. From my position I could not see this animal so I concentrated on the two before us. Just ahead was an open space where we could stand. My scout and I reached it and straightened up with relief. Without taking my eyes off the two rhino, I motioned to the scout to keep an eye on the third animal. At my slight motion, the pair in front of me became suspicious and swung around to face us. They had been mating for I could see the foot dried mud marks of the bull on the back of the cow.

I fired at the cow. She slumped heavily to her knees. The bull tore around in a circle giving me a chance to reload. Then he charged. A bullet from my right barrel hit him above the brisket. He never flinched and came on with head down. Suddenly I heard crashing in the bush on our left. The third rhino was also charging us from that direction.

I did not dare to take my eyes off the oncoming bull. I fired again. The shot hit him fairly below the ear and he went down. At the same moment I heard the third rhino right at my side. He tore past me and I saw my scout hanging on his horns. I reloaded again quickly. From the angle where I was standing it was almost impossible to deliver a killing shot without hitting the boy. I waited a fraction of a second and then fired for the rhino's shoulder. The animal dropped and the boy shot off his head like a rider whose horse has refused at a jump. The boy lay motionless and I could only think, "My God, I've shot them both." I was positive that my bullet had passed through the scout's body before hitting the rhino. I did not even have the courage to go over and examine the boy but stood there clutching my gun and staring at them.

Then I saw the boy move. I can think of no sight that has ever given me greater joy. I ran over to him, my first move being to examine his body for a bullet hole. There was none. I must have missed him by a fraction of an inch. The horns had not gone through his body. As the rhino lowered his head for the toss, the boy had been able to grab the foremost horn and hold himself clear of it while the animal carried him past me. I consider this one of the narrowest escapes I have seen in my years of hunting.

The next day, my scout was joking and laughing with his friends and seemed to have forgotten the incident completely.

By November, my work was finally finished. The rhinos had been dealt with in the districts that the government wished to have cleared of brush. I had killed 163. Such numbers may indeed appear incredible, but my records are on file with the game department in Nairobi, for the department received all hides and horns. I make no statements that cannot be substantiated by the government files.

My boys and I started back toward Machakos. We could walk freely through the brush now for there was little chance of meeting a rhino. Walking in a single file, we topped a little rise. I stopped in astonishment and I could hear the amazed boys gasping with surprise as they joined me.

Three months before we had crossed the same country that lay before us. Then it had been a maze of thorn bush and acacia, cut by a tangle of narrow rhino trails. Now it lay bare as a polished table. Mr. Beverly's labor gangs had been moving steadily behind us, cutting down the bush and clearing the land. What a short time before had been as wild a bit of Africa as God ever made was now farming country. Not a tree or bush remained. Now that the scrub was gone, I could see the white network of rhino trails criss-crossing over the whole land. Already the grass was beginning to obliterate them. The freakish beasts that had traveled those trails for centuries were now dead and gone. Here and there on the plain I could see piles of their whitened bones. In other spots were great black rings, showing where the labor gangs had piled the brush into heaps and burnt it.

As though in a trance, my scouts and I walked easily across this open country. It seemed only yesterday that we had crawled along these dim, white trails on our hands and knees beneath a canopy of brush. Now native huts were beginning to appear and we passed women breaking ground for their shambas. Civilization had moved on another few miles into the jungle. In a few generations the rhinos that had killed women gathering brushwood and set the village dogs barking at night would be little more than a legend— a story to tell children around the fire at night as we tell our little ones tales of dragons in the long ago.

This was not my only rhino hunt. As more and more demands were made by the natives for fresh land, I was sent back time and time again. At the time of this writing I have shot over a thousand rhino. Is it worth killing off these strange and marvelous animals just to clear a few more acres for a people that are ever on the increase? I do not know. But I know this. The time will come when there is no more land to be cleared. What will be done then? In the meantime the inevitable clash between men and beasts presents a problem and a headache.

13

Game Ranger—a Variety
of Rogues

I most certainly do not wish to give the impression that the game
department's main interest was the elimination of marauding
animals. Conservation was also of prime importance. Some eighty
miles south of the Makueni district lay the Makindu area, which
also was so heavily infested with tsetse fly that domestic cattle
could not live there. However, in part of this district there was so
much lava rock that it was calculated that the cost of uprooting
bush among the stones would be prohibitive. This section was set
aside as a game reserve, particularly to preserve the rhino.

I was appointed game ranger of this district, a position which I
still hold. My duty was to protect the rhinos from poachers, both
white and native. I had developed a great affection for these pug-
nacious beasts while I was hunting them, so I accepted the position
gladly. However, several personal complications presented themselves.

If Hilda and I lived in Makindu, we would have to sell our house
on the Ngong Road. This in itself was not too great a sacrifice. Now
that the children were growing up, the house had become too large
for us. Our two girls had married and moved away. One was living
in England, and the other was traveling around the world with her
husband, who was in the British Army. My eldest boy, Gordon, had
also left us. Gordon had once planned to follow me as a professional
hunter. He had shown great promise and I was most proud of the

lad. But he had married and with the responsibilities of a family upon him had decided to take up a steadier business. He had turned to farming, being particularly interested in the government's efforts to reclaim some of the vast areas that have been destroyed by erosion. Our family had been farmers for many generations in Scotland and I went to Africa to escape it. Yet my eldest son, living in the finest hunting country left in the world, had deliberately abandoned the profession of hunting to return to the traditional family occupation. Well, every tub must stand on its own bottom and I was glad that the boy had found a livelihood that interested him.

My second son had established himself as an architect and was absorbed in the new building developments that were going up all over the country. But the two youngest boys were still with us. Hilda was afraid the lads would not wish to move to Makindu, as all their interests were centered in Nairobi. After considerable discussion, we decided to sell our large house and buy a small, modern home near Nairobi where the boys could live. I would stay in Makindu and Hilda would divide her time between Makindu and the Nairobi house.

Hilda accompanied me to Makindu to help set up my home there. I liked the place the first time I saw it. The village is a small stop on the Nairobi-Mombasa Railway and was once the headquarters for the railroad personnel. Later, the offices were moved to Nairobi, but the very comfortable houses, originally built for the railroad officials, still stood. They were mainly deserted. Hilda and I rented a nice house and moved in. From our front porch on a clear day you could see the snow-topped peak of Kilimanjaro; sometimes it seemed to be floating among the white clouds. When we went to bed at night, we could hear the laughing wails of hyenas as they fed in the bush and often we dropped off to sleep listening to the throb of drums in the nearby native villages. Ostriches wandered within a hundred yards of our house and it was a poor morning when you could not sight a herd of giraffes teetering along through the bush on their long legs.

Mulumbe acted as our head boy, bringing three of his wives with him to keep him company. The rest he left in his village to attend to his shambas. We also had a boy to do the cooking and take care of the house. As I had, in addition, my government game scouts, quite a little community sprang up around us.

I was very happy in Makindu. Hilda and I had all the comforts of home and yet had the feeling of living in the bush. The days were full. We generally woke at dawn. A native boy sat outside our door and as soon as he heard us stirring ran for the kitchen. A few seconds later we would hear a discreet tap on our door and the boy would enter on silent, bare, black feet, carrying a tray with our morning tea. Under Hilda's training, he always dressed in a clean white robe with a red fez. Hilda once tried having the boys wear shoes, but a bush native wearing shoes is both clumsy and noisy, so she quickly abandoned that plan.

Our meals were always excellent. The local natives brought us fresh eggs every morning; we had a plentiful supply of bacon in our storehouse, and occasionally Hilda would vary our menu with sand grouse or quail if I had been out on a shoot the day before. As a Scot, I liked porridge for breakfast and Hilda always saw to it that I had a plentiful supply.

After breakfast, I'd light my first pipe of the day while the boys took the tarpaulin off the lorry and put in our rifles and water bottles. Then we started off for the reserve just as the sun came up. There are no proper roads through the reserve, but I had made a series of car tracks that took their place. I always drove, watching the soft dust in the tracks ahead for spoor. My scouts, with old Mulumbe, rode in the back keeping a sharp lookout over the countryside.

The reserve is too large to keep under a complete supervision. But by studying the signs, you can tell how matters are going. The sight of vultures circling in the sky always calls for an investigation. It means something has died—possibly from natural causes but also possibly because of the activity of poachers, either black or white. When we came on a herd of oryx, Tommies, or giraffe, I stopped and studied them through my binoculars. If one of the animals lagged behind the others, I investigated, for he might be suffering from some disease that could spread to the rest of the herd. If he seemed seriously ill, I shot him and took blood samples. These samples were later checked in Nairobi.

I varied my patrols according to the time of year. During the rainy season when the grass was lush, the game spread out all over the reserve. During this time, it was impossible to keep too close track of the animals, as often my tire tracks were nothing but ribbons of mud and not even the heavy lorry could get through. But I was not too disturbed at such times, for I knew that if I could not get through, neither could any other lorry, so poaching by Europeans was well-nigh impossible. Neither could the native poachers do much damage, for the animals were so scattered that it was difficult to approach them.

When the rains were over and the grass began to dry up, the game gradually concentrated in certain areas where the grass was still high. Although a few weeks before the grass had been up to the little Tommies' shoulders, now it was grazed as close as a golf green. More vigilance was necessary, because the animals could be easily seen and offered a better target. The rhinos that had wandered freely over the whole area now tended to gather about a few mud wallows and water holes. I tried to keep a check on these wallows and frequently examined them for spoor, both animal and human.

I would return to Makindu about eleven o'clock. Often there would be two or three natives sitting on the porch of my house, wrapped in their blankets, waiting for me. Some of them might be sick and want help. Others would have some complaint—usually that a rhino from the reserve had been damaging their shambas. I'd promise to investigate the matter. After lunch, Hilda and I usually took a siesta until the sun had dropped slightly. In the late afternoon, I would check on the natives' complaints, sight in some new guns, make minor repairs on the lorry, or do any of the countless small tasks that a game ranger is called upon to perform.

Sometimes I felt as though my main duty was to wage a constant war against the attacks of civilization. There was a very fine stand of eucalyptus trees along the banks of a stream in the reserve where the native women often come to gather dry sticks for firewood. One day I received a message that a Nairobi concern had asked for a permit to cut down this grove for lumber. With the increasing native housing developments in Nairobi, the demand for lumber is growing critical. I pointed out that this grove tended to hold up the banks of the stream and if it were destroyed, the district would be flooded during the rainy season. The permit was refused but I know that the lumbering concerns will try again. Already much of Kenya has been permanently ruined by the ruthless destruction of natural resources. Yet the constant cry is that the natives must have more houses and more land for their shambas. Where it will end, I do not know.

Hilda took frequent trips to Nairobi to see how our boys were coming along, and occasionally—but not often—I accompanied her. Our home there is very pretty and modern and Hilda has done wonders with the flower gardens and lawn. But I am not fond of modern Nairobi. I dislike the noise and crowds, and I feel out of place there. After a few days, I begin to grow restless and eager to return to Makindu again. The train passes through Makindu at eleven-thirty at night, but I had only to signal with my torch from the train window and in a few minutes Mulumbe, with some of my boys, would appear at the station platform to give me a hand with my luggage. The natives in Makindu are the Wakamba, and in that district at least they are unconcerned with politics, preserving their old customs much intact.

True, we had occasional troubles in Makindu. For instance, in addition to Mulumbe, I had another very experienced tracker, a Wakamba named Machoka. There was considerable rivalry between these two men but it never flared into open antagonism. When I returned from one of my trips, Machoka's son told me that his father had died during my absence. I asked the young man if he had called in a doctor. "No, bwana, Mulumbe was jealous of

my father and had a witch doctor put the spell of feteena on him,"
replied the youth bitterly. "No white doctor could have saved him."

Nevertheless, the Wakamba are a fine people, one of the greatest
hunting tribes in all Africa. Today, natives are forbidden to hunt,
and so one of my main duties at Makindu was to prevent native
poaching, especially on the reserve.

Now it may well seem unreasonable of the government to forbid
the Wakamba to practice their ancient art. Yet there are definite
reasons for it. Today, with their numbers increased tenfold, if every
Wakamba were allowed to shoot game as he wished there would
soon be no game (or sheer havoc). Also, the natives were beginning
to commercialize their hunting. Obviously, this practice had to be
stopped.

I had not been in Makindu more than a few days before I began
to find evidence of poachers. While on patrol, I found a dead
baboon, killed by an arrow. The animal had been skinned, which
struck me as curious, because baboon hide is worthless. Then I
found numerous native hides cunningly concealed along the banks
of streams or beside water holes. These hides were usually little
nests built in thorn trees, barely large enough to hold a man and,
as they were constructed of the branches of the tree itself, very
hard to find. A poacher would sit in his hide until an animal came
down to drink. Then a well-placed poisoned arrow would do the
business.

One afternoon while my scouts and I were going through the
bush, we came on a tiny boma such as poachers build for a camp.
We could hear natives talking inside. As we came up, the poachers
heard us. Instantly every man was on his feet, grabbing for his bow
and arrows. One of my scouts shouted, "This man is an ivory
poacher—not a game ranger." His quick thinking may have saved
my life, for the Wakamba were quick and accurate with their
weapons and even the slightest scratch of a poisoned arrow may
cause death.

The poachers were more friendly after that. I sat down and talked
to them. I noticed they all wore caps made of baboon skin, which

explained the skinned baboon that I had found. During the rhino hunt, I had learned to speak Wakamba fairly well, so I could talk to them. I was particularly interested in one old chap who seemed to be their leader. After talking to him for a few minutes, I was sure he was a master bushcraftsman. He talked with authority and his statements rang true.

These men were not in the bush simply to obtain food. They were doubtless interested in shooting elephants and rhino for their ivory and horns. They had learned that certain corrupt merchants would buy these valuable articles from them for a shilling or so a pound. The merchants would then smuggle the trophies to Mombasa where they would be secretly loaded onto Arab dhows and exported at tremendous profit.

The little old leader of the gang offered to take me out in the bush and show me how they bagged an antelope. I went along with him. While crossing an open stretch of bush, we saw a rhino. The Wakamba said, "Would you like to see me kill that animal?" As he spoke he pulled a poisoned arrow out of his quiver. I hastily told him no. "Very well, then, I'll simply scare him," said the little man. Back went the poisoned arrow into the quiver and out came an ordinary shaft. I hurriedly said, "Don't hurt the beast." "Oh, no, I'll just drive him off," said the old poacher confidently. With the ease of long practice, he slapped the arrow into his bow and without even seeming to take aim, fired at the rhino. The arrow hit the brute on the base of his horn, giving him a severe blow but doing no damage. The rhino gave a snort and bolted off through the bush.

I soon found that these natives were bushcraftsmen indeed. With no equipment but their bows, arrows, and a rubbing stick for starting a fire, they could live indefinitely in the bush. In the dry season, they got water from the baobab trees. These huge trees usually have hollow trunks and they act as natural cisterns to hold rainwater. The poachers were experts at imitating the mating call of a cow rhino to attract a bull within reach of their deadly arrows. They also shot lions from their tree hides. Their poison was so potent that they could even kill elephants. The old leader assured me that an elephant, hit in the belly with one of their poisoned shafts, would drop dead before he could run four hundred yards.

"Sometimes we only hit an elephant in the shoulder or leg," the old man explained. "Then he may run for miles before the poison does its work on him. But that doesn't worry us. We wait a day or so, and then climb a tall tree and watch for the circling vultures. They guide us to the kill."

The Wakamba bows are so powerful that they can shoot an arrow through a Masai buffalo-hide shield and kill the man behind it. As the Masai shields were tough enough to stop an Arab musket ball in the old days, this gives some idea of the penetration quality of the Wakamba weapons.

The Wakamba poison is far more deadly than the much-touted poison used by the pygmies. The old leader told me that it is made from the sap of the mrichu tree. This tree is scientifically known as Acocanthera friesiorum. "We can always locate the tree because it is surrounded by dead bees and humming birds that have tried to drink from the mrichu's beautiful purple flowers," the old man told me. Poison makers boil the bark for several hours until there is nothing left but a black, tarlike substance. This is then mixed with other ingredients such as snake venom, poisonous spiders and the roots of certain deadly weeds. Occasionally a live shrew is thrown into the mess.

The poachers have an interesting way of testing the strength of their poison. Before setting out on a hunt, a poacher will slash the upper part of his arm and let a trickle of blood run down to his wrist. The poacher touches the trickle with the poisoned head of an arrow. Instantly the blood begins to turn black as the poison climbs steadily up the man's arm. Just before it reaches the open cut, the poacher wipes it away. The man can tell by the speed with which the poison climbs the trickle of blood just how potent it is.

After we had established friendly relations, I told the men that I was a game ranger. The poachers were naturally very depressed and obviously considered themselves betrayed. I could not find it in my heart to turn these men in. After all, they had hunted for centuries before the coming of Europeans and were obviously keen sportsmen. There is a fellow feeling between sportsmen no matter what their color. I did explain to them, however, that the killing of rhino and elephant for the horns and ivory could no longer continue. After listening attentively, the old leader said, "I understand. The elephants and rhino belong to the government. The rest of the animals belong to us."

This was not quite what I meant, since the government has jurisdiction over all game. But I did try to explain to them the difference between taking an occasional antelope for the family larder and killing game animals wholesale. I think I got my point across for we parted on friendly terms. I never ran into any of these men again in the discharge of my duties and I believe that we understood each other completely.

I do not mean to imply that I condoned poaching. I merely think that a certain amount of common sense must always be used in administering the law among primitive people. The policy of the government is to do everything possible to encourage the natives to live off their own herds and shambas rather than depending on wild game for food. Otherwise, natives all over the colony would simply start out with rifles to shoot game wholesale. If you passed a law saying that only primitive weapons could be used, a cry would go up from the village natives that they were being discriminated against in favor of the bush tribes like the Wakamba. The whole question is a very delicate political problem and no completely satisfactory solution can be found. My policy was strictly to forbid the killing of rhino or elephant. After I felt that I had the confidence of the local natives, I gradually discouraged the killing of meat animals. But I must admit that during the occasional periods of famine when the crops had failed and the people were actually faced with starvation, I was not as active in enforcing the law as I would be ordinarily.

To my mind, there is a vast difference between the native who will set an occasional snare or knock over an antelope that gets too close to his shamba and the professional poacher killing for

profit. I had no mercy for the professional. The amount of damage
these men do can hardly be overestimated. I once found the skeletons of twenty rhinos in an area of twelve square miles, all killed
by poachers within a year. It is true that I myself have killed many
more rhino than this, but only in districts that had to be opened to
cultivation. Even more serious than the amount of game killed are
the numbers of animals that escape wounded. If the poison used
is old or weak, the animal usually does not die. He becomes something of a rogue, with a fierce hatred of humans, ready to charge
anyone he sees. Such an animal almost invariably injures several
people before he is killed.

I must say that even the most hardened poacher is a master
craftsman and an excellent hunter. Although I realize that these
men must be arrested, it is hard to work up any hatred toward
them. My own hatred was directed toward the dishonest merchants who encouraged these men to kill rhino and elephant,
letting the poacher take all the risks while they reaped the profit.
Yet it is almost impossible to bring these merchants to justice.

Once after much time and trouble, I succeeded in tracking down
some of these merchants who had been paying my Wakamba
to poach, and I appeared at their trial in Nairobi. The man accused
of being the head of the organization was clever. He hired the best
lawyers in the colony. After a long verbal wrangle, he was ac-
quitted. The underlings went to prison. So I went back to Makindu
and spent my time running in the poor native poachers.

White sportsmen who violate the game laws are by no means
unknown. If the man has outfitted with one of the big Nairobi safari
companies, you don't have to worry about him. He will have a
reputable hunter with him who will see that the laws are strictly
obeyed. If the client wounds an animal either through careless-
ness or stupidity, the hunter will finish off the wounded beast. But
there are a few hunters who "free lance" and are not connected
with any big company. Many of these men are as good as the best,
but others are highly unreliable. No safari outfitter will employ
some of these hunters because of their reputations.

Some unscrupulous hunters will deliberately overshoot their

license and then, if they are caught, claim that they were forced to shoot the extra animals in self-defense and were simply waiting until they returned to Nairobi to turn in the hides and horns. There was even a case of a man who shot three cheetahs, claiming the animals attacked him. The cheetah is a long-legged cat, very gentle, and once much in demand among Indian rajahs who domesticated them and kept them to hunt antelope, such as greyhounds are kept to course hares. Cheetahs are so good-natured that even an adult animal can easily be tamed. I do not believe that in the entire history of Africa there has been a single case of a cheetah attacking a human being, yet this man had the insolence to claim that he was attacked three times by these beautiful creatures. Naturally, he was severely dealt with.

With admittedly dangerous game, the plea of self-defense is sometimes more difficult to disprove. I was much bothered by a resident hunter who was constantly claiming that every time he went on safari, rhinos charged him and he was forced to shoot in self-defense. Naturally, this hunter was not allowed to keep his trophies, but I had a strong suspicion that he simply liked to kill rhinos and shot them whenever possible. In a case like this, I was afraid that the testimony of his native boys might not hold up in court, as there might be a question of what constituted "self-defense." So I had one of my own game scouts dress up as a bush native and join the man's safari.

Shortly afterward, the scout reported to me that this man had shot a rhino. I reported the man. He was most arrogant, claiming that the testimony of a "bush nigger" would never stand up against the word of a white man in court. But I had a little surprise for the chap. My scout and I had carefully gone over the details of the shooting. As a result of my talk with the scout, I had hunted up the dead rhino and cut out the bullet. In court, I was able to testify that the angle of the bullet showed that the rhino could not have been charging at the time that the shot was fired. I even brought in a section of the hide to prove my point. The man was convicted and heavily fined.

A problem in trying to protect big game is that the beasts do not know the boundaries of their reserve and not infrequently wander outside, doing damage. At once a cry goes up that the reserve is a menace to the district and all the big game on it must be shot. When reserve beasts are doing local damage, they must be shot, but often they are falsely accused.

I soon found that one of a game warden's main duties is to destroy vermin. To my mind, the most destructive beasts in Africa today are not the big game animals but hyenas and baboons. The damage done by big game is spectacular, but the destruction caused by hyenas and baboons, while not so dramatic, is continual. A game control man is constantly called upon to destroy these creatures, usually in response to some desperate message from outlying villages. I quote the following letter as fairly typical:

Honored Sir:
We wish congratulate with you for the victory and end of badly war in Europe.
But now we have here in farm the war amongst the hyenas and the oxen; the oxen are worsted, every night one or two wasted.
Four cows of our squatters are yet finished and eaten. You could come up ask and see.
This people is badly impressionated.
I hope on your help and kindness.

Such letters may seem amusing, but the desperation back of them is very real.

Hyenas are by no means only scavengers. Although they are cowardly brutes, they will attack if the odds are with them. I talked to one lady rancher who was driven to absolute despair by the continual losses among her calves and cows due to hyenas. A favorite victim for these brutes is a female animal giving birth to young. At such times, the female is helpless and the hyenas know it.

Hyenas frequently run in packs and will then attack even unencumbered cattle. I once saw an amazing example of their determination. While sitting outside my tent one evening, I heard a noisy drumming of hoofs. I grabbed my rifle in one hand and turned an electric torch toward the sound. A terror-stricken ox blundered past my camp with a hyena on his back. The hyena had his teeth embedded in the hump of the ox. A string of a dozen or more hyenas followed behind.

I knew that only a lion has the knack of springing on an ox's back and so I could scarcely believe my eyes. Before I could fire, the ox had passed on. I shouted to one of my boys to carry the torch and we set out after the animal. Two hundred yards beyond my tent we heard a great commotion and the boy flashed his light on the scene. The ox was dead and the hyenas were tearing him to bits. I shot several of them before the rest moved off, growling angrily at being disturbed.

Later, I found that hyenas will sneak up to a sleeping animal and leap on its back before it awakes. Until then, I had not given hyenas credit for so much initiative.

Hyenas are the recognized garbage disposal unit of Africa. Natives find it easier to throw refuse into the bush than to bury it, so the hyenas are naturally encouraged to stay around villages. In many districts, they also act as undertakers.

I believe that this native custom of allowing hyenas to eat their dead encourages the animals to attack humans. There have been several cases on record where this has happened, generally when the person has been asleep. I knew one young native who received a terrible mutilation from a hyena. Together with several friends, he was sleeping by a campfire. Natives usually sleep in a circle around a fire, heads toward the blaze and feet out. This boy was partly wrapped in his blanket and wore no other garment. During the night, a hyena rushed in, tore off the native's testicles, and bolted off with them.

Poisoning is the standard way of ridding a district of hyenas. It is at first very efficient but soon the animals learn to mistrust any carcass where they can smell the touch of human hands. Many times I have shot antelope and poisoned the carcasses, only to find that during the night hyenas came up and smelled the animals but refused to eat. I prefer to use the set-gun with these pests. A set-gun is a gun lashed in place, with a string leading from the trigger across the animal's path. By building a thorn-bush boma with several entrances, each with its own gun, and putting a dead antelope in the middle as bait, you will often find a dead hyena at every hole.

Next to the hyena, the greatest pest in Africa today is probably the baboon. In many ways he resembles a degenerate human being. One could easily admire the animals, for they are both brave and intelligent, were it not for their idle cruelty. Baboons will often catch native chickens and amuse themselves by plucking the birds alive, merely to watch the poor creatures scream and struggle.

When baboons plan a raid on maize fields, they display great intelligence about the business. One baboon is sent up a tree to act as lookout. If a man comes near the field, the sentinel gives a short, barking yelp and the rest of the band race for the bush, not forgetting to carry off a few ears of maize under their arms as they go.

The alarm bark is only given if the intruder is a man armed with a bow and arrows. If a woman comes near the field, the baboons treat her with the greatest contempt. Indeed, an old dog baboon will often approach a woman in a very belligerent manner, scratching up the earth and making angry gestures. It is "on record" that baboons have attacked young native girls. I should consider this unlikely, as in my experience the sexual instinct of animals is only aroused by the smell of a ready female of their own kind; yet this belief among natives is very general.

Male baboons are very plucky. When the band flees, the males invariably bring up the rear. I know of no dog that can tackle a male baboon and survive. The monkey grabs the dog, buries his long canine teeth in the animal, and then pushes him away with his arms. The strength of a big male baboon is prodigious and he can rip out a large chunk of flesh by this process. The teeth of a baboon are actually larger than those of a lion and extremely dangerous weapons.

Poison is the usual method used to destroy baboons. As with hyenas, this is effective only as long as the monkeys have never seen its effects. But as soon as a few animals die, the rest become cautious and refuse to touch poisoned bait. Although they do not have a particularly keen sense of smell, they are very wary and soon learn to eat nothing left lying around the ground. But they are too smart to be killed by set-guns and shooting them is a long and tedious process once they are on the alert.

Another form of vermin that government hunters are occasionally called upon to destroy are man-eating lions. I have read with great interest several excellent accounts of hunting man-eating tigers in India. I must say that I have been very much astonished at how the business is handled in that country. Apparently after a tiger has killed and eaten four or five hundred people, some young subaltern, tourist, or local sportsman decides to have a go at the animal. In Kenya, a man-eater is regarded as a dangerous menace that must be killed immediately. There is no element of sport in the hunt. As soon as a man-eater is reported, the game department instantly gives the animal top priority above every other consideration. An experienced hunter is promptly sent out with instructions to destroy him by any method he thinks best. Traps, poison, and set-guns are frequently used. The man-eater seldom has a chance to make a second kill.

Most man-eaters are either old beasts that cannot hunt wild game or lions that have become injured in some fashion. They may have been hit by a native arrow or crippled by the sharp horns of an antelope. But it sometimes happens that a perfectly normal, healthy lion will kill a human being, generally by chance. If he happens to like the taste of human flesh, he will then become a man-eater. This most often occurs in districts where cattle have taken over a range and driven off the wild game that are a lion's natural food. In trying to get at the cattle, the lion may kill a herdsman, just as he would knock down any obstruction that stood in his way. If for some reason the cattle then managed to escape, the lion may return to his kill and begin feeding. This combination of circumstances is rare, but when it occurs the lion almost invariably becomes a man-eater. However, once a lion definitely acquires a

liking for human meat, he will go to the most amazing length to
satisfy his craving. I have even known confirmed man-eaters to
charge through a herd of cattle in order to get at the herdsmen.

There seems to be a tendency among lions in certain districts to
become man-eaters—a peculiar hereditary taint that cannot be explained. It is true that a man-eating lioness will train her cubs to
be man-eaters. Young lions do not kill instinctively and will learn
to hunt whatever game their mother shows them. But this tendency
toward man-eating seems to crop up only every third or fourth
generation. It occurs especially in the Tsavo district which has been
famous for its man-eaters ever since 1890. Today, most of the lions
have been shot out of this section, yet there still are occasional
reports of an odd man-eater.

Generally poison is the best way to dispose of a man-eater. Lions
are extremely susceptible to strychnine, the poison taking effect
in a matter of seconds. To an old-time hunter like myself, the use
of poison can never be pleasant, eliminating as it does all last
vestiges of sportsmanship and skill on the part of the hunter. Yet
I freely admit it is murderously efficient and must be employed
in certain cases.

If a man-eater kills a native and leaves part of his victim un-
eaten, he will almost certainly return to the body just as he does
in the case of wild game. If the hunter poisons the body, he is virtually certain of getting the lion. This sounds like a grisly business
but it must be done. The natives themselves are most practical
about such matters as the following story will show.

Captain Tom Salmon, a friend of mine who is ranger of a district
near Makindu, received a report that a lion had killed the mother
of a local native chief. He went at once to the village and the chief
took him out on the spoor of the man-eater. They found the
woman's arm along the trail and then later came on her partly-
eaten body. Tom saw that there was no tree where he could put
up a machan, no brush near for a boma, and the ground was baked
too hard by the sun to make it practical to set out spring traps.
After considerable hesitation, he asked the chief if he could poison

the body, explaining that otherwise the lives of other people would surely be sacrificed to the lion.

The chief consented, and Tom made several incisions in the body, putting a small capsule of strychnine in each. Then he and the chief retired.

They returned the next morning and found the lion lying dead across the woman's body. He had swallowed one of the capsules inserted in the left buttock and died almost instantly. Tom turned to the chief and explained how grateful he was for the man's co-operation.

"The government will now see that the remains of your mother receive the best possible interment," he assured the chief. "No expense will be spared. Any stipulation you care to make will be carefully complied with."

The chief scratched his head. "Well, I hate to see the old lady wasted like that," he finally said. "We've been having a lot of trouble with hyenas lately. Let's leave her out another few nights and see if she can't get some hyenas." I never heard the result.

Though my duties as ranger of Makindu kept me busy, I was still often sent out by the game department to control marauding animals. The offenders were usually elephants. Or sometimes the call came in the form of a native SOS like the following:

To Game Warden
    Sir,
    I am compelled of notifying your Excellence the ecceptional an critical situation of my people at Tuso. Many times they called on my praing me of adressing to your Excellence a letter for obtain a remedy and so save they meadows from total devestation. I recused for I thought were a passing disease, but on the contrary the invasion took fearfully increasing so that the natives are now disturbed and in danger in their own huts for in the night the elephants ventured themselves amid abitation. All men are desolate and said me sadfully "What shall we eat this year. We shall compelled to emigrate all." I am alarmed not quite for the Elephants. I am nothing to dead but I fear much that my people shell he truly obligate to exultate begging work and lating—I hope your Excellence will kindly provide for such a whip as I am sure is sufficient to expose and obtain.
    With my best gratefully and respectful regards,
                    Yours sincerely, A Mission Boy

The intelligence of elephants is astonishing. They seem to know perfectly when they are safe from a hunter. I was once sent by the game department to deal with a herd of elephants that were damaging coconut plantations at Lunga-Lunga, on the Kenya-Tanganyika border. The elephants spent the day in Tanganyika but would cross the border at night and raid the plantations on the Kenya side. Ordinarily, killing off these raiders would be merely a routine job, but a delicate legal point was involved. The Kenya game department could not authorize a hunter to enter Tanganyika territory without considerable legal complication. By the time all the red tape had been cleared up, the plantations would be destroyed. It was, therefore, my task to kill the raiders on the Kenya side. This could only be done at night, since the elephants seemed to understand that they were safe in Tanganyika and always crossed back before dawn.

Now it is almost impossible to hunt elephants satisfactorily at night. The game department presented me with this problem and then told me to do what I could.

I traveled south with Mulumbe to Lunga-Lunga. The village is near the Indian Ocean and some fifty miles south of Mombasa. A little stream called the Umba winds past the village, and the coconut plantations bordered this stream. The palm trees overhung the banks and made a beautiful sight, but when I arrived many of the trees had been torn down by the raiding elephants and the plantations were in a sorry state. Trees that had taken years to grow had been snapped off like twigs and the ground was littered with broken coconut husks and bits of palm fronds.

I spent some time with Mulumbe spooring the elephants and learning their habits. They were young bachelor bulls, probably driven out of a larger herd by the bigger bulls when they grew old enough to show an interest in the cows. These young bulls had formed a sort of club, wandering about the jungle together until they grew strong enough to challenge the older bulls for the cows.

I knew that there was no use trying to shoot the raiders at night. They must be held in the plantation until day. This would be difficult, for at the first alarm, the whole herd would bolt for the safety of the Tanganyika border. After considerable thought, I decided on a plan. The plantation that the herd had been despoiling did not measure more than five hundred yards long and some two hundred yards wide. I told the local natives to make a long pile of brushwood along the Tanganyika side of the plantation. The elephants would cross this on their way to the palm trees, but when they tried to return the natives were to set fire to the dry wood. I doubted that the herd would dare to rush through the leaping flames in order to reach Tanganyika. If we could hold them until dawn, I could start shooting.

I sat up for a while that evening in the doorway of my thatched hut, watching the palm trees sway in the evening breeze and thinking of the old days in Scotland when I was a lad. Many a midnight expedition I'd planned then, setting snares for hares or netting partridges. Now I was doing much the same, except that the game was somewhat bigger. Finally the constant hum of the mosquitoes drove me inside to my cot.

About three o'clock in the morning, I heard the excited voice of a native calling to my gunbearer. I leaped out of bed. The elephants had returned and were feeding in the plantation. Mulumbe and I were ready in a matter of moments. We started out, following the lead of the local native who had been sent to fetch us. It was as dark as the inside of a bottle of ink, but the native ran through the night as though it had been broad daylight. Mulumbe followed him easily, but I stumbled into every pot hole we crossed, praying that I wouldn't twist an ankle.

The herd was on the other side of the Umba. We waded across the sandy bottom of the stream. The Umba is full of crocodiles but in the excitement of the moment we never thought of them. When we reached the far bank, I could plainly hear the crashing of elephants among the palms. Such sounds at night are always amplified. Now natives began to appear from all sides out of the darkness, eager for the hunt to start. I organized a firebrand brigade and stationed them along the pile of brushwood. When all were in place, I gave the signal to light the fires.

The dry wood caught like petrol. In a moment a wall of flames leaped up along the south side of the plantation as far as a man could see in either direction. What a sight! A herd of some twenty elephants stood before us, frozen at the sudden sight of the flames into motionless statues. Many of them still had their trunks raised in the act of ripping down the palms. Along the line of burning brush, the naked Negroes danced and yelled, waving their burning torches and screaming at the elephants that retribution was now about to overtake them. The elephants made not a sound. They were obviously thinking out a way to escape the semi-circle of fire.

The herd could have turned and run toward Kenya, later swinging around to avoid the flames. But I was counting on their using all their power and thought to return directly to Tanganyika. I was right. After a few moments of indecision, the herd charged us, making a determined effort to break through into their home territory.

This was the crisis of the whole hunt. If the herd once succeeded in getting past us, we had lost them. I did not dare to fire at them. The sound of shots when they were already panic-struck would only drive them on to fresh desperation. Mulumbe was great. Snatching a burning torch from one of the natives, he shouted to the firebrand brigade to follow him. Completely regardless of danger, he rushed at the herd, waving his torch and yelling like a siren. The others ran after him, hurling their torches at the oncoming elephants. The bulls hesitated and then turned back toward the plantation.

How I longed for the dawn to come! Never had hours seemed longer. I was continually looking oceanward for the grayness that precedes the break of day. Finally I heard the cooing of doves in the trees and knew that I had not much longer to wait. The natives were getting tired, but I urged them to fresh efforts. They piled more wood on the fires and renewed their yelling and torch waving.

About five-thirty the herd made another attack on the fire. This time they divided into two groups and came at the line of burning brush from different directions. The natives snatched burning embers from the fire regardless of the pain and flung them at the approaching elephants. Again the herd was turned. I could hear one group splashing in the Umba, evidently intending to wade up the stream to safety. This was all to the good as far as I was concerned. The sound of their splashing told me their position.

It was now light enough to see. I caught a glimpse of brown bodies moving quietly through the plantation toward our left. The other group was planning to swing around the far end of the fires and escape. Doubtless they reasoned that by dividing into two parts and striking at either end of the fires, one or the other party stood a good chance to get through.

Now was the moment to attack. I sent Mulumbe to deal with the herd on our right in the Umba. I jumped the burning wall of bush and moved forward to intercept the other group. Walking was easy. The ground had been trodden flat by the elephants during the night as they milled around in the darkness. I moved slowly, taking what cover I could. I saw five bulls ahead of me. They were about forty yards away. Two of them dropped instantly to my right and left barrels. While I was reloading one of the three remaining spotted me. He left his friends and charged. That is the worst of a double barrel. Often the time it takes to unload and reload may mean the difference between life and death. The bull's skull was getting unpleasantly close when I finally managed to get my breech shut and fired. He fell without a quiver.

The other two bulls stood with upraised trunks, trying to scent me. Then they both suddenly wheeled and bolted back toward the Umba. I followed them. Ahead I could hear the yelling of the natives. Then came the crack of Mulumbe's magazine rifle, followed by the "flup" of a bullet hitting home. He was also in action.

The yelling of the natives grew louder. Suddenly I realized that they were screaming in terror, not excitement. I ran toward the sound. I arrived in time to see a single elephant bull pushing in the front of large low-roofed native huts. The great rump of the beast was toward me. His head was held low as he shoved forward with his forehead. I saw the withies used to weave the walls of the hut strain and then give away. Natives bolted out of the cracks like rabbits out of a warren when a ferret is put in. They ran in all directions. I shot the bull through the shoulder. He turned and ran toward the palms, blood gushing from his trunk. Before he had covered half the distance he fell with a groan. He was dead when I came up to him.

I headed toward the place where I had last heard Mulumbe shoot. On the way, I passed four dead elephants—evidence of Mulumbe's work. A few seconds later I came up to him. He grinned and held up four fingers. The rest of the herd was now bunched together among the palm trees. Together, we approached them cautiously.

The whole plantation was full of shouting natives. Suddenly Mulumbe stopped and waved his hand in a beckoning motion. He meant the herd was coming toward us. We stood waiting.

In a few seconds, a group of elephants appeared among the trees. There were only four of them. We started shooting. The elephants stopped, milling about for a moment. We got three. The remaining bull managed to slip into the stream. We later found that this bull had waded past us, taking advantage of the high banks, and escaped to Tanganyika. He never returned to the plantation.

In all, eleven elephants were accounted for. Their ivory was of a particularly fine quality and wonderfully free of cracks and blemishes. As they were young animals, the tusks were not large, averaging about thirty pounds.

On rare occasions, a bull elephant will become insane and is then properly known as a "rogue." But I am always very suspicious of reports concerning rogue elephants for any bull will go temporarily mad during "must." With elephants, not only the cows but also the bulls come into season. When a bull is in season, he is said to be in "must." A bull in "must" is very nervous and irritable. A musky fluid is discharged from two tiny holes in the bull's head near his ears. The odor of this fluid tells the cows that the bull is ready for breeding. I am told that cows become very solicitous over a bull while he is in "must," perfectly realizing that he is in a very overwrought condition. They crowd around him, making soothing little noises and stroking him with their trunks. In case of danger, they hurry him away, knowing that in his hysterical state he cannot be trusted to take care of himself.

Natives attacked by a bull in "must" often claim that he is a rogue. He is not. The state will pass and the bull will become normal again. A true rogue is permanently insane, and when such an animal appears he must be killed as quickly as possible.

In my experience, an elephant never becomes a rogue unless he has been injured in some fashion, usually by a hunter's bullet or by a native's arrow. I know of only one exception to this rule and that was an elephant suffering from a natural deformity.

In 1945, I was asked by the Wakamba to kill a bull elephant that had attacked several people and was doing great damage to the native crops. The natives were in such dread of this beast that they called him "Saitani"—meaning "the devil" and believed that he was possessed by an evil spirit. They assured me that the beast was supernatural because he left a peculiar spoor quite unlike the footprint of any other elephant.

I traveled some 130 miles south of Nairobi to the Chunya stream where the animal lived. Very unwisely, I went alone, leaving Mulumbe in charge of my native scouts at the Makindu reserve. I thought this "Saitani" would simply turn out to be another marauding elephant and I could settle with him easily.

When I arrived at the village that had been the scene of the bull's latest raid, the anxious natives showed me his spoor. The tracks were certainly unusual. In all my experience as an elephant hunter I had never seen marks like them. Apparently the animal was what might be termed "club-footed." This deformity probably explained why he was shunned by his own kind and forced to forage alone.

The bull had been raiding the natives' watermelon patches. He had developed an interesting way of handling the slippery melons. Because of their shape, the melons were difficult for him to pick up with his trunk, so he would first step on a melon and squash it slightly. The partly flattened melon gave him a better purchase.

Usually a raiding elephant will not visit the same village twice in succession, but this animal had grown so aggressive that he would stay near one village until he had completely wiped out the shambas before moving on to a new locality. The natives assured me that Saitani would be back that night. I decided to meet him.

As I have said, night shooting is virtually impossible. But this seemed to be an exceptional case. If I could drop the bull that evening while he was in the shambas, it would save me many a long hour of tracking and I would be on my way back to Makindu in the morning. So I decided to make the attempt.

I had a powerful, five-cell electric torch with me and I showed a native how to use it. When I nudged him, he was to turn the light on the bull and hold it there while I fired. Then I went to bed. Tired by my long day, I fell asleep almost instantly.

I had hardly dozed off when an excited native rushed to my hut screaming that Saitani was in the maize fields. I grabbed my rifle and started out, followed by my assistant with the torch. All around us came the sound of excited natives jabbering in their huts. I could hear them barricading themselves, although the flimsy structures would not do them the slightest good if the rogue actually wanted to attack.

Then, through the noise of the terrified natives, I heard another sound. The steady crunch, crunch of an elephant feeding. I went forward slowly, slipping off the safety catch of my rifle as I did so. The thick darkness of the night seemed to press down on us from all sides but I was guided by the crackling and snapping of the maize stalks ahead.

We reached the edge of the field and began to thread our way through the tall stalks. The stalks were so close together that we had to force our way through them. Then I could see the dim outline of a huge mass against the dark sky. As quietly as I could, I moved towards it.

Suddenly the noise of feeding stopped. The bull had heard us and was listening. I could picture him standing motionless, probably with a maize stalk in his mouth, his huge ears spread out to catch the slightest sound. We were about fifteen yards away. I nudged my boy to flash the light on him.

Forgotten were all my instructions of the afternoon. The nervous boy simply flicked the light on and off. The bull had not known where we were before but the sudden beam of light betrayed us. Immediately he charged. I heard the maize stalks crackling like thorns in a fire as he dashed through them. My boy bolted through the maize, screaming with terror. I hesitated for a moment. I could see nothing, only hear the beast rushing down on me. There was nothing for it but to run. Run I did.

I tore through the stalks, expecting every second to have the bull on top of me. Being chased by an elephant at night is a horrible experience, for he can follow you by scent while you might as well be blind. When I reached the edge of the maize field, I stopped to listen. Everything was quiet. I sneaked back to my hut, perfectly willing to concede the rogue round one.

The natives were now surer than ever that the rogue had supernatural powers which were stronger than the medicine of the white man. But I was prepared to argue that point with the beast if we ever met face to face in the daytime. I dispatched a message to Hilda, asking her to send me Mulumbe as quickly as possible. As soon as he arrived, we started out on the rogue's deformed spoor.

The bull had gorged himself on maize during the night and so had not stopped to graze as would an ordinary elephant. The trail led straight through the brush and I knew we were in for a long trek. At first, tracking was simple. The soil was soft and we could see the deep imprints of the rogue's deformed foot always ahead of us. He had also dropped great masses of dung at more or less regular intervals. The temperature of the dung tells how long it is since the animal passed by. If the stuff is soft, it often means that the quarry has become alarmed and is on the alert. If there is a great pile of dung in one spot, the animal has stopped there for a long time to rest, and the chances are better of catching up with him. The contents of the mass are also important. A large amount of undigested food may well mean that the quarry is nervous and the hunter must be especially careful.

In tracking, I often vacillate between overoptimism and extreme discouragement. Now I expected at any moment to hear the noise of the elephant feeding or catch a glimpse of his great body through the bush. The hunt seemed almost too easy. I began to count on returning to Makindu that afternoon.

Then we hit a ridge of bare rock that stopped Mulumbe as quickly as a lost scent stops a hound. The ridge rose high out of the brush, naked except for a few rocks and pebbles. Mulumbe would find an occasional pebble that had been disturbed by the rogue's great feet, but it is astonishing how a huge animal like an elephant can walk over stones without seeming to move them. Finally we abandoned the ridge and going down to the edge of the brush on the far side, worked back and forth until we picked up the trail again. But even here it was heartbreakingly slow work. The ground was hard, gravelly soil and there were almost no signs. Crawling on his belly like a snake, Mulumbe would slip under the scrub and find marks that I never would have suspected could be there. When an elephant moves through brush, the undergrowth snaps back into position after him, so little disturbed that you would swear nothing had ever passed through it—least of all a beast the size of a motor lorry.

Just as I had been full of hopes a short time before, I was now completely discouraged. Finding one elephant lost amid the forests of Africa appeared a hopeless undertaking. I plodded on automatically after Mulumbe, thinking of my many past failures and sure that this would prove to be another of them.

We struggled through a clump of sansevieria. This horrible plant has leaves that end in spines so tough and sharp that they are often used as phonograph needles. Ranches plant sansevieria around their gardens, and it forms a very effective cattle-proof hedge. Many a cow have I seen minus an eye because the animal grazed too close to a sansevieria hedge. The suffering of two men who must force their way through a plantation of this devilish stuff may well be imagined. Here and there we came across bleached balls of the white pith. The interior of the plant is full of moisture and an elephant gathers the dagger-typed leaves with his trunk as though they were clover, sucks out the juice and then spits out the chewed remains. The rogue had evidently passed through the plantation just ahead of us.

We kept going until we hit a well-used game trail, trodden bare, and followed it through the brush. Suddenly Mulumbe stopped and pointed down. There, sure enough, was the familiar spoor of the deformed foot.

We had him. Mulumbe went first, following the spoor, while I kept watching ahead in case we came on the rogue unexpectedly. Then we heard the well-known sounds of an elephant feeding in the bush. The bull was moving about, pulling down especially tender branches as tidbits while he waited for it to grow dark enough to return to the village shambas. I could hear the old fellow's belly rumbling and a sudden gushing noise as he urinated.

The game trail led through a gap in a narrow belt of bushes. The rogue was on the other side of the bushes, not fifty yards away. In my eagerness, I pushed Mulumbe aside and started toward the gap almost at a trot.

Suddenly I felt Mulumbe give the back of my jumper a quick tug. I stopped. I could neither hear nor see anything. Mulumbe was holding his head sideways, one ear toward the ground. He was listening. Sound carries better through the earth than in the air, and he had instinctively bent his head to pick up some faint noise. He was sticking his tongue in and out rapidly, the bush alarm signal.

Then through the gap in the bushes ahead of us came a big cow rhino. She was plastered with mud from a wallow and her wet horns glistened in the setting sun. She came straight down the trail for us. She had not seen Mulumbe and me. She was listening to the noise of the elephant feeding. One of her ears canted in the rogue's direction. She was not alarmed but merely moving out of the bull's vicinity.

If it had not been for Mulumbe, I would have met the rhino

head-on in the gap. I had been saved from that mistake, but another problem instantly confronted me. The cow was moving down
the game trail where we were standing. If I fired at her, the elephant was sure to bolt. Yet I could not allow her to get too close.
It looked as though the Saitani had indeed some mysterious jungle
god looking after him.

The rhino came closer and closer, still listening to the feeding
elephant. I stood absolutely rigid. The rhino was so close that the
slightest motion would have provoked a charge. Mulumbe, standing
behind me, was magnificent. He never moved a muscle as the rhino
came on.

I decided to shoot her when she got to within five yards of us.
A wisp of withered grass lying on the trail marked the spot. She
continued to come on. Then she stopped. She stood listening to the
rogue. Then she moved forward again.

When I was a boy in school, we used to amuse ourselves with a
silly game. We would concentrate on the back of a boy's head
sitting a few rows in front of us and try by projecting thought
waves to make him turn around. I now tried to make the rhino
turn by concentrating on her. She seemed completely indifferent
to my mental vibrations. Suddenly, when she was less than a yard
from the bit of grass, she turned and moved off into the bush on
our right. I heard Mulumbe expel his breath with a long sigh.

Nothing now stood between us and the rogue. I moved forward
to the opening in the brush. There was the elephant some thirty
yards away. A bush stood between us. I began to work my way
around it. I was halfway around when the noise of feeding stopped.
He had heard me. At a time like this, the wise thing to do is to
stand motionless. I could not. I was under too great a strain. I ran
around the bush and saw the bull standing there with his ears out
and trunk up, trying either to hear or scent me. He offered a perfect
heart shot. As I raised my rifle, he decided to run. For an instant, his
ears flapped back against his body—perfectly marking the heart
shot, for an elephant's heart lies some four inches behind the point

where the edge of his ear touches his body. I fired both barrels, one after the other, into his body.

He bolted off through the bush as though I hadn't touched him. I stood waiting, knowing what must happen. Within fifty yards, he dropped to his knees. I reloaded and moved up carefully, but there was no need for another shot. The rogue was dead.

His tusks were nothing, weighing only forty pounds each, but I saved the deformed foot to prove to the natives that their Saitani was truly dead.

14

Guns, Men, and Fear

The most powerful big-game rifles made are the giant .577 and the .600. The .600 bullet weighs 900 grains and strikes with an impact equivalent to four tons. If you hit an elephant on the head with one of these bullets, he will be knocked back on his hunkers. Then you can finish him off with your second barrel. No elephant can withstand the impact of such a bullet if it is well placed.

Frankly, I do not use these extremely heavy guns. I am somewhat ashamed to admit the reason. I learned to shoot as a boy by rule of thumb. I was never told that a gunner should make a point of holding the butt of his rifle firmly against his shoulder to reduce the effects of the recoil. When using a shotgun or a light rifle, this is not too important, but when firing an extremely powerful rifle, the "kick" can be very punishing if the gun is held loosely. I have many times resolved to force myself to remember this important point but in the excitement of a hunt I always forget.

Because of this shooting fault, I have mainly relied on a .500 d/b hammerless ejector fitted with 24-inch barrels and weighing 10 pounds 5 ounces made by Holland & Holland. In my opinion Holland & Holland are the best in rifle makers, just as I would give honors to James Purdey & Sons for the best in smooth bores. My .500 has never let me down. It is quite adequate for all big game, including elephant. I have never seen it fail to stop a charge—if it had failed even once I would not now be writing these notes. As a result, I have never felt the need of burdening myself by carrying one of the heavier guns which, excellent though they may be, are cumbersome things and do give the shooter a certain amount of punishment.

I am convinced that it is extremely unwise for any man to hunt elephant, buffalo, or rhino with a gun of less than .450 caliber. A light rifle simply will not stop a charge. While I was on a hunt in Southern Tanganyika, I met a Dutch sportsman named Lediboor who was very eager to get an African elephant. The man came from Java and had shot several Indian elephants. He proudly showed me his gun—a .405 caliber he had used with great success in Ceylon.

I told the man frankly that his gun was too light for African big game. All African animals, even antelopes, are remarkably tenacious of life. They will take punishment that would quickly finish off Asiatic, European, or American game animals. But it is one of the hardest things I know of to try to convert another hunter to your way of thinking. He will listen politely and then, whether rightly or wrongly, will continue to cling to his own belief. Lediboor had shot elephant in India with his .405. Therefore the gun could stop African elephants.

A few weeks later, Mr. Millar, a tsetsefly research official in the Kilossa district, happened to pass by my camp and told me that Lediboor had been killed by his first elephant. Lediboor had sighted a herd and climbed a tree to get a better shot at them. He dropped one and feeling very elated, started toward the beast. The elephant was only stunned. He leaped up and charged Lediboor. All that Mr. Millar could say was that judging from the mangled remains, Lediboor had not suffered.

Elephants have a variety of ways of killing a hunter. Sometimes they will trample him. On other occasions, an elephant will pick a man up in his trunk and pull him over a tusk. Another beast may kill by braining the man with one blow of his trunk. Once an elephant has killed a man by one method, he tends always to use the same system on other hunters.

No man can guard against every possible accident while in the bush. Nevertheless, I still maintain that an experienced hunter like Lediboor, if armed with an adequate rifle, might well have been alive today. I have occasionally read accounts by hunters who claim to have fired both barrels of a powerful express into a charging elephant only to have him still come on. I can only say that either the man was using too light a weapon or he did not hit the animal in the right place.

An elephant is so huge that there are only a few places on him where even the heaviest rifle bullet will bring instant death. The old-time ivory hunters liked to aim for the ear orifice or just ahead of it. When a herd of elephants are feeding undisturbed, the ear gusset is unquestionably the best target. The next easiest shot is through the heart. A heart shot does not have such sudden results as a well-placed ear shot, but the animal will usually drop within a hundred yards.

The frontal skull is my favorite target. An elephant hit there crashes to earth on his knees. This is my favorite shot, possibly because I have used it so much, and with telling results. When the elephant is ten yards or so away it is very effective. The bullet crashes through the skull and enters the brain, bringing instant death. But at less than ten yards, the great difference in height between a man and an elephant makes this shot difficult and frequently impossible. The hunter is forced to shoot upward, and the bullet enters the elephant's head at an angle, missing the brain. When this happens the hunter rarely has time to fire again, for the elephant can whirl around in a flash and be off—or the reverse, as the mood takes him.

I was once hunting a herd of elephants that had been driving natives away from a water hole during a period of drought. I was stalking two bulls when a third suddenly appeared less than five yards in front of me. He seemed to have risen out of the ground. The bull saw me and stood glaring. I was too close for the frontal skull shot. I was not in position for either the ear or the heart shot. There was only one thing left to do. I fired about a foot below the level of his eyes, the missile in its course passing through the trunk and penetrating the brain. He died before he could take another step toward me. This is doubtless a very killing shot but not one that I would care to attempt too often.

I remember another occasion when a trunk shot was not so successful. That was a hunt from which I very nearly never returned. Mulumbe and I were tracking some bull elephants that had been plundering potato fields. While we were working our way through the cover, I heard a noise like a whip crack just ahead. One of the bulls had broken off a branch while feeding. We started toward the noise. I had taken only a few steps when Mulumbe stopped me. He pointed with his pursed lips. There, not twelve feet away, lay an elephant as if dead.

He was fast asleep. Some men had said that elephants never sleep lying down. This is not true. I have several times come across a herd of elephants lying on their sides fast asleep and snoring. But I knew that even a sleeping elephant can get to his feet with marvelous quickness once he is alarmed. From my position, I could see only this beast's rump. I would have to make a long detour through the dense bush to get the shot that I wanted. I started moving slowly. A thick patch of brush lay ahead. As quietly as possible I began to work my way through it.

I heard and saw nothing. But suddenly the whole wall of brush seemed to be coming down on me. Instinctively I looked up. As I did so, a sapling hit me in the face, striking my right eye. Half blinded and in great pain, I saw a thin, brown shape wriggling through the branches toward me. It looked like a great snake. The tip was not a foot away. It was the elephant's trunk. He had leaped to his feet and charged so swiftly and silently that he was on me before I knew it.

I did not have time to raise my gun. Pointing the muzzle toward his trunk, I pulled the trigger. The recoil of the .500 nearly dislocated my thumb. But the blast of the explosion turned the bull. There was a terrific crashing in the bush and then he was gone.

I had hit him. Blood from his trunk blotched my rifle barrels and sprayed over my jumper. He had been in the act of grabbing me when I fired.

For some time I could do nothing but sit and nurse my throbbing eye. When the pain had somewhat stopped, I determined to continue tracking the animal. After such a close call, a hunter must push on or he stands in considerable danger of losing his nerve permanently and never daring to go out again.

Mulumbe and I started out on the blood spoor. It soon stopped. I had merely nicked the elephant. He was going all out, headed for the deepest part of the forest. Truth compels me to admit that he proved too fast and smart for us. When evening came, we were obliged to give up and return to the village, shooting him the following day.

I have often heard the remark made of a successful hunter, "He does not know the meaning of fear." This was certainly never true of me and I doubt if it is true of any man. But a professional hunter after dangerous quarry is playing a very involved and intricate game. He must keep a dozen or more details constantly in mind— the wind, the nature of the cover, the condition of the spoor, the characteristics of the game, the peculiarities of this individual animal, and his own powers and shortcomings. He must constantly remember to move noiselessly, and this means that he must watch where he puts his feet and at the same time keep an eye on the bush ahead for a possible ambush. He must have his rifle constantly at the ready, safety catch off, and, if possible, never put himself in a position where he cannot instantly bring up the gun and fire. A true hunter loves this game of wits—it is the breath of life to him. If he concentrates on his work, he has no room left in his mind for fear. He is putting into practice the thousand and one little details of hunting that he has spent many long hours pondering over by his campfire or discussing with other hunters. As every hunt is different from every other, the hunter is constantly trying out new little techniques. In his eagerness to see how these techniques work, he seldom worries over danger.

I cannot recall ever having felt fear during an actual charge. The action is so fast and furious there is no time for it. I should say that the most fear-producing time in hunting is when you or your client has wounded a dangerous animal and the beast has taken to the bush. You start after him. The trail is plain—often a clearly defined blood spoor. It leads to a bit of virtually impenetrable bush. You know that somewhere in that cover the wounded animal is waiting for you. In the bush you will be at a tremendous disadvantage, often crawling on your hands and knees. The beast may well be on you before you can get your rifle up. For a moment, you hesitate. Better to let the animal alone and go away. That is the crucial time. You must force yourself to take the plunge. Once in the cover and actually trailing, the feeling passes and you are once more an expert technician working out a difficult problem.

I remember being called in by the game department to dispose of a pair of bull elephants that had taken to raiding native shambas in southern Kenya. One of these bulls was a very old animal. The other was a youngster. It not infrequently happens among elephants that a deep friendship develops between an experienced old bull and a young male. These two friends will desert the herd and live together in the jungle, forming a sort of partnership. The younger animal contributes his strength and keener senses while the old bull has his knowledge of bushcraft and the wisdom of years.

Previously natives knew all about this elephant custom. When they found the spoor of two bulls together in the jungle, they would race back to their village, dragging a hooked stick to mark their trail. Then they sent a message to the nearest white man interested in hunting. The hunter quickly took up the spoor, hoping that one of the beasts would be a century-old monarch with a fine pair of tusks.

Mulumbe and I went to the village where the bulls had been raiding. After talking to the natives, I had no doubt that these two animals were experienced marauders. They would circle the shambas downwind before staging a raid, testing the breeze to make sure that all was clear. They always left the shambas well before dawn and traveled to the thickest part of the bush during the day. By spooring them, we found that they also were in the habit of moving downwind of their lie-up place and checking the breeze before going into it. This was doubtless to guard against a possible ambush. Their lie-up was in the heart of a great swamp, full of stinging nettles, bogs, and patches of dense bush. They seldom used the same trail twice when going from their lie-up to the shambas. I had no doubt that the older of the two was responsible for these elaborate tactics and the younger bull was merely a very willing pupil.

Two of the locals, who were professional honey gatherers and claimed to know every foot of the swamp, volunteered to guide us. Now I dislike hunting with untrained natives. There is a popular belief that all natives are natural bushcraftsmen. Nothing could be farther from the truth. Whenever possible, I much prefer to go into cover with only my gunbearer.

However, in this case I had no choice so we started off with the two honey gatherers as guides.

Before long we came on the raiders' spoor in some trampled vegetation. There is always something exciting about coming on fresh spoor, no matter how much you have hunted. The sight of those great imprints makes the jaw muscles tighten and chills run up your legs. The prospect of action lies ahead and that is always thrilling.

In the swamp we began to encounter patches of vicious forest nettles. At the time, your mind is so keyed up with the excitement of spooring that you hardly notice the stings, but later the poison takes effect. You feel feverish and weak. The edges of the swamp were also full of biting forest flies, about the same size and shape as the clegs that used to drive horses nearly mad in Scotland during harvest time. These insects make no noise and can light on you with the softness of a bit of thistledown. Then suddenly they stab you with their bloodsucking proboscis. The constant irritation of these flies, coupled with the feverish effects of the nettle stings, tends to make a hunter careless. You push on regardless and often fall into an ambush. I was constantly forced to steady myself, much as a man who knows he has had too much to drink must take especial care with his speech and movements.

Then we heard the crack of a branch ahead. We were up to them. There was a quick check of rifles. Both Mulumbe and I were carrying .475 No. 2's. In this way there is no danger of mixing different caliber cartridges. The locals dropped back. I gave one of them my hat as I had noticed that branches kept rubbing against it and made a slight sound. Mulumbe tested the wind. It was shifty. We decided to make a detour and come in on a zigzag course.

All noises of the elephants' feeding had stopped. The jungle was absolutely silent. Mulumbe led me forward through the brush. Then to our right loomed up the outline of a great, brownish mass. Mulumbe maneuvered me into position for an ear shot. I fired a few inches in front of the ear. At the shot, the great animal dropped like a log. He was the old bull. I could not see his ivory but I did not want to go closer just then. I was waiting for the younger bull to move and betray his presence.

Mulumbe stood motionless beside me. For a few minutes there was no sound. Then we heard the other bull coming through the jungle toward us. He had heard the shot but did not know what it meant. He was looking for his friend, to make sure that the old bull was all right.

Try my best, I could not see a spot for a killing shot on him as he moved through the brush. I waited for him to come closer. Suddenly our two honey-gathering natives came up from behind and found the dead bull. They began to shout with delight. At the sound, the other bull instantly wheeled around and began to run. I had just raised my rifle for an ear shot as he turned. In desperation, I fired anyhow. Even as I squeezed the trigger, I knew my shot was too high. The bullet hit him in the top of the head as he bolted off.

Although, as I have said, no reputable hunter ever leaves a wounded animal if there is the smallest chance of tracking him down, it is one thing to know that such a code exists and quite another to put it into practice. When crawling through dense brush, you have a feeling of utter helplessness that can only be compared to the nightmare horror of being unable to run while some grisly phantom is bearing down on you. You are as helpless as a mouse caught in a tangle of flypaper. Thorns fasten in your clothes, and you must unhook yourself thorn by thorn. Vines wrap around your legs and if you try to take a quick step, you are apt to fall on your face. Your feet sink into the gluelike mud, and while you are struggling to extract one foot, the other becomes even more firmly planted. Then by the time you get that foot loose, your free foot has become stuck again. The flies dance around your head like a halo, stinging your face and through your khaki clothes. Nettle stings that you hardly felt an hour before now begin to throb while their poison makes you nauseated and dizzy.

But above and beyond all these troubles is the constant sense of impending death. Somewhere in the bush the wounded elephant is waiting. He is standing still, his trunk set to test the wind and his ears out to catch the faintest sound. You cannot keep downwind of him, for you must follow the spoor. A motionless animal has a great advantage over a hunter who must come to him. The animal waits, resting and preparing himself for the attack. Making no noise himself, he can easily hear his pursuer. He knows exactly where you are but you have no idea where he is. If you have to track the animal five miles, you are under a constant strain every step of the way. You never know when the attack will come. The quarry can choose his moment. You only know that the attack will be delivered at the moment when you least expect it.

At such times, the jungle is deathly still. Usually there is plenty of bird life about you, monkeys swing through the trees, small mammals scuttle through the underbrush. But as you come closer to the hunted animal all sounds gradually fade away. The whole forest seems to be silently waiting for the charge. There is no sound but your own breathing and the sucking noise of the mud as you go forward. You can smell your own sweat and the heavy odor of your gunbearer. Beyond that, there is nothing.

We reached a belt of brush so thick that we had to wriggle under it on our bellies. At such times, a man is in a bad way. He cannot see a yard ahead and cannot get his rifle in a position for a shot in case of a charge. I could see the soles of Mulumbe's feet ahead of me. I writhed along after them, praying every moment that he would come to a clear space and be able to stand. As we went on and on, I began to feel sick at my stomach. I could picture the bull standing somewhere in that bush, listening to us, biding his time before he rushed through the stuff as easily as a man running through tall grass. Finally, I began to wish that he would charge and get it over with. Anything was better than the constant suspense.

Mulumbe was at last able to get up on his knees. I saw him rise to a crouching position. He stopped. I crawled up beside him. He did not speak. He was looking ahead. There was the bull watching us. The animal did not realize that he had been seen. He was waiting for us to come a little closer.

He was standing in a very dense patch of brush. I could not see a good place to shoot. I did not know what to do. If I tried to provoke a charge, he might run instead of charging and then take up a better position farther on. So we stood watching each other, both waiting for the other to make the first move.

A fly decided the issue. One of the clegs lit on my cheek and bit me so savagely that I could not stand the pain. I jerked my head to dislodge it. At the motion, the bull instantly charged. Artists like to portray a charging elephant with ears outspread and trunk stretched forward. This is not correct. A charging elephant folds his ears back flat so he can go more easily through cover and his trunk is folded across his chest. In that position, he can strike either left or right with it and knock a man down. As the bull charged, he uttered a series of the most bloodcurdling screams. If he had come on me unexpectedly, those sudden cries would have doubtless paralyzed me for the few seconds needed for the bull to push his attack home.

I had no time to aim. I flung up my rifle and fired blindly between his small, bloodshot eyes. He reeled back at the impact. Before he could recover, I had dashed alongside and fired the second barrel into his ear. His skull rocked from the heavy bullet fired at such close quarters. Then his body relaxed and was still.

Although I have shot well over a thousand elephants, both on control work and during my old ivory-hunting days, my narrowest escape during elephant hunting came not from elephants but from nettles. This near disaster happened only a short time ago and I still remember it with a shudder.

I was shooting marauding elephants in the Meru district. They were spread out over a vast area. Much of this country was covered with vast patches of the giant stinging nettles. I had often encountered these nettles before and considered them merely another jungle nuisance. But never had I seen them so thick. Day after day I was forced to hunt among these terrible weeds and endure their stings. It was sheer joy to reach an area where the nettles had been trampled flat by the frightened elephants as they bolted away from us.

I returned to camp one evening after a particularly long day's hunt and sat down in my camp chair to enjoy a smoke. But I had no stomach for my friendly old pipe. This is always a danger sign with me. I could not eat my supper. As the evening went on, I began to grow feverish. I was so weak I could hardly make it to my camp cot. By morning, the nettle poison had done its work on me. I was semi-delirious and running a high fever.

I knew that I must get to a doctor as quickly as possible. My boys packed my lorry with the camp equipment and ivory. I told them to pile in the rear, but they refused. They preferred to walk. Frankly, the boys explained that in my condition they expected me to wreck the lorry and kill us all. I started off alone.

The track led down precipitous banks, across muddy streams, and over treacherous sand streams. Sometimes side tracks let off through the bush and in my confused state it was hard to remember which was the right trail. How I ever managed to get the lorry through will always be a mystery to me. I can only say that Providence was kind. Finally I arrived at the town of Meru, where there is a single hotel, known as "The Pig and Whistle."

Mr. Fred Davey, the proprietor, took one look at me as I reeled out of the lorry. Then he shouted to his boys to get a bed ready. He supported me into the hotel. The blessed relief of falling into that bed! Fred instantly sent a telegram to Hilda to "come at once. Husband dangerously ill. Bring big car and arrange nursing home Nairobi."

We were two hundred miles from Nairobi and at that time the roads were worse than bad. Neither Fred nor I expected Hilda before late afternoon of the next day. But my dear Hilda arrived that night shortly after twelve o'clock. She had arranged a room for me at the Maia Carberry Nursing Home in Nairobi, had installed a bed of overstuffed pillows in the back of her car, and had even remembered to bring along an extra boy to drive my lorry of ivory back to Nairobi.

All this was told me later, for when Hilda arrived I was hardly conscious. I could hear her voice but could not see her. Fred Davey had sent for a doctor. The doctor told them that I was weakening fast. They must get me to Nairobi as soon as possible if I were to live. We started back as soon as it was daylight.

In the Maia Carberry Home, I was put under the care of Dr. Gerald Anderson. His first report was far from bright. Had I arrived a few hours later, nothing would have saved me. Now he could tell within the next six hours if I would live or die. Hilda remained beside my bed, praying constantly during this time. I was packed in ice and injections of M & B 690 were given me to bring down my fever. During most of this time, I was only semi-conscious. I could hear faint, pleasant voices coming from far away. I felt no pain, no unhappiness, no regrets. I was floating through space on cushioned comfort. I was sure that I was going to die, yet I felt no fear.

Two days later, the doctor reported that I was out of danger. But I spent several weeks convalescing in the nursing home. Hilda stayed with me almost continually. Finally I was able to move back to our own house near Nairobi. But it was many months before I completely recovered from the effects of that terrible Meru elephant hunt.

15

Big Game Photography

At the present time big game photography has largely superseded big game shooting.

In my youth, the only animals that were photographed were dead animals. This made the problem of animal photography very simple. After your client had shot his trophy, he posed on the dead beast while you clicked the camera. But today people are determined to secure pictures of living animals. The animals seldom care to co-operate. A white hunter guiding a photographer has a difficult task.

At first, photography was combined with shooting. This never gave good results. A man must use either a camera or a gun—not both. The requirements of the two sports are very different. A sportsman wants his trophy. He cares nothing about weather conditions or the pose of the beast. A photographer must have the sun in a certain position and the animal out in the open so he can get a good, clear picture. In the early days, picture taking was considered incidental to getting good trophies. I grew up in this tradition and little thought that I would see the day when a good half of all safaris leaving Nairobi would be carrying cameras instead of rifles.

When the camera became as popular as the gun, I realized that it was up to me to learn the requirements of this new sport. Personally, I have never seen the picture that I thought could compare with a fine trophy, but as a professional hunter my task was to give my clients what they wanted.

Photographing game animals is frequently far more difficult than shooting them. Shooting an animal only takes an instant, but getting satisfactory pictures requires a long time. I have spent many hours racking my brain for every possible trick that could be used to keep animals still long enough for my clients to take their innumerable pictures.

Every sportsman wants to bag a lion. Every photographer wants pictures of them. I have always treated lions with great respect, as I consider them very dangerous animals. At first, I thought photographing them would be a well-nigh impossible task. But by using a few tricks based on lion psychology, the pictures can be taken quite easily.

My first photographic safari was to obtain pictures of lions on the Serengeti Plains. It was a motorized safari. By then the motorcar had almost completely taken the place of the old-fashioned foot safari, and we were able to whisk over the great plains that had once caused me so much suffering with comparative ease. When we came to a drift, we simply paralleled the gully until we found a place where we could cross, for miles mean nothing to a car.

After many failures, we finally reduced the problem of lion photography to something of a formula. As the method we used cast an interesting sidelight on the mentality of these big cats, I will describe it in some detail.

There was no lack of lions on the Serengeti. To see fifty of them in a day was common. They ranged from lordly old beasts carrying heavy manes that swayed back and forth with every step they took, down to young spotted cubs, playing about their mothers like kittens. Often we would see family groups of a dozen or more lying about in the shade of acacia trees. A noble sight. But for photographic purposes, the animals had to be coaxed out into bright sunlight or at least made to stand up so they did not blend in with the tall grass. To do this without alarming them was a problem.

We finally devised the following technique. Cruising around in our lorry, we would spot a pride of lions, generally lying near some brush. I would drive by them, being careful to move parallel to the pride rather than directly toward them, as a frontal approach tended to alarm the group. Moving slowly, I would stop the lorry between the pride and the bush. Unless this was done, the lions would grow restless and move off into the cover. But with their escape cut off the pride would stay where they were as long as they were not unduly alarmed.

We did not take any pictures at this time. Our maneuvering was only to gain the animals' confidence. The lions would regard us intently for a few minutes and appear to be thinking deeply. Finally, satisfied that we meant no harm, they would turn their heads away indifferently. We had now won the first round. Next we would leave the pride and drive across the plains until we sighted some antelope, one of which we would shoot for bait. A hook attached to a long rope was fastened to the bait so we could drag it behind the lorry. Towing the dead antelope behind us we would return to the pride, keeping upwind of them. At the right moment, one member of the party would release the bait and we would drive on downwind. Then we would stop and wait.

After a few minutes, the pride would scent the carcass. One after another would stand up, snuffing the wind with nostrils extended. At last one lion would start over toward the bait, slowly followed by the rest of the pride. The leading lion would sample the antelope while the rest stood and watched. Then in a few minutes the whole pride would be tearing at the animal.

This was round two. Now small liberties could be taken. We would approach the feeding pride slowly in the car and start taking pictures, edging closer and closer as the pride became more accustomed to our presence.

In the early days of lion photography, it was unwise for anyone to put his legs or arms outside of the lorry or even to speak. The lions would bolt at once. Apparently they did not connect the lorry with humans and possibly considered it simply another kind of animal. Later, when lions became more used to cars, this precaution was unnecessary.

We soon found that if we drove along slowly with a length of rope trailing behind the lorry, one or more lions would chase us and play with the rope like house cats playing with a dangling string. This trick always produced amusing pictures.

Individual lions varied considerably in their reactions to us. I remember in one pride that we photographed there was a big, black-maned male that was particularly bad-tempered. This old veldt veteran continually cuffed the other members of the pride about with no gentle blows and snarled at them unpleasantly. When we tried to take his picture he whirled on the lorry with an angry "woof" that made me reach for my rifle. One of his wives finally took the situation in hand. With true womanly intuition, she seemed to sense that we meant no harm. Not wishing to have a scene that would deprive the family of their dinner, she left the antelope and came up to the old male, purring ingratiatingly and rubbing her back under his heavy jowl. After being fussed over for a few minutes, the old male relaxed, showing his pleasure by urinating with spasmodic jerks. Satisfied, the lioness left him and returned to the bait—a perfect example of a tactful female quieting down an irritable male.

There was some slight difficulty and danger to lion photography in those early days, but now the whole business has become a joke. When the game in Kenya showed signs of becoming overshot, the government declared several large areas game preserves. Lions in these reserves, knowing themselves protected, became remarkably indifferent to humans. Lions are highly adaptable beasts. When they find that people are kind enough to shoot game for them in return for a few photographs, they become almost a parasite on humans. In some areas, lions virtually depend on photographic safaris to supply them with food.

In many reserves, lions have become so used to human beings that the sound of a rifle shot actually attracts them. They know the shot means that some photographer is shooting an antelope for them. These lions will trot after every lorry they see like big dogs, expecting the people inside to feed them. If the lorry stops, the lions often walk over and lie down in the car's shade rather than take the trouble to walk to the nearest bush. I have seen them mating within a few yards of the vehicle.

This naturally makes the task of photographing lions very simple. I once received a cablegram from a client who was flying down to

Kenya in his private plane with a group of friends. They particularly wanted lion pictures. I was to clear a small landing field on the veldt so they could land there and start out at once on safari. With a lorry and some boys I went to the place indicated and we set about clearing out the long grass. While we were engaged in this work, I saw a pride of eight lionesses and a fine old male walking past us. The plane was due to be along in an hour or so and I determined to give my client a real surprise. Jumping in one of the lorries, I drove out a few hundred yards and bagged a Coke's hartebeest. We dragged the carcass over to the edge of the landing field. The lions promptly trotted over and took possession. When the plane appeared and came down, the lions were just finishing. Far from being frightened by the plane, they trotted over to it and stood there as if asking, "Well, have you brought us any more meat?" The visitors, who had expected a long, hard hunt after lions, stood in the open doorway of the plane staring at the beasts, hardly able to believe their eyes. I must say that I enjoyed this little joke immensely, knowing that I had given my client a dinner-table story he could tell for many years to come.

Natives have a great dread of lions and find it hard to believe that the animals can become so tame. Sometimes when we were putting out a bait for photographers, a pride of lions would come up to us in the calmest and friendliest of moods, but our native boys would always run like hares for the lorry. Usually the sight of a fleeing figure will cause any carnivorous animal to give chase. Even a domestic dog will chase anyone who runs from him. But these lions were interested in nothing but the bait. I have heard natives tell each other that lions will not eat white people, only black. This was the only way they could explain their remarkable behavior.

As if photography were not enough, people began trying to make sound recordings of big game. I once guided a man and his stately wife who were keen on getting a recording of lion sounds. They had imported the last word in modern sound equipment, built into a special Bedford truck. I shot a zebra for bait and the man set up his microphone near the carcass. We hoped the instrument would pick up the snarling woofings and spitting noises lions make when they feed.

After a short wait, a fine pride came over to the bait. Our hopes were high as they began to feed. There was an elderly lioness in the pride and the others kept shoving her away from the kill. Finally the old lady got angry. Looking around, she saw the microphone and decided it was good to eat. Walking over to it, she grabbed the "mike" in her mouth and began to chew it. The man was furious. All his work was being ruined. He leaped up and down, waving his hands wildly, trying to make her let go. In his efforts, he knocked off his hat. The lioness promptly dropped the mike and, bounding over, grabbed the hat. This was the only hat my client had brought with him on the safari and his expression while the lioness was tearing it to pieces was indeed interesting. I burst out laughing. I just couldn't help it. I give the man full marks for the flow of unprintable words he got off his chest, much to the horror of his pious wife.

In one way, photographers are much like sportsmen. No matter how fine a trophy a sportsman secures, he always wants to get one a little bit better. So it is with a camera fiend. No matter what pictures he takes, he keeps trying for something more startling. The lengths to which these men will go is amazing. I took out one party that spent weeks photographing lions in every conceivable position. After they had pictured lions feeding at a kill, resting under thorn trees, and trotting after the lorry, they wanted the beasts to take still other poses. I tried every trick I knew. I hung an antelope carcass from a tree limb so the lions would jump for it. I had a carcass dragged past the lorry so the lions, following the scent, would walk parallel to the camera, thus affording a different type of shot. But all this had been done before by other photographic safaris and my party wanted to surpass their rivals. Finally one man had a brilliant idea.

"Why don't we get a picture of lions and humans at dinner together?" he suggested. "It'll be terrific! Never before photographed!"

No sooner said than done. We set up a table with a linen cloth and a vase of flowers. Places were laid and chairs put in place. Vegetable salad, fruit, and beer were the bill of fare. A zebra was shot and dragged alongside the table. I had it carefully staked down to make sure the lions did not pull it out of focus of the cameras. The three cameramen took their positions in the truck while the rest of the party sat down at the table.

I fired my rifle a few times to attract the lions. Shortly, a pride came hurrying along toward us. In a few minutes they were hard at work on the zebra. Now the cinema cameras began to purr. Shaking natives in white robes served the meal, their courage having been much strengthened by a liberal distribution of baksheesh. The two meals progressed within a few yards of each other, the lions caring not a whit what we did as long as we left them alone to finish their meal.

Such is lion hunting with a camera in Africa today—a long cry from the old times when lion hunting required a cool head and a steady aim if the hunter was to return from the bush alive.

Photographing other big game animals is by no means so simple a matter, especially as photographers are constantly demanding "action" pictures. I have guided many photographers, and no matter what they say when we start out, sooner or later they all want to photograph a charge. When a client hires me for a photographic safari, he usually begins by saying solemnly, "Now, Hunter, I want one thing clearly understood. I am not one of these people who like to kill poor wild animals. No, I merely want to take their pictures. We'll have no shooting on this safari."

For a while, everything goes smoothly. He sees his first rhino, his first buffalo, his first elephant. He runs thousands of feet through his cinema camera. Then he begins to grow restless. After all, the animals do not do much but stand around and eat. A little action is needed in the film. Finally, the man says to me with some hesitation, "Hunter, couldn't we get one of these beasts to charge us—just for the picture?"

"That can be easily arranged," I assure him. "But then I will have to shoot the animal."

I see the hesitation in his face. The man is sincere in his love for animals. But he can also visualize the picture on the screen—a charging rhino coming right into the camera lens! Such excitement! How his friends will exclaim over it! What cool nerve he had to stand there and take pictures during a charge! At last, he decides "just this once" to sacrifice an animal for the picture.

The favorite animal for "charging pictures" is the rhino. Elephants are too uncertain. Buffalo are too savage. But a rhino is formidable enough to make an excellent picture and yet can be easily handled. This is how the business is arranged.

We cruise around in the lorry until a rhino is spotted feeding in open country. The photographer gets out his camera, takes his light reading, and adjusts his filters. I get out my gun and wait until he is ready.

The next step is to get between the rhino and the cover, for when he is alarmed, he will run for shelter. When we get in position, my client focuses the camera. The rhino stops grazing and raises his head to see what is going on. Usually he trots over to investigate. It would be comparatively easy to frighten him away now by shouting or waving the arms. But we want a charge. I wait until the rhino has stopped to look at us and then I sway my body slightly from side to side. For some reason best known to the rhino breed, a sudden movement or a loud cry will panic them, but a slight movement brings them on.

Down goes the rhino's head and he comes for us. At the last moment, I fire and drop him in front of the camera. Using a powerful rifle like the Jeffery .500 I am sure of stopping him. Later, the photographer will explain, "I am opposed to killing wild animals but in this case there was a charge and the hunter had to fire in self-defense."

The position of the rhino's tail is a sure indication of his intentions. If the tail is held straight up in the air, the animal is frightened and seeking to escape. In case of charge, the tail goes down. When

I see a rhino's tail go up, I whisper to my client to make no move or sound until the animal can be coaxed into a charge.

All this is rather unfair to the poor rhino. So if a photographer wants charging pictures, I insist that he take out a regular shooting permit and licenses. After that, he is entitled to kill two rhino by whatever means he wishes.

One year I took out a young American named Walter Sykes who wanted rhino pictures. Walter was only sixteen years old but a very keen photographer. The boy should have gotten the best pictures of charging rhinos ever made, for in one day we had six charges, not one of them induced. I cannot speak too highly of this lad's courage. I have never had a client who kept a cooler head during times of great stress.

On this great day we were camped in the vicinity of Yaida. Walter had already taken some excellent pictures of rhino but wanted more. We agreed that I was not to provoke a charge and that if a rhino did come for us, I would try to turn him instead of shooting him.

Lorrying over an open plain studded with thorn trees, we spotted a browsing rhino. I stopped the car and we approached him cautiously, taking care to keep downwind. The bull continued to chew his meal, his molars making a noise like a hand decorticator. Walter lifted his camera and began to take pictures. Instantly, the rhino charged us.

When he was slightly more than twenty yards away, I shouted to turn him. If possible, I never allow a dangerous animal to come closer than twenty yards. At less than that distance, the momentum of his charge will carry him on top of the hunter unless your bullet hits him in exactly the right spot. At my shout, this bull twisted like a good forward in Rugby and went by on our right. Walter remarked, "I didn't believe those creatures could turn so quickly." I wish some of the men who claim that it is easy to jump aside and avoid a rhino's rush could have seen the way that animal spun around.

I do not know why the Yaida rhino were so aggressive, but we had five more charges. One I had to turn by firing my express across the animal's snout. He passed between my gunbearer and myself. After that experience, I was ready to stop but Walter still wanted one more picture. So, although it was getting late in the day, we continued to look for rhino.

We headed for a valley which might be called "Rhinos' Stronghold" as there were always plenty of them to be found there. We saw a large cow rhino standing under an acacia tree and Walter began photographing her. I saw the cow was beginning to grow restless and might charge at any moment. Then my native gunbearer pointed with his puckered lips to the left and right. Two more rhino were approaching us from opposite sides.

I had no wish to be "rhinoed" from three directions at the same time. I touched Walter on the shoulder and we began to retreat as rapidly as possible, walking backward. Suddenly the old cow charged us.

She was forty-seven yards away when she started—I measured the distance later. Walter instantly lifted his cinema camera and began to photograph the charge. I waited with my gun ready. I shouted to turn her. She came on. The gunbearer yelled and waved his arms. She paid no attention to him. Without taking his eyes from the finder of his camera, Walter muttered, "When I say 'Take her!'—shoot."

On such occasions, the white hunter must justify his client's faith in him. Walter had complete confidence that I could drop the cow at the first shot. I waited with my rifle ready as the animal came down on us. Moments, mere flashes of time, pass quickly in such emergencies. The beat of the rhino's hooves grew louder. Her head was down at a perfect tilting angle, ready for the toss. Walter refused to give an inch and kept his camera going. When she was twenty yards away I raised my rifle, waiting for Walter to give me the word to fire. He did not speak, the rhino came on. She was now less than fifteen yards away. I could wait no longer. My finger tightened on the trigger. At the same instant, Walter called, "Take her!" His voice and my shot came almost together. The heavy double rifle bellowed. The cow died in her tracks, the bullet striking her in the gradual slope between the ear base and the eye. She hit the ground with a crash and lay there, not a leg moving or an eye twitching. Walter, pale but unruffled, calmly remarked, "Sir, I have seen you in action."

Few visitors to Africa have had the luck of seeing as many rhino charges as did Walter Sykes. I know of no man who deserved the privilege more, for Walter was a plucky lad and a true sportsman.

There is a popular belief that photographing big game is a harmless amusement while hunting the animals with a rifle is a cruel affair. In actual practice, there is often not much difference between the two sports, because when a photographer wants really first-class pictures of rhino, buffalo, or elephant, he will almost certainly be charged sooner or later. Then the animal must be killed. Photographers seldom realize this simple fact. They think that an irritable cow elephant with a calf will understand their kindly intentions and allow unlimited pictures to be taken. This is rarely the case. The cow will give one or two danger signals. If the man does not instantly retreat, she takes matters into her own hands.

Nothing so infuriates big game as the steady purring of a cinema camera or the sudden click of a big still camera. If I wished to induce an elephant to charge, I can think of no better way to do it than suddenly to click a heavy camera at him. That fatal, mechanical note has brought on many a charge. Before I take a client up to a herd of elephants, I always explain that when I give the signal, he must instantly stop picture taking and move back. The man invariably promises in all good faith. There follows a long stalk in which matters always seem to work against the camera. The elephants are in thick cover, the wind does not coincide with the sun, or the animals keep their rumps to the lens. Then a big bull becomes alarmed. Suddenly he breaks out from cover, full into the sunlight. He stands motionless. His great ears are outstretched. His trunk is up, testing the breeze. I instantly motion my client to retreat for I know the bull will be on us at the first sound of the camera shutter. But the photographer sees a chance for the picture of a lifetime. He clicks the camera. At once, the bull charges and there is another elephant "shot in self-defense."

If a man sets out to do serious big game photography, during which he may incite a charge, he should take out a hunting license, exactly as if he were going on a shooting safari. This greatly simplifies matters. If the client points out an elephant he wishes to photograph, I simply say, "You are allowed one elephant on your license. If that elephant charges, do you want him to be the one?" If the client says yes, there is no problem. He can take all the pictures he wishes. When the charge finally comes, I drop the elephant. Any animal will attack you if you keep annoying him, so this arrangement is only fair.

Yet I must admit that animals are sometimes remarkably tolerant of picture taking. I have watched in amazement while a group of photographers ducked in and out of brush within thirty yards or so of a herd of elephants, taking light readings, changing lenses, and assuming the most incredible poses to get unusual "angle shots." The elephants must have known that they were there and still the big brutes put up with their antics very patiently. After considering the matter carefully, I am convinced that the elephants thought that the photographers were a herd of baboons. Elephants are short-sighted, so this is a natural mistake for them to make under the circumstances.

I do not mean to imply that every tourist who comes back from Africa with reasonably good pictures of big game animals has had to kill the animals to secure them. In many parts of Kenya, it is quite possible to secure good shots of game animals from a lorry, especially if your camera is equipped with a telephoto lens. At one time, pictures of buffalo were exceedingly difficult and dangerous to take. But a buffalo can run only about twenty-five m.p.h. and a lorry can easily keep up with a fleeing herd. From the safety of the cab, a photographer can take fair pictures of the animals with little danger. The photographer's main troubles are keeping his camera steady and avoiding dust. Once when I was guiding a safari sent out by the Colonial Film Corporation, we started after a buffalo herd over a very dry stretch of veldt. So much dust was thrown up by the galloping animals and the speeding lorry that we were driving in a kind of fog. One of the buffaloes, trying to escape, turned at right angles to the rest of the herd and blundered straight into our lorry. He landed straddled across the bonnet and rode there for some time before the driver managed to shake him off.

A sportsman's only desire is to shoot an animal, while a photographer often requires you to pose the beast for him. Since no one can tell exactly what a wild animal will do, this is often a difficult and delicate task. During one hunt, I was very nearly responsible for the death of a native in my efforts to pose a herd of elephants for a big film concern.

We had located the herd in the open and the cameras had been set up. The herd refused to co-operate. They crowded together in a bunch, rumps pointing outward. This made a miserable picture and the director told me to regroup them so their heads would be toward the camera. After some thought, I decided to send one of my native boys upwind of the herd to give them his scent. I believed that the sudden whiff of human smell would swing the herd around to us. I could not go myself as I had to stay by the camera crew with my rifle in case of a charge.

The boy I sent was a Masai, an excellent fellow and as plucky as all his people. The Masai are famous runners and this boy was especially fast, which turned out to be lucky for him. The boy circled the herd and moved slowly upwind of them. The elephants' trunks went up as they winded him and I waited for the herd to wheel around. Instead, a young bull backed out of the bunch. With an angry trumpet, he charged the boy.

He was too far away for me to shoot. The Masai ran for his life with the charging elephant gaining on him by the second. The boy threw down his blanket, his only covering, hoping the bull would stop to gore it. The elephant never paused. The Masai ran fast, but the elephant's feet simply skimmed the ground. There was no cover and I knew the boy was as good as dead.

Suddenly the Masai came to a drift some six feet wide. He

jumped it and kept on going. The bull could not make the jump. He was stopped more efficiently than if he had encountered a stone wall. He ran back and forth along the edge of the drift, trumpeting with fury and trying to find a way across. At last, he grudgingly gave up and returned to the herd. I am glad to say that the herd had turned around to the cameras so the photographers were finally able to get the pictures they needed.

The day may come when the camera will take the place of the gun in African hunting. In many ways, it will, no doubt, be a fine thing. Yet I am glad that I lived in a time when a man went out against the great animals with a rifle in his hands instead of a device to take pictures. Sometimes I think the animals themselves may have liked it better too.

16

The Most Dangerous Game

For many years clients have been asking me, "Hunter, what do you consider the most dangerous big game animal in Africa?" No man can answer this question exactly, but at the risk of some repetition, I will summarize my own thought about it. Much depends on circumstances. An animal that may be most dangerous in bush can often be easily shot on open veldt. Also, hunters vary considerably in their individual abilities, and an animal that one man would consider dangerous would not cause another sportsman much concern. For example, a man who can take quick "snapshots" with a rifle would find a charging lion less formidable than a hunter whose reactions are slower. Again, much depends on the hunter's past experience. Some hunters have specialized in one type of game and, knowing the animal's habits, are apt to consider it a fairly easy quarry. The same hunter, confronted by a different type of animal, will probably have a series of narrow escapes and naturally conclude that this new beast is very cunning and aggressive. Thus a man may have been a professional hunter for many years and still find it difficult to judge correctly the abilities of different types of big game.

Owing to constant hunting, many game animals have completely changed their whole character in the last fifty years. During the turn of the century, some animals were easy to hunt. Today, they are much more cunning and dangerous. I am thinking particularly of elephants. They have learned that man is their enemy and are not as trusting as they once were.

Some years ago, a friend of mine formed a partnership with a famous old-time ivory hunter who had killed well over two thousand elephants in his day. These two men were starting out on an ivory-hunting safari and my friend wanted me to accompany them, taking as my share one-third of the ivory shot. I refused. The old hunter was famous for shooting elephants with a very light-caliber rifle. I felt that the old man would simply anger and panic the elephants without helping us get any ivory.

My friend looked at me as though I were mad. "Hunter, this man has shot twice as many elephants as you'll ever kill," he told me. "Surely he knows more about the matter than you do."

"He made his reputation as an ivory hunter thirty or forty years ago," I explained. "In those days, elephants lived mainly in open country. As they had never been hunted, they had little fear of man. A hunter could lie out in the veldt with a light rifle and pick his shots. There was little danger of a charge. Now elephants live in bush. They know more about guns than many hunters and have learned how to set ambushes. Elephant hunting is far more danger-ous today than it used to be."

My friend would not be convinced. He set out with the old hunter. Several months later he returned to Nairobi. They had not taken enough ivory even to pay for the expenses of the trip.

Later, my friend confessed to me that there had been so many close calls with elephants that he considered himself lucky to get back alive.

I have hunted every type of big game in Africa, both as a white hunter and as an employee of the game department doing control work. I have not specialized in any one type of hunting. Yet, be-cause I lived during a period when it was necessary to shoot large numbers of game animals to make way for the rapidly expanding population, I have established records of one kind and another with several of the big game animals. I do not say this boastfully, as any experienced white hunter could, given my opportunities, have done as well or better. I mention the fact because I believe I have acquired more general experience with big game than most men. So, in giving my idea of the five most dangerous big game animals, I speak as a man who has hunted them all extensively. Yet I most certainly am not dogmatic in my listing, for as I have said, much depends on time, place and the individual man or animal.

First, let me say that any animal can be dangerous when cornered or wounded. I have seen water buck, sable antelope, and warthogs put up a desperate fight under such cimcumstances. So I confine my remarks to the "big five"—the outstanding big game animals of Africa. They are the elephant, the rhino, the buffalo, the lion and the leopard. These animals have been the cause of the vast majority of hunting fatalities on this continent.

The elephant is by far the most intelligent of this group. But unless he is a rogue, his very intelligence tends to keep him from being a menace to hunters. An elephant knows he is no match against a man armed with a rifle and so does everything possible to avoid man rather than attack him. I am not speaking now of an irritable cow elephant with a young calf or a herd that has been so badgered by hunters that they will charge anything on sight. I am talking about the average animal. In elephant hunting, the great problem is generally getting near enough to make the shot possible, not having to stop a charge.

Naturally there are exceptions. When an elephant knows he is being hunted and finds that he cannot throw the man off his spoor, he may set out to "hunt the hunter." At such times, an elephant is exceedingly dangerous, especially if he has been hunted before and knows something of men and their ways.

It did happen once that an elephant waited for me beside a trail after I had killed his two companions. I was lucky to kill him before he killed me. Also—and in my opinion this is of prime importance —a charging elephant will nearly always turn away from a shot, even if not seriously wounded. Few elephants will push a charge home once they feel the impact of a bullet. For these two reasons, I class the average elephant as the least dangerous of the "big five."

Now let us consider the rhino. Unlike an elephant, a rhino will frequently charge with no provocation whatsoever. In my opinion, this makes them a more dangerous animal. But a rhino will also generally turn away from a shot.

I have met with three rhinos in a simultaneous charge, killed the middle one (a cow), and watched her escort (two bulls) disappear into the bush on either side of me so rapidly that I could hardly see them go. If those rhinos had been buffalo, they would have pressed their attack home and one or the other would surely have tossed me.

I do not mean to say that rhinos will *always* turn from a shot. On another occasion, I was again charged by three rhinos under very similar conditions. I was using a .500 double-barreled express rifle at the time. I dropped the two leading animals with a left and right, then turned to grab my second gun from the bearer. The man had vanished. He had bolted when the rhinos charged, taking my spare gun with him.

The third rhino was on me. I have a vivid memory of the animal's face. His eyes were closed and seemed mere slits. At the last moment, I tried to jump aside. As I did so, I was shot into the air with a suddenness that surprised me. Fortunately, the rhino kept on going and did not return to gore me. In general, rhinos are one-way beasts. I have heard that rhinos close their eyes at the moment of a charge and my observations at that time would seem to bear out this theory. However, I have strictly guarded against any further investigations.

I mention this incident to show that no one can tell exactly what an animal may do, but I still claim that few rhinos will press home a charge in the face of gunfire. I, therefore, class them fourth on my list; more dangerous than elephant because of their aggressive natures but less dangerous than buffalo, lion or leopard.

Many sportsmen have classed the buffalo as the most dangerous big game animal in Africa. There is much to be said for this point of view. The buffalo will push home a charge in spite of a gunshot wound. He is often most aggressive and will charge with comparatively little provocation. When he charges, he presents his great boss to the hunter and only a very heavy-caliber bullet will stop him. If he knocks a man down, he will almost always come back to gore his victim. Also, the buffalo is a cunning antagonist. He will circle and stand by his back trail, waiting for the hunter. This trick is usually played by a wounded buffalo that knows he can go no further.

Unlike other big game, a buffalo has all his senses equally well developed. As I have said, elephant and rhino have excellent scent but poor sight. Lions and leopards have good sight but, for an animal, indifferent powers of scent. A buffalo can see, hear, and scent equally well. A terrible combination.

Why, then, do I not consider the buffalo Africa's most dangerous big game animal? The buffalo's very size counts against him. No beast weighing well over two thousand pounds can effectively conceal himself except in the very thickest bush. Also, a charging buffalo offers such a large target that a man is reasonably sure of hitting him somewhere. If you use a heavy enough gun, you are sure to knock him down. Then you can plaster him with your second barrel.

There is another consideration. When a buffalo charges, he seems to come like the wind but actually he cannot do over thirty-five m.p.h. Nor can he reach the top of his speed immediately. This gives a man time to get his gun up and take aim. For these reasons, I class the buffalo as the third most dangerous animal in Africa.

We now come to the great cats—lions and leopards. I consider the lion the second most dangerous game animal in Africa. His ability to conceal himself in the sparsest cover, and his great speed, which requires no build-up—he hits high gear at the first bound— are both factors. Moreover, he is a small target compared with a buffalo. Also, he comes at you in a series of great leaps that make it difficult to draw a bead on him. He is as courageous as a buffalo and will not flinch away from a shot. He comes all out, either kill or be killed. If he hits a man with the full force of his charge behind him, the man will probably be knocked unconscious.

This is lucky for the hunter, as then he will not feel the subsequent mauling.

As I explained in my chapter on photography, lions are exactly what you make them. A man can shoot lions from a lorry with virtually no trouble or danger. The same is true of killing them from a boma or machan. But following lions through bush is a very different matter. Here the lion has all the advantage. He knows where you are but you have no idea of his position. You must come to him—he will not come to you. Elephant, rhino, and buffalo can often be coaxed into charging, thus giving the hunter an advantage. A crouching lion waits until he is certain of getting his man. The reader must remember that I am talking now of a single hunter following a single lion. If you have beaters who will drive the animal out into the open, the whole affair becomes far more simple. I am also assuming that the lion knows he is being hunted and has not suddenly been bolted out of a donga by stones. But to go into the bush after lions with only your gunbearer is a very difficult and dangerous sport.

The courage and strength of a fine lion can hardly be overestimated. I once saw a lion charge a three-ton lorry. This animal was ten feet from the lorry when he sprang for us. He made a wonderful leap. His whole body was stretched out to the fullest and gave the impression of being streamlined. I have often had lions leap at me but never had such an opportunity to see their grace and perfect co-ordination. He hit the back of the lorry with such force that the entire vehicle shuddered.

From my position in the driver's seat, I could not see what was going on in the back. Taking my 30-06 Springfield that I use to shoot antelope, I got out of the cab and went around behind. There was the lion walking away from the lorry, obviously dejected and disillusioned.

If, hunted under fair conditions, the lion is the second most dangerous animal in Africa, what animal is the most dangerous? In my opinion, the leopard. I know that many white hunters will not agree with me, yet I hold to my verdict. I have shot a great many of these animals—how many I do not know because we used to hunt them for their hides and kept no records. Shooting leopards was considered a praiseworthy occupation when I first came to Kenya, because they were most detrimental to stock. Wounds made by a leopard's claws invariably became infected, as his talons, like a lion's, are coated with putrid meat from his kills. Even if a sheep or cow were only lightly scratched, the animal almost always sickened and died. Leopards also showed no hesitation about attacking any rancher who came to the defense of his herds. Many of the early settlers in Kenya had lost an eye or part of their face as a result of leopard attacks. A charging leopard always leaps for a man's face, trying to tear out his victim's eyes with his germ-laden foreclaws while his rear talons are equally busy. At the same time, he usually fastens his teeth in the neck or shoulder.

A friend and I were once hunting leopard in the Masai Reserve. We saw one of the creatures running up a steep, stony slope. My friend fired, hitting the cat in the flank. The leopard gave a bound and vanished among the boulders. We picked up the blood spoor and began working our way slowly up the hill, walking a few yards apart with rifles held at the ready. This is nerve-racking work, for we knew that the cat was waiting for us somewhere among the great stones and was sure to charge.

We had gone about twenty yards when the leopard suddenly burst from behind a boulder and leaped on my friend. The creature simply whizzed through the air—he was nothing but a yellow flash of light. My friend was a quick shot but he did not even have time to bring his rifle up before the cat was on him. I fired while the leopard was still in the air, "snap-shooting" as though my rifle were a shotgun. By great luck the bullet broke both of the leopard's shoulders and he fell dead on my friend. Later, we measured the length of his spring. My friend had been twelve feet from the boulder when the cat leaped on him.

If a leopard is to be hunted in any kind of cover, I prefer to use a twelve-gauge shotgun charged with heavy shot. When a leopard leaps for you, his strung-out body makes a very difficult target indeed. I have said that a charging lion is a difficult target but a leopard weighs less than half as much as a lion. Being smaller than a lion, he can conceal himself even more thoroughly.

Many people think that an animal is dangerous only in relation to its size and that a bull elephant is naturally a more formidable enemy than a two-hundred-pound leopard. Not at all. Man is a delicate creature, easily killed by any decently aggressive wild beast. A man being hunted by any one of the great game animals is like a rat being pursued by a dog. A small, quick little terrier is more dangerous to a rat than is a big, clumsy Great Dane or St. Bernard. A leopard is not so powerful as a lion but he is quite strong enough to inflict a mortal wound on a man, and that is a hunter's only consideration.

A leopard is a smart beast. When a leopard knows he is being spoored, he will often climb a tree and lie out on a limb over-hanging the trail. If the hunter does not see him, the leopard will usually let him pass. But if the hunter happens to glance up and their eyes meet, the leopard is on him like a flash. Most animals when they find themselves discovered will grunt or snarl and run on again. Not so with the leopard. The instant he sees a look of recognition cross the hunter's face, he charges instantly.

Twice I have been with hunters who walked under a tree where a leopard was crouching. In both cases, the cats gave no sign until the men happened to look up. Then the leopards sprang. Only the quickest of quick shooting saved the hunters from mutilation or worse.

Because leopards are as much at home in trees as on the ground, you must not only watch the cover on either side of the trail but also the limbs overhead. This more than doubles your difficulties.

A leopard's bushcraft is deficient in one notable respect. Although he may conceal his body perfectly in a mass of foliage, he often leaves his tail hanging down. I have shot a number of leopards that were waiting for me in ambush simply because they forgot to hide their tails.

In most other respects, leopards are very crafty. Their method of catching domestic dogs is a good example of their intelligence.

While leopards have a passion for dog meat, it is a curious fact that a leopard will run from a pack of dogs. Half a dozen little curs can hold the biggest of leopards up a tree indefinitely. But a leopard will go to any extremes to catch and kill a single dog, often actually enticing the dog into his power.

When a dog scents a leopard, he usually begins barking furiously, but takes care not to leave the safety of his master's tent or front porch. The leopard moves to a patch of open ground and lies down, apparently completely indifferent to the yapping dog. Then he begins to purr, waving his tail gently from side to side, and holding his head close to the ground as another dog would if he wanted to play. After a few minutes, the dog becomes curious. He moves closer to investigate, sniffing cautiously and still on the alert. The leopard, with hind legs tucked under him, is in a perfect position for a spring. But he does not appear to be crouching. He pays only occasional notice to the dog, looking around him and purring contentedly. Finally the dog is lured within range. Suddenly, and without the slightest warning, the leopard leaps for the unfortunate animal like a released spring. No dog, even the largest or fiercest, has any chance against a leopard. The cat has inch-long fangs and his claws as well. The leopard grabs the dog's throat, at the same instant fastening his talons in the dog's belly. As soon as the dog is dead, the leopard carries the carcass into the nearest thicket and devours it.

A leopard will almost always put the remains of a kill in the fork of a tree limb to protect it from scavengers. A large leopard can carry an animal weighing a hundred pounds up a tree trunk even though there are no branches to aid him. During the day, he will sleep in a tree some distance from the tree where he has left his kill, returning to feed on it after dark.

This fierce cat has at least one good trait. Unlike lions, leopards are not polygamous and have only one mate. There is strong affection between the couple. I once put out poisoned bait for a female leopard that had been killing a settler's stock. The next morning, I visited the bait and found the leopardess lying dead across the kill. Beside the dead animal was her mate, his head resting on her body in a caressing attitude. When he saw me he sprang up. He died beside his beloved consort.

Hunting a leopard in long grass, although not so dangerous as spooring the beast through jungle, is none the less a thrilling business. A leopard cannot be bolted out of grass with stones; he will not move even if you chance to hit him. A lion will nearly always betray his presence by growling, while a leopard remains absolutely silent until the moment of attack.

The elders of a Masai village once sent for me to destroy a cattle-killing leopard that had caused them great losses. Two young moran had spoored him down, only to be madly mauled. When I arrived at the village, I was astonished by the amount of damage this one animal had done. He would often kill five or six calves during the night, never touching the flesh but apparently killing merely for sport.

I set about tracking the animal. Near the village were several rock kopjes, made of colossal boulders that rested on top of each other in perfect balance, looking for all the world as if placed in position by mechanical means. With no frost or thaw to shake their balance, they had remained there for centuries and would, no doubt, continue to remain there for all time although it seemed that a puff of wind could topple them over. Between these great boulders were deep fissures, ideal dens for a leopard. I could see where he had walked among the huge, oblong rocks but I could not spoor him to his den. I lost his pug marks among the stones and returned to the village unsuccessful.

During the night there was a great commotion in the kraal. Cattle were stampeding and the natives yelling. When morning came, another calf had been killed, bitten through the throat as on other occasions.

I persuaded the owner of the calf to let me have the body as bait. My boys built me a machan in a convenient tree and I sat up to await the leopard's return.

At ten o'clock that night I saw a moving form loom up in the semi-darkness and creep cautiously toward the bait. It made no sound and its tread was deadly still. It was so large that I actually thought it was a lioness. It moved onto the bait and then squatted down. I could hardly see it against the earth. I decided to shoot as soon as it stood up again. Half an hour later, the cat rose and I could see his tail flicking from side to side. Taking aim, I fired low, as in the darkness you are apt to overshoot. The animal gave a tremendous bound and disappeared. I was satisfied he was hit but the light was so poor that I could only hope for the best. Taking no risks, I stayed in my perch until daylight.

When the dawn came, I examined the ground and found blood. The spoor was undoubtedly that of the cattle-killing leopard for I had examined his pug marks carefully while tracking him. My aim had not been good, otherwise he would have lain down within the first hundred yards. There was nothing for it but track him down to his den among the kopjes.

I set out with four moran, all carrying their spears and shields, and we tracked the blood spoor to the entrance of a small cave. Two of the moran cut a long sapling and began to probe in the hole while the other Masai stood by me with their spears at the ready. Suddenly a deep, coarse growl came from the cave, reverberating off the rocky sides. Immediately the leopard burst out like a bullet from a gun. As the leopard charged us he continued to utter a series of grunts, made by his breath's intake and output. He knocked down the two Masai with the pole and then leaped for one of the armed moran. The man met the charge with a spear thrust. He missed. In an instant the leopard was on top of his shield, mauling him about the face with his forepaws and biting him in the shoulder. The man fell to the ground with the animal still clinging to him. The other moran stabbed at the leopard, his spear passing so close to me that the razorlike head cut my trousers. Instantly the cat turned on him and seized the man by the arm. Down he went, with the leopard ripping him open with both forepaws and hind legs, his teeth still buried in the man's arm.

All this took but seconds, far less time than it takes to tell it. I pushed my rifle muzzle against the thick neck of the leopard and fired, blowing a hole through the mass of snarling savagery. So ended the worst cattle killer in that area.

I was astonished at the amount of damage this leopard had been able to inflict on the two Masai in a matter of moments. Knowing how rapidly wounds made by a leopard's teeth and claws infect, I lost no time in attending to them. The deep fang wounds on the moran's shoulder I syringed with T.C.P. disinfectant. The claw wounds I simply rinsed out with the same disinfectant. A week later both moran had gotten over their mauling.

All in all, I know of no beast that I would less wish to hunt in cover than the fast, savage, cunning leopard.

In many parts of Africa, the use of traps, poisons, and dogs have virtually exterminated the leopard. In my youth, we thought that the only good leopard was a hide stretched out for drying. But now we are discovering that the leopard played an important part in maintaining nature's balance. Leopards used to kill thousands of baboons every year, and now that the leopards have been largely wiped out baboons are proving to be a major control problem in many parts of the colony. The perfect way to keep them in check is by allowing their natural enemy, the leopard, to destroy them. So leopards are now widely protected and allowed to increase in numbers. Such is the strange way that man works—first he virtually destroys a species and then does everything in his power to restore it.

17

Homecoming

No matter how many years a Scotsman may spend abroad, to him Scotland is always home. Although it was now over forty years since I had left Shearington, I had never doubted that some day I would return. Often while sitting by a campfire in the Marenge Forest, listening to the distant chatter of monkeys and the occasional coughing grunt of a hunting lion, I would remember the cackling of wild geese as they flew over the Lochar Moss and the sweet scent of the heather in spring. That was my home. Africa was only a temporary adventure.

After my nearly fatal encounter with the stinging nettles, it began to occur to me that possibly I was getting along in years. Although now in my sixty-third year, my eye was still good and I could keep up with any man in the bush. When marauding big game was reported, I was still one of the men that the department sent out to deal with them. Old Mulumbe and I would get our guns and start out on the spoor of the raiders. It was rare when we were not able to report after a few days that the raiders were no more. Therefore, it came as something of a shock to me to realize that some day I would have to retire.

I finally mentioned the matter to Hilda. Although it was obvious that such a thought had never occurred to her before, still by a curious coincidence she had been corresponding with some of my relatives in Scotland. She suggested that we take a brief trip to Shearington, merely to look the place over. The more I thought about this plan, the better I liked it. Already I could see the blue

waters of the Solway Firth and the long stretch of the Bankend-
Annan Road, once traveled over by Mary Queen of Scots, leading
over the great moors that stretched away as far as a man could see.

We packed our belongings and said good-by to our friends. Our
children had all grown up and were either married or hard at work
in their various professions, so we had no ties left in Kenya.

We arrived in Scotland during the late spring, the pleasantest
time of year. We went at once to the old farm at Shearington.

As we drove up the well-remembered road, I was shocked by the
look of the place. It had fallen into ill repair. Stables and cowsheds
were shabby. Instead of the sleek horses of my youth, a row of
Ferguson tractors stood in the farmyard. I missed the pleasant odor
of clover hay. The place smelled of petrol. It looked more like a
factory than a home.

My parents were long since dead and the farm had been taken
over by others. Hilda and I talked to them. Their story was discouraging. Farm labor was almost impossible to get and wages were
high. In Kenya, you can hire a first-class native field hand for two
pounds a month. Here, men were getting nearly that much a day.
And reluctant to do the work. "They all want factory jobs," said the
new owner sadly. Gone were the red-cheeked maids and the farm
hands of old.

Much of the farm had gone back to turf. It was impossible to
work it without help. How well I remembered the farm in my
youth! My mother supervising a household of servants. Father out
in the fields with the men, bringing in the harvests. The farm had
been prosperous and happy for hundreds of years. Yet in a single
man's lifetime, everything had changed.

We lived in a rambling old house near the farm. Gloomily, we sat
down to supper that first evening. I could hardly believe my eyes
when I saw the change. In Kenya, we usually started out with a
good, rich soup, followed by the fish course, and then some first-rate
steaks with three or four vegetables—unless, of course, Hilda decided to vary the menu with spur fowl, sand grouse, or wild duck.
Dessert was pie, tropical fruits, a nice trifle pudding, or possibly

cake and ices. Coffee was then served by the houseboys in our living room.

Hilda is the best of housekeepers and for a moment I could not imagine why she did not have a nice kongoni or a Tommy chop or two for supper. When I looked up at her, I saw she was watching me anxiously.

"You must remember that we are only allowed sixpence worth of meat a week, John," she reminded me.

"Ah, well, then I'll be content with a nice omelet," I said.

"One egg a week, John," said Hilda sadly.

How could people live under such conditions? But I was not long at a loss. That very evening I got some wire and went out to set snares.

Everything had not changed. I still remembered the runs in the moorland that the rabbits used as passageways. I set ten snares that night. In the morning, I visited them. My hand had not lost its cunning and I had six fine, fat rabbits. I took more pride in those rabbits than if I had shot the same number of elephants with a hundred pounds of ivory in each tusk. After forty years I still could set a snare. I only wished that Tom Salmon could have seen that catch. Tom insists that the right way to set a snare is a fist and half a fist above the ground. The correct height is two fists. We had often argued the point over a glass of whiskey in Makindu, but the proof of the pudding is in the eating and there were my half-dozen rabbits neatly noosed.

On the way back, I felt that I was behaving selfishly in keeping all this good meat for Hilda and myself. I passed a farm and saw the lady of the house out sweeping the front steps. So I stopped and offered a rabbit.

She looked at the animal indifferently. "We don't have any pigs," she told me.

"You'd feed rabbit to pigs!" I shouted. "Haven't you ever heard of rabbit pie?"

"Oh, we don't eat them any more," the lady explained. "I know people used to eat them in the old days but we're above that now."

I went out after rabbits and hares several times after that, but my interest in the sport began to wane. I could not find for love or money any boy to carry my game bag. A string of rabbits becomes heavy after a time. I cannot imagine why I never noticed that as a boy.

I got out my old rod and went fishing. I caught but few trout, nice little things weighing a pound or so. But it took a long time to get them. I remembered the narrow wooden bridge which spanned the Lochar stream in the tidal reaches where as a youth I fished for sea trout, freshly run fish from the Solway which rose greedily to gaudily colored flies. A bonnie Scotch lassie passed by. She stopped while I inquired about the place. "You mean the murder bridge," she said.

"Tell me more," said I. "Did you no hear," she vouched, "that a man found his woman love out with another man and waylaid them in the bridge. He saw a knife and bolted, but the woman stood and had her throat cut from ear to ear, her body heaved into the Lochar stream, the assassin followed suit. His corpse was found and placed in a pig sty overnight. You're no going to fish there surely." Shades of my forefathers! My thoughts hied me back to less savage places in Kenya. I remembered fishing for barbel on Lake Edward near the source of the Semiliki River. Barbel run ten to fifteen pounds and you can catch a dozen within an hour. Then there are the great Nile perch in Lake Rudolf, weighing as much as two hundred pounds and more. A small perch, say one about fifty or seventy-five pounds will give you a noble battle. This trout fishing seemed like a waste of time.

But the fondest memory of my youth was shooting. So one morning I set out with my Purdey for a day on the moor.

I tramped over the old, familiar fields, but somehow they had grown much smaller than I remembered. My eye was used to the great expanses of veldt in Kenya and these tiny patches seemed no bigger than a native's shamba. The distant hills, that once had been great mountains with their peaks close to the sky, were now nothing as compared to Mt. Kenya or Kilimanjaro. Also, I missed the game.

You could walk all day in Scotland and see nothing but an occasional roebuck and plenty of stoats and weasels—vermin were in possession.

Then the sound of grouse calls reached me. In an instant I was a boy again. The cries came from a heather-covered moor. To reach it, I had to climb a gate and cross a pasture. As I mounted the gate, I saw a small herd of cattle in the field, presided over by an old bull. I noticed in passing that the animal had a fine spread of horns.

I was halfway across the field when I heard the roll of hoofs coming toward me. For the moment I was back in Kenya again. How many times have I heard that thunder as a buffalo charged! I glanced around and saw the bull was charging me—head down, neck out. A noble sight.

Suddenly I realized that I had no rifle. The bull was only some fifty yards away and coming on with admirable ferocity. I never like to turn my back on a wild animal, but in this case there was nothing for it but to run. I ran.

Fortunately, the gate was not high and I vaulted over it just as the bull's horns hit the wood. He broke one of the center bars and then stood there, bellowing. He pawed the dung on the ground— just as a rhino will scatter his own droppings. I have seldom seen an animal with so much spirit.

When I returned to Hilda, I announced my intention of taking a rifle with me in the future. Hilda pointed out that farmers might object to having me shoot their pedigreed cattle.

"It's a fine country when a man can't protect himself from wild beasts," I protested.

"After all, John, you were trespassing," Hilda said gently.

Trespassing! I hadn't heard that word for forty years. Yet there was no doubt that Hilda spoke the truth. It was probably illegal even to shoot grouse. We were back in civilization.

Hilda was watching me with a troubled eye. Finally she said, "John, we've had a very nice holiday. But don't you think it's time we got back to Makindu?"

Here indeed were welcome words. Hilda, as always, was quite

right. We packed up our belongings and took the next ship back to Kenya.

We landed in Nairobi, and I dropped in to talk to my old friends. I was rather surprised to hear that everything was going well in the Makindu area, although we had been away for several months. However, I was sure that there would be several things that needed looking into. We took the train south that evening. From the car window, we saw the herds of game scattered out across the plains— stretching away as far as the eye could reach toward the setting sun. A welcome sight.

Although we had been away so long, I had not bothered to notify the boys that we were returning. As the train pulled into Makindu, I signaled with my torch and then turned to supervise the unloading of the luggage. Before we had got more than one or two boxes out, Mulumbe came trotting down the trail with three of my boys.

We sat on the porch that night, listening to the wild laughter of the hyenas and the distant sound of native drums. Mulumbe had already sent one of his wives to notify the native women to bring eggs and milk in at dawn.

The sky was thick with stars and the scent of the night-blooming flowers was heavy in the air. Hilda and I raised our glasses and drank a toast to Africa. We had come home.